BRITAIN AND THE REGENCY OF TRIPOLI

BRITAIN AND THE REGENCY OF TRIPOLI

Consuls and Empire-Building in Nineteenth-Century North Africa

Sara ElGaddari

I.B.TAURIS
LONDON • NEW YORK • OXFORD • NEW DELHI • SYDNEY

I.B. TAURIS
Bloomsbury Publishing Plc
50 Bedford Square, London, WC1B 3DP, UK
1385 Broadway, New York, NY 10018, USA
29 Earlsfort Terrace, Dublin 2, Ireland

BLOOMSBURY, I.B. TAURIS and the I.B. Tauris logo are trademarks of
Bloomsbury Publishing Plc

First published in Great Britain 2023
This paperback edition published 2024

Copyright © Sara ElGaddari, 2023

Sara ElGaddari has asserted her right under the Copyright, Designs and Patents Act, 1988, to be identified as Author of this work.

For legal purposes the Acknowledgements on p. viii constitute an extension of this copyright page.

Series design by Adriana Brioso
Cover image: A Sand Wind on the Desert, 1821, by Denis Dighton. (© Heritage Image Partnership Ltd / Alamy Stock Photo)

All rights reserved. No part of this publication may be reproduced or transmitted in any form or by any means, electronic or mechanical, including photocopying, recording, or any information storage or retrieval system, without prior permission in writing from the publishers.

Bloomsbury Publishing Plc does not have any control over, or responsibility for, any third-party websites referred to or in this book. All internet addresses given in this book were correct at the time of going to press. The author and publisher regret any inconvenience caused if addresses have changed or sites have ceased to exist, but can accept no responsibility for any such changes.

A catalogue record for this book is available from the British Library.

A catalog record for this book is available from the Library of Congress.

ISBN: HB: 978-0-7556-4089-8
PB: 978-0-7556-4093-5
ePDF: 978-0-7556-4090-4
eBook: 978-0-7556-4091-1

Typeset by Newgen KnowledgeWorks Pvt. Ltd., Chennai, India

To find out more about our authors and books visit www.bloomsbury.com and sign up for our newsletters.

CONTENTS

List of Figures	vii
Acknowledgements	viii
Chapter 1 INTRODUCTION	1
Chapter 2 BRITISH IMPERIAL HISTORY BEFORE 1839	7
Chapter 3 TRIPOLI: THE END OF A DYNASTY	19
Chapter 4 TRIPOLINE NOTABLES	35
Chapter 5 THE BRITISH CONSUL AT TRIPOLI	55
Chapter 6 AN IMPERIAL BRIDGEHEAD	77
Chapter 7 SURVEYING NEW FRONTIERS: INTELLIGENCE-GATHERING AND INTERVENTION	95
Chapter 8 CONCLUDING REMARKS: CONSULS AND EMPIRE-BUILDING IN NINETEENTH-CENTURY NORTH AFRICA	117
Annotated Index of Names	123
Notes	131
Bibliography	169
Index	195

FIGURES

1	Map of the Regency of Tripoli, 1707	3
2	Author unknown, *Marina di Tripoli; Tripolis*. Colour illustration of the harbour, fortress and hinterlands of the city of Tripoli, c.1780–90	20
3	W. H. Bartlett and J. C. Varrall, *Tripoli*. Black-and-white illustration of the city of Tripoli and its surrounding areas, 1830	21
4	W. H. Smyth, *Plan of the Harbour of Tripoli*. Map of the city and greater area of Tripoli, showing the Menshia ('The Meshiah') – cultivated gardens – that extended from the city walls eastward and south into the desert, 1826–35	25
5	W. Balten and W. Crane, *Tripoli*. Depiction of the fortress and harbour of Tripoli	26
6	A. Earle, *Prime Minister to the Bay of Tripoli*, 1815–17	45
7	A list of the agents officially appointed to Tripoli during the reign of Yusuf Qaramanli	56
8	G. F. Lyon, *Triumphal Arch: Tripoli*	59
9	A. Earle, *not titled (Mustopha, Head Dragoman to the Consul of Tripoli)*, 1815–17	62
10	Tonnage of cargo arriving and departing at the ports of Tripoli and Benghazi for the purpose of British trade, 1823–31	85
11	Quantity of vessels arriving and departing at the ports of Tripoli and Benghazi for the purpose of British trade, 1823–31	85
12	Robin Hallett, *Map of North and Central Africa, with Trade and Traveller Routes*	103

ACKNOWLEDGEMENTS

I would like to begin by thanking Colin Heywood for his support and the University of Hull for awarding me a full scholarship to support my earlier doctoral research and, in turn, making this book possible. I also want to thank the Department of History for their annual research allowance that facilitated research trips to London. I thank my former supervisors David Starkey and David E. Omissi for their time and input, particularly David Omissi for his comments on the early chapters of this book.

I would like to especially thank Alex Kazamias and Richard Pennell for their generosity with both their time and effort in commenting on my research ideas and chapter drafts. I would also like to express my gratitude to Zoë Laidlaw and the late Chris Bayly for their time and comments on my work.

During the course of my research, I benefitted from invaluable input from the audience at seminars as visiting research fellow at the University of Turku in Finland. In the UK I would also like to thank Keith Hamilton, former chief historian at the FCO; Mohamed Ben Madani at *The Maghreb Review*; James Cronan of The National Archives at Kew; and Mauro Nobili for their well-timed advice and discussions. Thanks to Rachel Heeter Smith at the Department of History, University of Illinois at Urbana-Champagne, for generously sharing her work with me, to Joachim Östlund and Gustaf Fryksén of the Department of History, Lund University, and also to Maria do Carmo Strozzi Coutinho at the Centro de História e Documentação Diplomática, Rio de Janeiro, for their assistance.

For the use of images in my work, I would like to thank Torbjørn Ødegaard, Bridgeman Images, the National Gallery of Australia, the Royal Geographical Society and, finally, the Institut Cartogràfic i Geològic de Catalunya, Barcelona.

For everything else, I would like to thank my family – especially my husband, Andrew, and my daughters, Inés and Riva.

Chapter 1

INTRODUCTION

This book interrogates British imperial activity and ambition in the Regency of Tripoli, an Ottoman province of North Africa, in the early nineteenth century. While charting changing British strategic priorities prior to the British invasion of Aden in 1839, the central focus is the ways in which British power, influence and prestige were established in the Regency of Tripoli. Through diplomatic and consular channels and individual enterprise, the British consul cultivated a protected and influential presence in the Regency. Alongside the successive missions of the African Association to explore the course of the Niger and the African interior, British naval activities along the coast, an expanding network of vice-consular representation in and beyond the Regency, and the development of health programmes by the British consul, all contributed to an evolving but powerful imperial bridgehead in Tripoli in the first half of the nineteenth century. The history of Libya in the early nineteenth century is part of a wider history of British pre- and early colonial engagement in the Middle East. This modern history is one of Ottoman decline and growing rebellions across Ottoman lands. At the same time, British ambitions in the region were primarily driven by cultural and commercial motives within a Mediterranean and wider global context of Anglo-French power rivalry and, at home, a recurrent impulse by the Foreign Office to check its overseas expenditure.

The following chapters will set out the significance of the Regency of Tripoli for British strategic concerns, as well as for British imperial ambitions as defined by the consul as the most senior imperial agent. Building on the concept of 'informal empire', the interests, actions and influence of an autonomous British consul 'acting on the spot' are set out – through the expansion of a vice-consular network and the creation of an influential imperial presence in the Regency. In so doing, a fuller picture is developed of the extent of British engagement in Tripoli, and a revised framework is proposed within which British imperial activity in Tripoli during the first half of the nineteenth century can be usefully analysed.

Drawing primarily on the consular correspondence of British agents in Tripoli during the reign of Yusuf Qaramanli from 1795 to 1832, there is a much needed re-interpretation of both British policy in the region and Tripoli's engagement with the outside world – especially the emerging European powers during the long process of Ottoman decline.[1] Moreover, the dominant view in the historiography of British imperialism in the Regency is challenged. The presumption that Tripoli, because of its relative unimportance, cannot reveal much about British strategic concerns, policy and ambitions in the Mediterranean, Africa and the Middle East during the post-Napoleonic era is no longer tenable.[2] The despatches of British consuls to Tripoli enable us to provide a fuller account of the Regency's relations with its neighbours, Europe and the United States – as well as British imperial policy formulation in the region – whether through the government or individual agents. This is because the agents, driven by both a high sense of duty and personal ambition, were able to reconstruct a relatively detailed depiction of the local social, economic and political life and their own evaluation of their contribution to the effective exercise of British influence in and beyond the Regency of Tripoli. The letters and reports provide an important new dimension to our understanding of Tripoli and British imperial activity when carefully read alongside other sources.

By the early 1820s British policy in the Mediterranean – as manifested by both agents overseas and the government in London – was at a crossroads. Historically shaped by rivalry with France, the course of Britain's future role in the Mediterranean and the 'East' was also directed by concerns over the future of the Ottoman Empire and fears over Russia's ambitions in the Balkans and the Middle East. Since 1795 the Regency and port of Tripoli came to serve a strategically important place in intelligence-gathering and supply for the British government and Royal Navy. With the accession of a friendly Qaramanli dynast, who looked to establish a new era in foreign and commercial relations with Europe and the United States, Britain relied on its consul general to represent, protect and promote British interests in the Regency and wider region. As the most senior imperial agent, the consul ensured that treaty agreements were honoured, and prioritized the protection of British subjects and commercial interests. As the 'man on the spot' the British consul came into his own, and using his abilities fostered the growth and operation of an influential imperial bridgehead that countered the ambitions of rival states, including France and the United States.[3] In this atmosphere of alarm and competition, the consul at Tripoli exercised, in contrast to his counterparts elsewhere, a high level of autonomy that was reflected in both his initiatives in Tripoli and in his influence and intervention in the politics of the Regency.

The paradigms of 'formal' and 'informal' empire cannot sufficiently account for the place and role of Tripoli in Britain's imperial designs in the early nineteenth century. This is because the activities of European agents, particularly those of the British consuls, did not contribute towards the creation of an 'informal empire', but rather towards a more disparate network of alliances and activities that culminated in the construction of an imperial bridgehead at Tripoli. A colonial bridgehead can be 'a commercial, settler, missionary or proconsular presence or a combination of all four. It might be a decaying factory on a torrid coast or, at its grandest, the "Company Bahadur".'[4] Central to the concept of a bridgehead is the notion of a physical 'presence', the importance of access to central resources – military, financial and diplomatic – as well as the importance of context and environment over policy.[5] The network of privileged relationships and the activities pursued by British agents in Tripoli during the reign of Yusuf Qaramanli contributed to a British imperial presence in a strategic North African port. An imperial bridgehead stresses the core characteristic of a privileged and, by implication, protected presence of an external power in the territory of a 'peripheral' country.

The Regency of Tripoli

As a province of the Ottoman Empire, with key trading ports connecting the ancient trading routes in the African interior to the shores of the southern Mediterranean, the Regency of Tripoli (see Figure 1) reflected a diverse collection of ethnicities, cultures and languages. The ruling Qaramanli dynasts were of Kuloghlu origin and the dynasty was established in 1711 by Yusuf Qaramanli's (1766–1838) grandfather, Ahmad Qaramanli, who reigned until 1745. The Kuloghlu as a distinct social and ethnic group came about as a result of intermarriage between the Ottoman Janissary forces and the local Arab populace. As Figure 1 illustrates, the location of the port of Tripoli, at least since the fourteenth century, was key to its historical prominence and commercial livelihood. Tripoli's position as a frontier state, between Ottoman, African and European worlds contributed to its identity and global outlook. The Regency and its ports acted as a conduit, entry and exit point for the trans-Saharan caravans, Christian and Muslim traders and the annual Hajj pilgrims en route to Mecca and Medina. Tripoli's liminality provided it with strategic advantages and made it a desirable location for the pursuit of economic ambitions.[6]

Figure 1 Map of the Regency of Tripoli, 1707, four years before the establishment of a Qaramanli government and dynasty by Ahmad Qaramanli. Available online: http://upload.wikimedia.org/wikipedia/commons/2/22/Royaume_de_Tripoli_1707.jpg.

In the sixteenth century, Tripoli had been under Spanish rule from 1510 to 1530, until it was taken over by the Order of the Knights of St John. The occupation by the Knights of Malta in turn was brought to an end on 13 August 1551, when Ottoman forces invaded Tripoli and made the city-state an Ottoman province until the founding of the Qaramanli dynasty at the beginning of the eighteenth century. Until 1711, the Ottoman Porte maintained a series of governors in Tripoli to see to its effective administration, its revenues and ultimately to secure Tripoli against continuing attacks by Spain and the Order of Malta.[7]

From 1676, as a result of continued disruption to their shipping in the Mediterranean, England and France began a series of bombardments against Algiers, Tunis and Tripoli. In this context, and with a weak central government, Ahmad Qaramanli capitalized on the growth in the autonomy of the role of the governor and, in July 1711, mounted a coup and established his authority over the Regency of Tripoli.[8]

The eighteenth century marked a shift in commercial relations between Europe and North Africa, as European states began to obtain their staples from the New World rather than from the traditional 'grain stores' of North Africa and the Middle East. At the same time, the ties between the Ottoman provinces and Istanbul became increasingly symbolic, with dwindling support from the local elites in North Africa. While local rulers, including the Qaramanli in Tripoli and the Mamluks in Egypt, had focused on consolidating their power and building stronger ties with Europe, the shifts in global commerce prompted a decline in revenues. The Ottoman Porte undertook numerous direct military expeditions to states such as Tunis (1713 and 1794), Tripoli (1794) and Egypt (1786) in failed attempts to reinstate central authority over its rebelling provinces. There was also another military expedition, in 1756, by Algiers at the instigation of the Porte, to execute and replace Ali Pasha with a new beylical system of governance.

Meanwhile, the Russo-Turkish War of 1768–74 highlighted Britain's position on the Eastern Question, and in particular that its relationship with the Ottoman Porte was ambivalent at best and occasionally strained, particularly during the embassy of John Murray (1712?–1775) from 1766 to 1769. Throughout the eighteenth century, Britain sought to maintain, through the Levant Company, its commercial relations with Turkey and all the ports where 'Levantine' consuls were posted, including to 1825, the North African Regencies.

The Regency of Tripoli held a position of advantage among its North African neighbours as it was a key meeting point and conduit of the four major trade routes crossing the Sahara, as well as connecting to a fifth route through the east of the Regency which linked Wadai to Kufra and, eventually to Benghazi on the coast (see Figure 12 on page 103).[9] These ancient caravan roads provided the lifeblood for the economic and social life of North and Central Africa during the nineteenth century. They connected the powerful Kingdom of Kanem-Bornu to Tripoli and the Mediterranean Sea, as well as to the urban and commercial centres that included Timbuktu, Lake Chad, Gao, Kano, Ghat and Murzuq.

A staple, and substantial source of income for the Regency of Tripoli, like its neighbours, was derived from the trade in slaves from the interior. The capture of

Christian, White slaves onboard seized vessels or from piratical raids on coastal populations in the Mediterranean was conducted to a much lesser extent than the trade in Black slaves from the African interior. Nevertheless, the capture of White slaves provided the incentive for a Royal Navy brokered treaty with Algiers, Tunis and Tripoli outlawing the practice in 1816, as well as providing the pretext for a full blockade and bombardment of Algiers, led by Edward Pellew (1757–1833), in the same year.

Yusuf Qaramanli's government (1795–1832) benefitted from the advantages of courting both France and Britain through offering both powers favourable terms of trade. The gradual decline in revenues from prizes since the seventeenth century was ameliorated by the continued trade in African slaves and other goods from the interior, while the export of livestock and provisions steadily increased to satisfy the demand of the reinvigorated British garrisons throughout the Mediterranean following the end of the Napoleonic Wars. Despite having maintained a close relationship with European states, the Regency of Tripoli began to struggle with what appeared to be a terminal decline in its economic resources. In turn, the social and political fabric of the Regency came under increasing strain.[10]

What did remain constant for Tripoli was its advantageous position as gatekeeper to the interior, as well as its established connections with both European and African powers. By 1818, Yusuf Qaramanli had clearly defined what he wanted to secure for the future of his Regency and dynasty. His government needed to diversify its revenue base by expanding trade, developing agriculture and lowering Qaramanli's formerly exorbitant demands for annual tribute from parties that desired trade with, and through, the Regency. Within the boundaries of his territories, the Pasha periodically deployed his military assets to quell internal insurrections by various Arab tribes and installed a governor in Murzuq (the urban centre of Fezzan) that was loyal to Tripoli. In an apparently desperate attempt to bolster his government, he also ordered short-sighted military incursions into the sovereign territories of Kanem-Bornu.[11]

Meanwhile, in a still heady atmosphere of great-power rivalry, Britain desired the security of its existing empire, and its newly found regional influence. Beyond ensuring the regular supply of its naval bases across the region, from Cádiz to Valletta, Britain was concerned to check the ambitions of France and Russia in the East. These priorities, however, brought an unexpected role as a mediator with the Ottoman Porte over rebelling Greek subjects in the Ionian Islands. Britain's involvement was designed to avoid any further European wars and to maintain the integrity of the Ottoman Empire, despite the waves of rebellion sweeping across the provinces of the Ottoman Empire.[12]

In focusing on the relationship between Britain and Tripoli, the spotlight is turned to three consuls to Tripoli – Simon Lucas (1793–1801), William Wass Langford (1804–12) and Hanmer Warrington (1814–46), who were appointed as successive 'Consuls General & Agents' during the reign of Yusuf Qaramanli.[13]

Consul Warrington's term witnessed a profound change in British relations with North and Central African states. The consul's activities in the Regency interrogates our understanding of the role of the 'man on the spot', and in turn, the creation of a powerful, influential and interventionist British presence in the region through the operation of an imperial bridgehead at Tripoli.

In contrast to Egypt, the Regencies to the west have not attracted the same attention because of their ambiguous status on the periphery of empires. This, in turn, reflects the schism created by imperial history in its treatment of colonial and non-colonial territories. The prospect of increased trade and profit remained a prime motivating factor for British agents in these 'ambiguous regions'.[14] The consuls to Tripoli were no exception. Apart from a few works, there is a need for a more in-depth interrogation of the diplomatic relationships and connections between France, Britain and the North African states in the early nineteenth century.[15] The history of economic development and political and social change cannot be understood in isolation from Tripoli's engagement with the newly ascendant powers in the region – Britain and Egypt.

British interests during and after the tumultuous years of the Napoleonic Wars remained diverse, with the British government facing an array of competing priorities across the globe. This 'European' change coincided with a time of economic and political upheaval in Tripoli, and in North and Central Africa more generally, as well as in the eastern Mediterranean. The decline in the caravan trade, and in turn in revenue for the government of Tripoli, necessarily changed the dynamics of the relationship between Britain and the Regency. The concerns of the British government over French and Russian ambitions in the region remained justified, while in Tripoli a power vacuum was created that the British consul exploited for personal and official ends.

Chapter 2

BRITISH IMPERIAL HISTORY BEFORE 1839

Throughout the turbulent wars of the Napoleonic era (1803–15) and in the cautious post-1815 political climate, British priorities focused on the protection of British subjects and interests, which included the maintenance in the supply of provisions from North Africa, including the Regency of Tripoli and Egypt. Britain's efforts initially concentrated on countering French manoeuvres in Egypt and Napoleon's ambitions in the Levant. As fierce competition over access to resources and valuable trade routes continued into the nineteenth century, Britain initially occupied Aden in 1807, more than thirty years before the widely recognized occupation of 1839.[1] Britain's 'will to empire' was shaped in the eighteenth century by the desire to commercially expand, fierce rivalry with other European powers and by an ever-increasing global portfolio of geostrategic concerns, not least the security of British Empire in India. By the early nineteenth century, Britain's growing overseas interests and concerns reflected its power, prestige and influence across both the Old and New Worlds. Despite a vagueness of purpose in its overseas policy, pre-emptive interventions nevertheless became the norm for an expansive empire with the greatest military largesse ever witnessed in the modern era.

The Seven Years' War

The Seven Years' War (1756–63) brought about a profound and irrevocable global change in the Ancien Régime system. The conclusions of the Treaty of Paris at the end of the war replaced Spanish influence with British global ascendency. The independence of the North American colonies thirteen years later, in 1776, forced a change of course in British strategic priorities and at the same time reasserted the primacy of empire in India. Despite the loss of its American colonies, by the close of the eighteenth century, Britain had solidified its position as one of the foremost colonial powers alongside France, the Netherlands, Spain and Portugal. The inconsistent policy of evacuating the British naval fleet from the Mediterranean in the final decade of the eighteenth century was a result of the 'vacillation' of the government, prompted by the reconquest of Corsica and Elba by Napoleon Bonaparte.[2] Through the War of the Second Coalition and the Treaty of Campo Formio in 1797, France had also acquired Corfu and the neighbouring Ionian

Islands, while Britain at the time only had Gibraltar as a base for its Mediterranean expeditions.[3] As 'irresistible' as imperial and military expansion became, British activity was paradoxically a result of a lack of an explicit or coherent policy in the region beyond the protection of loosely defined 'British interests'. The protection of existing strategic concerns, however, usually necessitated invasion, occupation or annexation. In turn, the numbers of British subjects and interests inexorably increased across the globe. By the turn of the nineteenth century, the rise of the 'Eastern Question' and the future of the Ottoman Empire inevitably focused the gaze of the British government upon the 'East'. This focal point of imperial power and ambition was sharpened by French motivations in the Middle East and Asia, and crucially, access to resources and commercial wealth through the gateway of Egypt. As Consul Lucas wrote, in April 1797 to the Duke of Portland, William Bentinck:

> The growing power of this Bashaw [sic] must require a little more attention from the different European powers, this free trade and commerce in the Mediterranean and Levant Seas ... the Americans, have concluded their Treaties with all the Barbary states ... [and] now bids fair to rival the French in very lucrative trade.[4]

Invasion of Naval Commerce

A notable feature of the late eighteenth and early nineteenth centuries was the use of navies as instruments of state policy.[5] Britain's Royal Navy was no exception. A clear policy shift was prompted following Russian annexation of the Crimea in 1783, in response to the conclusion of the Treaty of Kuçuk Kainarji of 1774, whereby the British government prohibited British seamen from entering Russian military service.[6] Thereafter, Russia continued in its policy of aggressive expansion to acquire more territories, including Georgia in 1804 and neighbouring Qajari provinces.[7] In the Mediterranean, despite some failures, such as the evacuation of Toulon in December 1793, Britain's occupation of the island of Corsica in June 1794, 'foreshadowed in Minorca and Gibraltar – of an Anglo-Mediterranean order in the making'.[8] The increased targeting of British commerce also necessitated a greater British naval presence in the Mediterranean.

In some measure, the nineteenth century represented, for Britain, a continuation of the concerns and priorities of the late eighteenth century, with a focus on India and access to its resources. The ascendency of the British Royal Navy globally and in the Mediterranean confirmed Britain's sense of cultural and military superiority in the region. British control of commerce and traditional patterns of trade from the Middle East and Asia across to the Americas underscored its global hegemonic position. Since the eighteenth century, British chartered companies, including the East India Company, the Levant Company and the Royal African Company, dominated trade in the region. Following the conclusion of the Seven Years' War in 1763, Britain also asserted its control of trade across the Red Sea. At the same time, following the loss of its colonial possessions in the West Indies, France moved to counter British influence in the Middle East and Asia, and directed its energy to the occupation of Egypt. As the gateway to India, the British government and its agents stationed in Egypt attempted to counter these French manoeuvres in the region, and in 1799, a British military force occupied the island of Perim (Mayyun, Yemen), a strategic port at the southern entrance to the Red Sea. Britain's exploitation of commerce was reinforced in treaty provisions, primarily through preferential tariffs and duties on the import and export of goods. When force was required, European powers, particularly Britain and France, resorted to blockading harbours and ports. The blockade system became a notable feature of the early nineteenth century and, after being deployed successfully in Malta in 1798, was later used against North African states, including Algiers and Morocco, to force those powers to accede to terms they would not have otherwise accepted.[9]

On the ground, at outposts throughout the world, the government relied on the initiative and influence of its locally stationed agents. In turn, favourable treaty provisions relied on the character and diplomatic skills of individual agents. Local powers, from time to time, were forced to acquiesce diplomatically or by force when a demand from a European power would not be accommodated.[10] In August 1816, a joint Anglo-Dutch squadron bombarded Algiers and forced the Dey, Omar Agha, to agree to an end to the capture and enslavement of White slaves and to release the thousands held in Algiers. Just over a decade later, in 1828, two British ships of war blockaded the port of Tangier to obtain compensation in a case which, according to the British government's own legal counsel, was one without merit. Although the Sultan of Morocco, Mawlay 'Abd al-Rahman was well within his rights to detain two British ships with uncertain papers, the Royal Navy continued to blockade the port until the Sultan acceded to Britain's demands.[11] This tactic later made way to the 'gunboat diplomacy' so prevalent in the late nineteenth century.

In July 1798, the Battle of the Pyramids was accompanied by the arrival of Napoleon in Cairo and marked the start of France's 'Eastern project' or 'Oriental Expedition' and military campaign to Syria.[12] The Napoleonic expedition to Egypt and Britain's subsequent occupations of Alexandria, Aden and Perim signified a new era in British and French colonial ambitions and the rise of European cultural imperialism. For France, the possession of Egypt could revive the trade route through Suez, strengthening the connection with India and countering the 'growing commerce of Atlantic born trade'.[13] Access to the Middle East and Asia hinged on access to the overland routes through Egypt. Napoleon's ambitions stoked British fears about losing its strategic advantages and ultimately, India. France's occupation of Egypt from 1798 to 1801 served to emphasise Egypt's deeply symbolic and strategic purpose for Britain. As a consequence of Napoleon's invasion of Egypt, the Porte issued a declaration of war against France, while Britain hastened to form an alliance with Turkey and Russia against French policy in Egypt. Napoleon and the French Directory's decision to seize Egypt was fundamentally about countering British power and imperialism in the region.[14]

Militarily, Britain became entangled in Egypt following the Battle of the Nile in August 1798. The scene of the naval operations in Abukir Bay marked the return of Britain to the Mediterranean and its 'resumption' of control of the Mediterranean from the 'Straits to the Levant'.[15] Crucially, the success of the British naval fleet checked Napoleon's ambitions in the East and India.[16] The victories of the Royal Navy were followed in the same year by Britain's reoccupation of Minorca and the blockade of Malta, which had the unilateral support of the Porte. In expression of Britain's closer friendship with Turkey, pro-Ottoman diplomat Sir Sidney Smith (1764–1840) was appointed as minister plenipotentiary to Istanbul.[17] Meanwhile, in Tripoli, Nelson demanded an end to friendly relations between Tripoli and France, and the expulsion of all French subjects and agents in the Regency. On 28 April 1799, Nelson wrote to Yusuf Qaramanli:

> I was rejoiced to find that you [Yusuf Qaramanli] have renounced the treaty you had imprudently entered into with some Emissaries of General Buonaparte – that Man of Blood, that Despoiler of the weak, that Enemy of all good Musselmen; for like Satan, he only flatters that he may the more easily destroy; and it [is] true that, since the year 1789, all Frenchmen are exactly of the same disposition.
> … It is now my Duty to speak out and not to be misunderstood. That Nelson which has hitherto kept your Powerful Enemies from destroying you, can, and will, let them loose upon you, unless the following Terms are, in two hours complied with – Viz., That the French Consul at Tripoli Vice Consul and Every Frenchman are delivered on Board Her most faithful Majesty's ship 'Affonço'.[18]

The following month, in May 1799, Britain roundly defeated France's staunch ally Tipu Sultan at Seringapatam. Naval power was vital in establishing British hegemony in far-off lands separated by expansive seas. In the same month came the turning point in France's Eastern campaign when French forces were beaten in the Siege of Acre. Acre was significant as the gateway into Palestine and symbolic of the continuance of Napoleon's expedition to the Levant. Despite the resounding destruction of France's naval strength in the Mediterranean, Napoleon still believed in the superior strength of his land forces.[19] Smith, with the assistance of General Louis-Edmond Antoine le Picard Phélippeaux (1767–99) led an Anglo-Turkish defence of Acre and caused French troops to withdraw, retreat to and successively evacuate, Jaffa, Gaza and Al-Arish.[20] The initial British occupation of the island of Perim in 1799 and Aden in 1807 – Perim was subsequently reoccupied in 1857 and Aden in 1839 – was designed to counter the threat posed by Napoleon's ambitions in the east.[21]

The two-year British blockade of Malta in 1798–1800 ended in the evacuation of French troops from that island on 5 August 1800, and Malta was promptly placed under British administration. The combined British occupation of Malta and the destruction of the French fleet at Abukir signified the end of Napoleon's campaign in Egypt and Syria. While the Treaty of Amiens which concluded the following year marked a temporary peace, the treaty provoked an outcry in Britain in its stipulation that Britain withdraw from Malta. This public reaction highlighted the British government's adjustment of its affairs in the Mediterranean.[22] By the time of

Napoleon's retreat from Russia in 1812, however, France had lost 'all power to dispute the control of the [Mediterranean] sea' and 'this Important Intelligence has been communicated to His Highness [Yusuf Qaramanli] and the same has been rendered as public as possible'.[23] In addition to Gibraltar, British influence was now also firmly established in Sicily and Malta. After 1814, Malta gave the British fleet a 'central position in the Mediterranean from which it could strike at every coast, and from which it could easily withdraw westward should its position become untenable'.[24] The successive invasions of Egypt in 1801 and 1807, the arrival of Mohamed Ali (1769–1849) as Pasha in Egypt in 1805, the occupation of Malta and later Sicily in 1806, and entanglement in the Peninsular War (1807–14) emphasized Britain's rapidly expanding role in the politics of the region as well as marking a period of upheaval for Europe and Russia. This is exemplified in the Treaties of Tilsit concluded in 1807, whereby Europe was divided between Russia and France and where France gave its support to Russia in its conflict with Turkey. As a result, these agreements 'virtually gave the French a free hand in Europe and the Russians in Asia'.[25]

By 1808, Britain's naval superiority was utilized by Foreign Secretary George Canning (1770–1827) in an array of political negotiations, including British diplomatic efforts to restrain Spanish and French ambitions during the Peninsular War.[26] In 1809, Britain took possession of the Ionian Islands. The occupation of the Ionian islands enabled a further extension of British influence into the eastern Mediterranean. For Ionians, a new constitution for the islands was drawn up in August 1817. The earlier capture and occupation of Malta and Sicily signified the 'huge explosion' of British power in the region.[27] Three years previously, in March 1814, British troops occupied Parga in the northwest region of Preveza in Greece, before eventually handing the town to Ali Pasha (1740–1822) of Ioannina/Tepedeleni's troops, in a political settlement that was hard to justify given the numbers of Christians that felt they had no choice but to flee. Those Christians sought refuges in places such as Kalamas 'as late as August 1829'.[28]

While merchant companies appointed by royal charter no longer held sway in the trade of the Mediterranean or the Middle East, on the back of the might of the Royal Navy, Britain's sense of moral and cultural superiority was reinforced through a succession of treaties of peace and commerce. Diplomatic protocol, outlined in those same treaties, detailed the preferential political and commercial treatment demanded by Britain. British agents, including those in North Africa, did not hesitate to suspend cooperation at the slightest provocation or perceived lack of due respect. The diplomatic mission of Sir William à Court in 1813–14 to the Regencies of Algiers, Tunis and Tripoli emphasizes Britain's exploitation of its dominant position to obtain peace settlements in its own national interest and to the distinct disadvantage of the other signatories. To their own detriment, in 1813, the Regencies of Tunis and Tripoli acquiesced to much smaller debt settlements than originally owed by the Spanish government.[29] On 5 May 1822, when asked to clarify points of the settlement and Convention reached with Tripoli, Sir William à Court confirmed to Robert Wilmot Horton: 'The Convention, I am ready to admit, was a disadvantageous one to the Bashaw [sic], but it was one the nature of which he certainly never misunderstood.'[30]

Britain and North African states were heavily reliant on the slave trade as the principal source of their revenue. British agents at stations along the west African coast took firm advantage of the trade to the Americas and the West Indies. Despite the rising public anti-slavery sentiments across Britain, the wealth accruing from the slave trade was integral to the maintenance and growth of the British Empire. In turn, the British government prioritized the maintenance and oversight of its forts along the Gold Coast (all located in modern-day Ghana) and granted the Royal African Company the funds for the repair and upkeep of these forts.[31] The British settlements continued to be governed by the Royal African Company until 1821. Despite anti-slavery legislation being passed by British Parliament in 1807 – the Slave Trade Act – British agents continued to monopolize the slave trade from West Africa.[32] As an eighteenth-century pamphleteer extolled,

> How great is the importance of the [slave] trade to Africa ... so that both for exports and imports, the improvement of our national revenue, the encouragement of industry at home, the supply of our colonies abroad, and the increase of our navigation, the African [slave] trade is so very beneficial to Great Britain, so essentially necessary to the very being of her colonies, that without it neither could we flourish nor they long subsist.[33]

While maintaining a powerful influence on the commerce of the Mediterranean and the slave trade out of West Africa to its colonies in the West Indies and the Americas, the British government and philanthropic societies supported and funded successive missions and naval initiatives to survey, map and acquire knowledge of the countries and peoples across the globe. With commercial dominance a primary concern, merchant companies constituted an important arm of British colonial power and influence. These companies cemented British hegemony by altering traditional trading patterns from the Middle East, in staple goods such as cotton and coffee and opening new markets of export in South America and British colonies in the West Indies. The amount of freedom permitted to the Levant and East India Companies was symptomatic of Britain's unwillingness to define a clear set of policies for its overseas engagements. This lack of articulation of a 'foreign policy' of sorts enabled British imperialism to spread in unexpected ways through individual initiatives of British agents, from La Plata to Africa to Burma over the course of the nineteenth century. Correspondingly, however, the sheer scale of British activity across the globe made the task of management from London impossible. The British government's attempts at reform and regulation of companies, agents and branches of the government proved to be a long process which was never completed before the final loss of India in 1947.

Rebellions of the Ottoman Pashas

After the 1790s, British imperial manoeuvring in the Mediterranean and beyond – including in the Red Sea – is best understood within the context of the 'Eastern

Question'. The losses incurred by the Russian annexation of the Crimean Peninsula in 1783 and the port of Ochakov (Ochakiv, Ukraine) in 1791 marked the beginning of a gradual erosion of the sovereign integrity and political stability of the Ottoman Empire. Moreover, the losses incurred by the Porte laid the foundations for the growing power vacuum in the eastern Mediterranean. The 'Eastern Question' that occupied ministers in London into the nineteenth century centred around the future of the Ottoman Empire and its provinces. At the same time, Britain was concerned to counter Russian imperial ambitions in the eastern Mediterranean. Russia continued to intervene in the affairs of the Porte and wanted to secure control of the Straits – the Dardanelles and the Bosphorus.[34]

The British government was deeply concerned over the increasing instability of the Ottoman Empire and about both French and Russian ambitions in the region. In Tripoli the rebellion against the rule of the Ottoman Porte began in 1711 with the establishment of a local dynasty, the Qaramanlis, and again in 1795 with the ousting of Ottoman officer Ali Borghul and the reinstatement of dynastic Qaramanli rule in Tripoli. With much relief, on 6 February 1795, Consul Lucas wrote to Henry Dundas informing him of the fortunate occurrence for 'European trade' that 'we are not only freed from the despotism of an arbitrary Tyrant [Ali Borghul], but once more restored to the peaceful enjoyment of our former rights and privileges, by the restoration of the lawful Princes of the Qaramanli Family to the Throne of their Ancestors'.[35] Rebellions by Pashas and Beys were also underway in other Ottoman territories, including Osman Pazvanoğlu (1758–1807) in Bulgaria, who repeatedly rebelled against Sultan Selim III until his (Pazvanoğlu's) death in 1807. As early as 1793, Pazvanoğlu led military expeditions throughout Eastern Europe, along and beyond the course of the Danube and as far north as Bucharest. Meanwhile, Ali Pasha of Ioannina challenged the authority of local Beys loyal to Istanbul and by 1809 had firmly established his rule in southern Albania and over extensive territories in modern-day Greece. His powerful reign continued until 1820 when Sultan Mahmud II besieged Ioannina with 20,000 Turkish troops. Meanwhile in Egypt, Mohamed Ali (1769–1849), asserted his absolute authority in March 1811 by ordering the massacre of the mamluk ruling elite in the citadel of Cairo. As the Pasha, he had transformed Egypt from an Ottoman province into an expansive empire. Along the coast, another provincial ruler, Hussein Dey (1765–1838) of Algiers, also fought to assert his independence from outside influence, particularly following the demand for the settlement of debts from France in 1827, until the formal occupation of the Regency by French forces in 1830. In the same year, the Pasha of Tripoli militarily prepared the Regency for what was believed to be an imminent invasion by French and Egyptian troops, as part of a greater scheme to conquer all the Regencies of North Africa. On 10 March 1830, Consul Warrington, in a letter to R. W. Hay, described the escalating situation in Tripoli:

> It is true that Merchandise was relanded at Leghorn [Livorno], having been previously shipped for this Port [Tripoli], merchants have arrived to endeavour to close their accounts, and I apprehend His Highness [Yusuf Qaramanli] must have more solid grounds from the steps He is adopting. Hagge Mohamed and

the Reis [of the] Marina depart for the Cyrenaica and Bomba, Sidi Amor for the Gulf of Syrtis [Sirte] and I should suppose their united numerical Force will be 70,000 men.

Secret Divans are held, about 2 million of Dollars have been subscribed, and everything indicated, an honorable Resistance to the Invasion of Mohamed Ali.[36]

These rebellions and campaigns signified an end to the central authority of Istanbul over its provinces in Eastern Europe and North Africa, an increase in European and Russian rivalry and the rise of Britain as the dominant imperial power in the Mediterranean.[37]

In the aftermath of prolonged European wars and with the growing rebellions of Ottoman provinces, the Congress of Vienna in 1814–15 provided a much-needed peace establishment for Europe and a European consensus on subjects of political and public concern. The Congress presented a united European front to move against depredations made on the commercial shipping of European states and agreement to stop the enslavement and trade of White (Christian) Europeans. This 'crusade' was, very possibly, a mask for 'another extension of an English presence' in the Mediterranean and is discussed further on with reference to the British and Dutch expedition in 1816 against Algiers.[38] The five-power alliance of Britain, France, Russia, Prussia and Austria that emerged in 1815 marked the end of the age of war and European revolutions. The termination of the Napoleonic wars also saw the 'restoration of the old pattern of Mediterranean trade' – Livorno and Genoa recovered while Malta and Gibraltar suffered.[39] Meanwhile, the dependence of the British garrisons on the regular supply of goods and livestock from North Africa continued. The foreign policy of Prime Minister Lord Liverpool (1770–1828) was committed to the restoration of European affairs to their pre-revolutionary state.[40] This was a divergence from the consensus to reduce overseas (naval) spending by the government and underscored Britain's continuing commitment to facilitate British commercial interests in the southern Mediterranean.[41] By 1815, Britain emerged as a fiscal-military state where 'governments in London had ten times the revenue enjoyed by their predecessors a hundred years earlier'.[42] Despite suffering a defeat in February 1808 following the French invasion of Spain, Britain had secured its position as a global maritime power and its Mediterranean fleet continued to dominate the waters of the Mediterranean.[43] In 1816, this naval might was exemplified in Britain's sustained bombardment of Algiers by Lord Exmouth (1757–1833) and the peace terms subsequently forced upon Omar Agha, the Dey of Algiers.[44] Surprisingly, this British expedition against Algiers, in alliance with the Dutch, marked the first major bombardment by the British navy and procured the release of 1,200 slaves.[45] This bombardment is significant because it was the first time the British navy had successfully 'batter[ed] a fortified Mediterranean bastion into compliance'.[46]

As early as 1817, the British government also found itself concerned by the activities of US warships in the Mediterranean, and the government readied a British warship in expectation of a confrontation with an American naval force. The United States wanted to stake an interest in the commerce of the Mediterranean and identified a suitable base in the port town of Derna and Gulf of Bomba, territories contiguous to the Regency of Tripoli. In the wake of the growing desire to gain a foothold in the Mediterranean and the American-Tripoline wars of 1801 to 1805, Earl Bathurst (1762–1834) viewed the continued stationing of a powerful US squadron in the Mediterranean with 'much alarm'.[47]

While Mohamed Ali strove to develop the economic infrastructure of Egypt, the British government viewed Egypt not only as a crucial supplier of grain provisions for the nearby British garrisons, but also, following its occupation of Egypt in 1807, as a vital component of its future strategy in the Mediterranean and the Middle East. Britain's growing interest was as much about control of trade in the Mediterranean as it was a reflection of its geostrategic concerns in the region.[48] Preferential treatment for British trade and matters of political protocol were enshrined in treaties of peace and were strictly enforced. A system of blockade was successfully utilized by the Royal Navy in North Africa to coerce local powers into acquiescing to both commercial and political demands.

In addition to the protection of a growing portfolio of commercial and political concerns, by the 1820s, British priorities included a concern to protect a rapidly increasing number of British subjects, largely made up of Maltese and Ionians, in the eastern Mediterranean and Ottoman North Africa.[49] Growing philhellenism in Britain helped to direct British policy in the Aegean – from the lack of popular support for any significant involvement in the Russo-Ottoman conflicts – to mass public sympathy in the cause of Greek independence.[50] These were all factors that contributed to British policy responses and British cultural imperialism in the early nineteenth century. This public interest in the future of Greece was as passionate and influential as the anti-slavery movements calling for the abolition of the slave trade, and the imperative to intervene in Greece was supported by the overwhelming strength of the Royal Navy.[51]

Others contend that Britain's policy towards the Greeks was one fired by the public imagination as well as by influential political figures such as George Canning. While the massacre of 20,000 Greeks in Chios in 1822 is immortalized in Eugène Delacroix's 'Massacre at Chios', the equally infamous massacre which preceded it in 1821, of mainly Muslim and Jewish citizens of Tripolitsa (Tripoli in the Peloponnese) by Greek rebels, was not an event that Britain wanted to recognize or address.[52] Differences in the opinion between government ministers continued and precluded a clear policy in the eastern Mediterranean and eventually, in 1828, precipitated the Russo-Turkish War. The Battle at Navarino the previous year highlighted further divisions between the Royal Navy and the government on how to address the issues raised by the Greek revolt in 1821. Finally, in Navarino Bay (1827) the Navy's 'patience with the slow grind of policing Ionian neutrality had run its course'.[53]

The Greek Wars of Independence (1821–32) were symptomatic of the wider Eastern Question that preoccupied Britain, and which had come to the attention of the government as early as 1770 with local revolts in the Morea, followed by the rebellions of once loyal provinces such as Tripoli in 1793, Egypt in 1810 and later Algiers (1827–30). By September 1829, and by the Treaty of Adrianople, Sultan Mahmud II recognized an autonomous Greece. Despite the British navy strengthening its Mediterranean fleet following the St. Petersburg Protocol (1826), the government still feared the activities of Russian troops building up 'along the Danube'.[54] Problematically, however, in the eastern Mediterranean, while Britain remained determined to counter Russian and French threats to its naval power in the region, the British government remained ambivalent about its role in the Greek Question because of continuing fears over Russian intervention in Greek affairs.

Naval Power and Commercial Enterprise

The size of the British fleet stationed in the Mediterranean rose from fifty-four ships of the line in 1792 to ninety-four by 1836, with only an additional ten new vessels dispatched outside of the Mediterranean. The increase in the size of the Mediterranean fleet emphasized the growing range of British interests and activities in the region, as well as its political concerns and territorial acquisitions.[55] In 1816, the Congress of Vienna witnessed the restoration of France as a European power while the congress underscored the earlier consensus of 1815 and drew up a protocol against depredations on European commercial vessels in the Mediterranean. A further proposal to form a dedicated maritime league to destroy corsairing was rejected by the foreign secretary, Viscount Castlereagh (1769–1822), because of British fears of the longer-term consequences of the presence of Russian warships in the Mediterranean.[56]

British activities, naval expansion and commercial ambitions in the Mediterranean encompassed the political, naval and philanthropic spheres. In the tradition of the merchant adventurers and the philanthropic work of the African Society, a series of exploratory missions, naval surveying and acquisition of antiquities were successfully undertaken over the course of the nineteenth century. The British consul at Tripoli also identified a ready source of timber supplies for the British dockyards in Malta, and consequently obtained the agreement of the Pasha to exploit the forests in the east of Regency. Consul Warrington, in March 1821, wrote to Earl Bathurst on the suitability of the timber for the Royal Navy:

> The Timber is equal to the Building of the largest ships, situated near the sea, and 1,000 ship Loads might without difficulty be embarked. In the commencement of this object I secured this Forest from the Bashaw [sic] provided the British Gov.t wished to extract Timber from that Quarter.[57]

The idea of introducing new initiatives was part of the civilizing mission of Britons and Europeans overseas and justified much of British agent's activities at remote outposts. Britain continued to exploit the slave trade despite the growing abolitionist movements at home.[58] The pursuit of commercial revenues and trading agreements favourable to British interests – the expansion of wealth and influence – motivated the government to continue to support its 'men on the spot' stationed across the globe. Agents such as Consul Warrington did not hesitate to threaten the dispatch of ships of war or naval bombardment if the ruling Pasha would not acquiesce to British demands.[59]

Appointed by the African Association, British adventurers over the course of the eighteenth and nineteenth centuries sought to explore and gain knowledge of new and uncolonized territories. This drive for knowledge contributed to the launch of successive missions in the 1820s from Tripoli, including to identify the origins of the Niger River. Earlier expeditions were similarly motivated, including James Bruce's mission in 1768 to trace the source of the Great Nile, and later, in 1795, Mungo Park's exploration of West Africa. In February 1773 Bruce obtained a firman allowing 'British ships to operate between India and Suez, and for British merchants to trade across Egypt'.[60] Following this mission, Bruce returned to Egypt in 1786 on the assurance that, as the newly appointed British consul general, he would 'secure an agreement with the new Pasha for the safe passage through Egypt of British and Indian trade and passengers'.[61] Through accounts of travels in the late eighteenth century, Egypt had captured the British imagination, and the imperial gaze was to remain on Egypt until the nationalization of the Suez Canal Company in 1956 which, in the words of the British Prime Minister Sir Anthony Eden, was to disrupt 'the economic life of Western Europe'.[62]

Britain's geostrategic concerns, and its vast portfolio of responsibilities, inevitably led to both government and agents posted throughout the world, to pursue a myriad number of ambitions. 'Men on the spot' such as Henry Salt (1780–1827) in Egypt, Hanmer Warrington (1776–1847) in Tripoli and Sir Thomas Reade (1782–1849) in Tunis, all used their initiative and influence in the promotion and expansion of British influence. Perhaps inspired by Egyptian and European cooperation, British enterprise in Tripoli also focused on a health and vaccination programme to cover the Regency and Central Africa.

A notable feature of British imperialism overseas was the convergence of political pressure, economic imperative, strategic concerns and individual lobbying of agents that could lead to the 'pre-emptive annexation of economic deserts on geopolitical grounds'.[63] The lawyer and economist Charles Robert Prinsep (1789–1864) and Consul Warrington repeatedly made the case for a permanent British settlement in the Regency of Tripoli.[64] The multiplicity of demands on Britain to protect its commercial shipping and British subjects throughout the Mediterranean required that the naval bases also be maintained to an operational standard during times of peace as well as war. These competing priorities inevitably blurred the line between intervention and non-intervention in the region for the decades to come.[65]

The 1830s marked a colossal enlargement of Europe's zones of influence, occupation and rule and the commencement of an era of free trade. By 1830, Malta's trade had doubled following its occupation by British forces.[66] However, the continuing political crises sweeping the Ottoman Empire and the increasing power of Mohamed Ali in Egypt continued to occupy the attention of British government.[67] In a direct challenge to the Royal Navy, the French invasion of Algeria in 1830–31, signified the growing threat of the French fleets in the Mediterranean.[68] As a consequence, the British government responded decisively in 1831 by increasing its naval spending.[69] On the other side of the Mediterranean, Greece finally achieved independence in 1832. Despite its fears over Russian activity and influence in the eastern Mediterranean, Britain failed to assist Turkey in 1832 following Mohamed Ali's invasion of Syria. As a result, Sultan Mahmud II was forced to sign the Treaty of Hünkâr İskelesi (Unkiar Skelessi) that effectively provided Russia with a legal basis to intervene in future Ottoman affairs.

The fate of the Ottoman Empire was bound to the changing global political environment and European power politics. Britain's lack of a coherent policy towards Turkey contributed to its downfall. For Britain, its burgeoning global empire made imperial expansion irresistible, even if the immediate goals of conquest were not clear. British interventions in North Africa and the Middle East prior to 1839 are crucial to understanding British expansion. Ottoman provinces, such as the North African Regencies, including Tripoli, provide an opportunity to closely examine British activity over the course of the eighteenth and early nineteenth centuries. In turn, this enables a better understanding of British imperialism in the Middle East, particularly in the Fertile Crescent and Yemen in the modern era.

Britain's will to empire, to spread civilizing values, gave both the government and its agents a deeply ingrained sense of moral and cultural superiority. The Greek cause for independence against the 'despotic' rule of the Ottoman Empire continued to capture the British imagination. Greece, however ancient, was symbolic of Britain's inheritance of a superior system of governance that was to the British public, more just, more civilized and essentially everything that the 'barbaric' Ottomans were not.

In the end, British and European pre-eminence was not the result of 'commercial success or scientific prestige but of a series of forced entries or forcible overthrows'.[70] Britain's unplanned 'systems' resulted in political engagement and naval responses primarily directed by resistance, opposition and resilience. The combined effects of imperial agency, global developments as well as individual enterprise contributed to the shape and pace of British interventions in the Mediterranean. Fortunately for Britain, many crises proved themselves 'unusually amenable' to solution by sea power that placed 'pressure upon small states who were refusing or delaying redress to British subjects for alleged injuries'.[71] Nevertheless, the principle of interference in a sovereign power's territory by a foreign state, such as that of Russia in Turkey, was not a precedent that the British government could allow. In 1840, the Convention of London 'abrogated the main features of the Treaty of Hünkâr İskelesi which recognised the "ancient rule" that while Turkey was at peace no foreign warship should be admitted to the Straits'.[72] With the support of the Royal Navy, Britain's commercial ambitions and political interests in the region continued to grow, and Aden was consequently reoccupied in 1839.

Chapter 3

TRIPOLI: THE END OF A DYNASTY

Give a Turk money with one hand & you may take his Eyes out with the other.

– Richard O'Brien to Thomas Jefferson,
US Minister to Paris, 8 June 1786.[1]

We know little and understand less about the political, commercial and diplomatic connections between the Regency of Tripoli and Britain during the first half of the nineteenth century. Nor do we fully appreciate what factors made Tripoli an attractive base (as Figures 2 and 3 illustrate) for Britain to pursue its regional, political and commercial interests. In the final decades of Yusuf Qaramanli's reign, Tripoli became preoccupied with seeking new trading partners in Europe. Yet the Regency still retained its African orientation and its close economic ties with Central Africa, as well as its close identification with its immediate neighbours, especially Tunis and Egypt.

Tripoli supplied crucial provisions to the British Navy in Mediterranean entrepôts such as Minorca, Malta and Sicily, as well as military bases on Spanish territories that continued after the Treaty of Amiens (1802) and the termination of the Revolutionary and Napoleonic Wars. In practical terms, Tripoli served as a crucial point of supply and intelligence-gathering for Britain, and as a source of renewed imperial ambition for European powers, as well as for the United States of America. The British bridgehead in the Regency acted as a counterweight to French imperialism in the region and continued after 1814 in its efforts to protect British interests in the Levant and India, as well as to pursue its own imperial designs on the African continent.

Tripoli, as a port city, played a vital role in shaping British imperial strategy in the region, through contributing to the maintenance of Britain's naval garrisons as well as providing a base from which to develop British influence globally. What factors were unique about Tripoli which enabled a British imperial bridgehead to develop there during the rulership of Yusuf Qaramanli, and how did the Regency unwittingly permit British interests to override its own in the economic and political spheres? As an autonomous city-state, the Regency's economy and political stability was deeply affected by a series of exogenous shocks that in turn

Figure 2 Author unknown, *Marina di Tripoli; Tripolis*. Colour illustration of the harbour, fortress and hinterlands of the city of Tripoli, c.1780–90. Institut Cartogràfic i Geològic de Catalunya, Barcelona.

affected British activity in the region. At the same time, the Qaramanli government was under pressure to reduce its role and financial reliance on the slave trade. In a context of dwindling revenues in Tripoli, what steps, if any, did the Pasha take to address economic decline across the Regency? Crucially, to what extent did factors such as disease, famine, civil unrest and external intervention adversely affect the stability of Yusuf Qaramanli's government?

Focusing primarily on the Pasha of Tripoli's relationship with European powers, particularly Britain, the correspondence of the British consul provides an insight into how Tripoli asserted its autonomy vis-à-vis Istanbul and of the practice of autonomy by the Regency. Tripoli, like its neighbours, was tied to the European arena, as much as to a Mediterranean or African one, because the Regency looked both land- and sea-ward for its economic, social and political development.[2] The prospect of new commercial opportunities and access to the resources of the 'Great Sudan' proved a decisive driving force in the growth of Britiain's presence in Tripoli, and in the launch of successive exploratory missions from the Regency. Here is an account of the economic and political challenges faced by Tripoli during the reign of Yusuf Qaramanli, who ruled as Pasha from 1795 to 1832, as well as Tripoli's changing relations with European trading powers.

Figure 3 W. H. Bartlett and J. C. Varrall, *Tripoli*. Black-and-white illustration of the city of Tripoli and its surrounding areas, 1830. Institut Cartogràfic i Geològic de Catalunya, Barcelona.

The correspondence of the British consul from the Regency highlights Tripoli as an area of growing strategic importance for Britain. The letters and reports of the consuls at Tripoli, and the unique insights from those closest to the Pasha, overcome some of the challenges that persist of 'an important analytical space between general analyses of the growing capitalist world system ... and, on the other, the history of specific cultures or communities'.[3]

Tripoli's prominence in the political arena of North Africa, as well as its connections with its neighbours, made it an attractive base for any enterprising imperial state. At the time of Yusuf Qaramanli's accession as Pasha on 11 June 1795, Tripoli was considered as one of a triad of strategically important port cities, along with Algiers and Tunis. This relationship is explicitly reinforced by the accounts of Consul Simon Lucas and later, Acting Consul Bryan McDonogh. In fact, following the Sultan's firman in 1795, according to Lucas, Yusuf Qaramanli considered himself 'as far superior to any of the other States, in which he is now confirmed, by the Grand Signor's late favourable reception of his Ambassador, and restoring this State to its former Titles of Capitána or Chief of [the] three States'.[4] In April 1797, Consul Lucas wrote once more to the Duke of Portland, William Bentinck:

> The [Turkish] Ambassador is soon expected here with the Sultan's Grand Firman, or Decree, wherein he restores Tripoli to it ancient title of Capitana, or Chief of the three Barbary states – Algiers the Second, & Tunis the Third.⁵

The visit of an Ambassador from Istanbul was perhaps in no small part due to the failed coup by an Ottoman officer, Ali Borghul, which had led to Yusuf Qaramanli's father fleeing the castle in July 1793. Five years later, in 1802, Acting Consul Bryan McDonogh wrote to Lord Pelham, the Home Secretary, to inform him that Yusuf Qaramanli as Pasha was on 'the best of terms' with all the neighbouring states of Africa, and, in particular, had especially friendly relations with Algiers and Morocco.⁶ McDonogh added that Morocco and Algiers were in the habit of sending Yusuf Qaramanli annual presents of 'three or four ships loaded with grain'.⁷ The Pasha utilized this to the best commercial advantage and would sell these cargoes to the British garrison at Malta.⁸ Nine years later, in 1811, Tripoli's friendly relationship with Morocco was reinforced by ties of kinship between the Saif al-Nasser tribe of Fezzan and the Emperor of Morocco. On 10 July 1811, Consul Langford informed Lord Liverpool of the departure from Tripoli of a new bride for the Emperor.⁹ As well as being a niece to the late wife of the Emperor, the sixteen-year-old bride was also, according to Langford, a 'Grand Daughter of "Shake Seffannafsar", who has a considerable command in this "State".¹⁰ On the following day, the girl was conveyed to Morocco on a vessel chartered by Yusuf Qaramanli.¹¹ The Saif al-Nasser tribe remained of key importance for the British consul in later years.

Tripoli's place of pre-eminence, as emphasized by the Grand Signor's earlier Firman, was subsequently challenged by Algiers after 1802. This challenge, however, did not affect Tripoli's strategic relevance to the British consul and government. In negotiations for peace in London between the American and Tripoline Ambassadors, the latter proposed 'ninety thousand pounds sterling ... But he could not answer for Algiers: They would demand more.'¹² In other words, the inability of a Tripoline ambassador to represent Algiers' demands presents the possibility that the supremacy granted Tripoli was at best contested by Algiers and, at worst, was merely symbolic of the relationship that the Porte hoped to foster with Yusuf Qaramanli. Nevertheless, the American secretary of state underscored the importance of all three port cities for Britain and for its commerce in the Mediterranean, reporting that 'it is supposed that the peace of the Barbary States costs Great Britain about sixty thousand guineas, or two hundred and eighty thousand dollars a year'.¹³

An Autonomous Regency

Contrary to both popular belief and historical accounts, the Regency of Tripoli was autonomous from Istanbul in its political and economic decision-making. The Regencies of Algiers, Tunis and Tripoli by the early nineteenth century were effectively independent, and the Sultan's nominal authority was both ancient and obsolete.¹⁴ Although the Regency of Tripoli possessed a shared history as an Ottoman eyalet (province), Yusuf Qaramanli as Pasha paid no tribute, symbolic or real, to the Ottoman Porte. Whilst it is unclear when the practice of paying tribute had ceased, an account left in 1823 by the Tripoline ambassador to London confirms that this was the case in Tripoli by January 1823.¹⁵ Tripoli's perception of its independence is relevant as it allowed the Pasha to pursue his own commercial policies in the Mediterranean, as well as forging new diplomatic and commercial relationships with European states.

Tripoli maintained close relationships with its neighbours, especially Hammuda Pasha of Tunis, and, following the coup in Egypt, with Mohamed Ali and his son Ibrahim Pasha.¹⁶ Tunis in particular serves as a good example of the dynamic and close relationship that North African states could maintain with each other. In 1793, this unity was emphasized in a violent resistance to the centralizing policy of the Ottoman Porte that aimed to bring the Regencies back under the direction of Istanbul. Following the coup in Tripoli by the Ottoman officer Ali Borghul, Hammuda Pasha had sent his prime minister Mustafa Kogia, with a formidable force of 20,000 troops, 'well provided with stores and ammunition', to support Hamed Qaramanli (elder brother of Yusuf Qaramanli) in ousting Borghul and to reinstate the authority of the Qaramanli dynasty in the Regency.¹⁷ On the arrival of those troops into Tripoli on the morning of 9 January 1795, Ali Borghul fled the city, and Tunis was also able to reclaim the nearby island of Djerba. Consul Lucas provided a dramatic account of the events which then ensued:

> The Troops began to flock to the Gate by thousands in order to plunder the Town, nor was it in the power of their General to restrain them; but the Tripoleens very courageously not only refused to open the Gate but manned their Walls and Batteries ... The Tuniseans, who retreated but soon returned with two field pieces to force the Gate; which they must have done, had it not been for the courage and humanity of their Bey or second in command of the Camp who placed himself at the mouth of the Gun as they were going to fire it – during this time Sidi Hamed the oldest Brother, who is now our Bashaw and Sidy Juseph his Brother (our late brave Besieger) now our Bey, or next Heir to the Throne, were entreating the General of the Camp to recall his Troops and prevent the total destruction of their poor devoted city and the remainder of its Inhabitants, who were already reduced to the utmost misery and distress by the tyranny of their late Oppressor, and that a proper contribution should be levied on the People to reward the Troops as a compensation for what they might have made by plunder – the Troops were accordingly recalled, and Sidi Hamed the Bashaw entered the Town that evening amidst the acclamations of his poor subjects.¹⁸

Yusuf Qaramanli's first minister, Mohamed D'Ghies, otherwise known as the Minister for Foreign Affairs, and his family, maintained a 'confidential correspondence' with Ibrahim Pasha, held contacts 'high in the Algerine government', and had the personal confidence of Hussein Dey.¹⁹

In late January 1795, Hamed Qaramanli briefly took the seat of power, until he was replaced by his brother, Yusuf, less than five months after ascending the throne. Yusuf Qaramanli 'had been frequently applied to in private by the principal people, to save his country from total ruin, by resting the ruins of the Government out of his Brothers hands, and placing himself on the throne'.[20] Indeed, his elder brother was in a 'constant state of inebriation' and 'having but a very weak understanding gave himself entirely up to his pleasures'.[21] Yusuf then 'shut the Gates against that Drunkard ... and in less than half an hour he was seated on the throne, and proclaimed by the unanimous Voice, and to the great Joy of all his loving Subjects'.[22] Yusuf Qaramanli took the reins of government after more than five years of civil unrest, with the populace of Tripoli deeply impoverished and living in fear of further military incursions within the city walls. As the new Pasha, Yusuf Qaramanli was determined to reassert political authority and civil order. Tripoli's population was between 25,000 and 30,000 citizens, excluding Fezzan, whose number alone totalled 15,000.[23] The greatest proportion of foreigners in Tripoli were Maltese subjects, estimated in 1824 by Consul Warrington at 1,200 and then in 1828 at 2,000. There was also, according to the correspondence, a sizable Jewish population.[24] The city played host to an ever-changing collection of European agents, as well as merchants of France, Genoa and Naples. There were also Sicilians, Greeks, Turks, Sardinians and Corsicans living or conducting business within the city walls. Consul Warrington's 1844 account *A Short Account of Tripoli in the West* does not contradict the figures provided by the Tripoline ambassador to London in 1822, but the consul was specific about the population of the 'town of Tripoli' itself rather than the greater Tripoli area. He stated that Tripoli 'contains 12,000 Turks and Moors, about 1500 Christians, and Jews, say 2000'.[25]

In the sphere of education, the Regency had two well-established universities located not far from Tripoli, in Tajoura and Zanzour. The former, approximately 30 miles west of Tripoli, was the largest with 400–500 students in 1814. Both universities instructed in the disciplines of grammar, rhetoric, logic, law, mathematics and the Qu'ran (and commentaries thereon).[26] While notables of Tripoli did attend universities in the Regency, it was not unknown for them to send their children to be educated in Europe. Mustafa Kogia, a close friend and confidant of the minister for foreign affairs, sent his son to a boarding school just outside London. Children of members of the Tripoline elite were also sent to be educated at schools in Brixton and Hazelwood (in Birmingham) in England.[27] This is an example of the less tangible but nevertheless felt affinity towards England, and all the benefits it had to offer to future members of the highest political echelons in Tripoli.

Meanwhile, those families who had amassed a fortune in estates in and beyond the Regency also had a vested interest in the security and prosperity of Tripoli, and, by extension, of the Qaramanli government. Yusuf Qaramanli, like his predecessors, ensured that trade throughout the Regency was regulated at the ports and at the land gate of the Menshia. The Menshia was an area that effectively included the cultivated 'gardens' of consumable produce such as dates and citrus

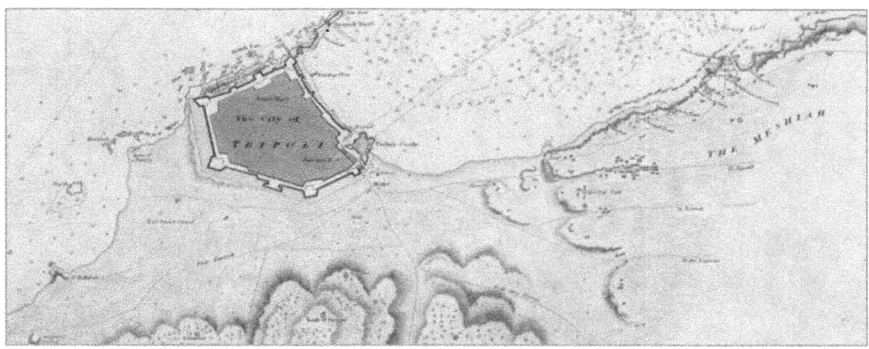

Figure 4 W. H. Smyth, *Plan of the Harbour of Tripoli*. Map of the city and greater area of Tripoli, showing the Menshia ('The Meshiah') – cultivated gardens – that extended from the city walls eastward and south into the desert, 1826–35. Institut Cartogràfic i Geològic de Catalunya, Barcelona.

fruits, and extended from the city walls into the country (as shown in Figure 4). During periods of unrest, these gardens also provided shelter for inhabitants fleeing the confines of the city. Foreign governments and individual merchants were levied with a percentage on goods that entered either at port- or land-side, and Britain claimed to possess the lowest burden of duty at 3 per cent.[28]

Lord Richard Grosvenor (1795–1869), on a visit to Tripoli in 1830, wrote in his journal that these gardens helped to set Tripoli apart from the other 'Barbary' states of Algiers and Tunis.[29] While Grosvenor was impressed with the gardens, he also noted the favourable defences (see Figures 2 and 5) and position of the city:

> The breeze ... bore upon its wings such fragrant odours from the gardens about the town of Tripoli, that, although we were full ten miles distant, they pervaded every part of the ship. Tripoli is well fortified to seaward, and has a small harbour to the eastward, protected by a low reef of rocks. It is capable of containing vessels of considerable burthen, having nearly sufficient water for a line of battle ship.[30]

Prospects as a British Colonial Settlement

Neither religion nor country of origin presented a bar to participation in the commercial or political life of Tripoli.[31] During the reign of the Qaramanlis, a Scottish renegade could rise to the trusted position of admiral-in-charge of the Raises (Captains of the Marine); an Italian could cultivate a career as personal agent and broker to the Pasha himself; and a Gibraltarian Jew could establish a successful career in trade with the Regencies of North Africa. Peter Lyle, in May 1794, had 'turned Turk' and became known as 'Murad Rais' following his embezzlement of part of the cargo of the *Hampden of London*.[32] Leon Farfara had

Figure 5 W. Balten and W. Crane, *Tripoli*. Depiction of the fortress and harbour of Tripoli [sketch and lithograph]. From R. Grosvenor, *Extracts from the Journal of Lord R. Grosvenor. Being an Account of His Visit to the Barbary Regencies in the Spring of 1830*, n.l.

once been a broker to the Pasha and had maintained the position until his untimely death in 1805.[33] Saverio Naudi had also acted as Qaramanli's broker in the 1820s and, in November 1825, was accused by the European consuls of 'undesirable' interference in the Pasha's relations with the Regency of Denmark.[34] Since at least the consulship of Richard Tully from 1783 to 1793, to that of Langford's in 1812, Abraham Abd' al-Rahman had been an established merchant with commercial interests in Tripoli.[35] According to Consul Lucas, Abd' al-Rahman was also once broker to his predecessor, Consul Tully.[36] It was this same openness to outsiders that made the Regency of Tripoli vulnerable, as well making the city an accessible and attractive base for foreign agents. These unique circumstances were utilized by Consul Warrington in particular, and, under his guidance, allowed a British imperial bridgehead to flourish. This pluralism was also reflected in the judicial processes of Tripoli. The Qadi and Government of Tripoli did not distinguish between their Tripoline subjects or foreigners when resolving legal issues. This approach was confirmed in a letter from the Pasha to the British consul in December 1831, when he wrote that the 'same justice' was dispensed to individuals, whether Turk, Christian or Jew.[37] This practice was in accordance with established customs, Muslim religious observance and the diplomatic protocol of other nation's jurisdiction over their own subjects in the Regency. Details of cases involving British subjects emerge on an infrequent basis in the consular diary.[38] Indifference to background and origin did not apply, however, in the upper echelons of the Qaramanli government, which constituted Yusuf Pasha's inner council of advisors and confidants in the Diwan.[39] The consul's time, beyond his political responsibilities, was more preoccupied with trade and shipping. The grievances that did arise entailed complaints or requests for redress over seized goods or perceived wrongs committed against merchants (and in particular against the Maltese due to their preponderance in the city). The production, import and sale of wine or other forms of alcohol was subject to strict regulation, as was the export or trade in specific local produce such as dates and olive oil.

By 1825, the imports to Tripoli from the Central Sudan were valued at £40,000 pounds sterling.[40] While gold dust came from Timbuktu, the trade in slaves, and other goods including various grains, gum Arabic, civet, olive oil, saffron, madder root, soap and senna came from the Sudan.[41] The early nineteenth century encompassed a period where slaves represented the 'single most valuable commodity in the trans-Saharan trade'.[42] At the time the three most important routes for the caravan trade into Tripoli were, as Figure 12 illustrates: Timbuktu–Ghadames, Bornu–Murzuq and the Kano–Ghadames route. All of the northbound trade of these routes, from across the Sokoto Caliphate, ended in Tripoli. A later Wadai–Kufra route was also developed that terminated in the east of the Regency, in Benghazi. The most important of these routes was the Kano–Ghadames way.[43]

The external pressure to reduce and ultimately end its participation in, and profit from, the slave trade contributed to Tripoli's growing economic and political instability. In the meantime, the trade in slaves from the south and southwest – the greatest majority from the Sokoto Caliphate and Bornu – remained a lucrative source of revenue for the Regency and its cooperating European agents. It has been conservatively estimated that between 1810 and c.1830, between 3,000 and 6,000 slaves reached Tripoli, not including the thousands that perished along the caravan routes to Tripoli.[44] Some of these enslaved were sold in the local market, and the rest transported overseas. The terms and scale of this trade in slaves began to shift because of the pressure exerted by European states, Britain's Slave Trade Act of 1807 and by British naval strength in the Mediterranean. While Yusuf Pasha initially maintained the stable government installed by his grandfather Ahmad Qaramanli in 1711, the changing local environment and European political climate began to create a series of ruptures in the traditional sources of income for the government's treasury and politically within the Diwan itself. Various expeditions were led against perceived French threats to British trade and empire (namely the invasion and occupation of Alexandria in 1801 and 1807) as well as against individual local powers, including Pellew's bombardment of Algiers in 1816.[45] These political and economic pressures resulted in part from the British government's responses to populist humanitarianism at home and emphasized the growth of the anti-slavery movement 'from below'.[46]

For Britain, the crippling cost of the Revolutionary Wars and the loss of the thirteen American colonies contributed to Britain's concern to protect its remaining Empire in the east, and British agents were to take the initiative in pursuing new avenues of exploration and revenue. While consuls were limited in the pursuit of their own commercial interests, for private gain, well before the consular reforms of 1835, the Colonial Department did not object to the exploration of commercial opportunities on behalf of the government. Consul Warrington, from the time of his appointment in November 1814, helped to define his career by seizing on the opportunity to foster Tripoli as a friendly base from which to launch British scientific and commercial expeditions into Central Africa. The consuls' dispatches to the Colonial Department routinely emphasized what would be of interest to government and to British society at large. Consul Langford in 1810 produced a report on the state of 'Corn', 'Cattle', 'Horses', 'Money', 'Tripoli Coin', 'Coast', 'Winds' and 'Current' in the Regency.[47] Consul Warrington later made a similar attempt, although in a letter to the secretary of state on 27 July 1815, he went much further and provided his opinion on the desirability and suitability of forming a new British settlement, not unlike the existing colonies in the West Indies, in Tripoli. In 1815, in a letter to Bathurst, Warrington wrote:

> In short the enlightened (comparatively speaking) Political Views of this Bashaw [sic] ... little difficulty would attend the British Government forming a Settlement on this Coast, should it at any future time be desirable. The Climate & Capability of the Soil is so well known to Your Lordship that I shall suffice it in only saying that it would produce every Article which is now grown in the West Indies.[48]

Britain's interests, as described by the consul, did indirectly impact on the government of Tripoli. Warrington gained an unusual amount of influence over Yusuf Qaramanli, and in so doing, undermined his rulership over the Regency until the Pasha's death in the summer of 1838.

'This Regency Is in an Alarming Position'

One of the first serious challenges which Yusuf Qaramanli faced, after taking power, was a five-year war with the United States. Although American shipping in the Mediterranean had been established by 1786, it was not until 1801 that 'any naval forces were available for warlike operations in the Mediterranean'.[49] Subsequent wars with Algiers and the forced voyage of the USS *George Washington* from Algiers to Istanbul, on the orders of the Dey, were immediately followed by a declaration of war on the United States by Tripoli on 12 May 1801.[50] The United States responded by ordering the dispatch of a squadron under the command of Commodore Richard Dale (1756–1826). This squadron blockaded two Tripoline cruisers under the command of Murad Rais in the Bay of Gibraltar, then proceeded to capture the Tripoline vessel *Tripoli* and blockade the port of Tripoli.[51]

The evidence suggests that the growth of the Pasha's naval forces began to stagnate between 1802 and 1828.[52] By 1828, Warrington wrote that although 'the capabilities of the place renders [it] very formidable if properly fortified', the Pasha's naval force now consisted of '2 Corvettes of about 300 Tons, 6 Brigs from 300 to 120 Ton, 5 Schooners from 180 to 80 Ton, 10 Gun Boats 5 Carrying 24 & 5, much smaller Guns'.[53] In contrast, in 1802, Acting Consul McDonogh had written that Yusuf Qaramanli had a strong maritime force and that he had brought all the chiefs to subjection; which happy event for this country opened a [illegible] intercourse through the dominions of Tripoli for the caravans that annually pass from Mecca and Fezzan to the different states of Barbary ... His Excellency the Bashaw is at present on the best of terms with all the surrounding African states, particularly those of Morocco and Algiers.

The Bashaw of the Regency has within these few years become rather formidable in his Forces. He can send to the field in a few days notice 20,000 horse, and 30,000 fighting men, which he had on a late occasion assembled on the plains near the city of Tripoli; for the sole cause of a false report that came from Malta by [a] Danish frigate that the Swedes and Americans have 20,000 men to land in the territories of Tunis and March them to Tripoli. His Excellency has in constant service 12,000 horse, and about 15,000 Levant Turks.[54]

While the American blockade of the port of Tripoli that began in 1801 was initially directed against corsairing activity by the Pasha's Raises, the dispute rapidly escalated following the US bombardment of Tripoli in July 1804.[55] As a consequence, the USS *Philadelphia* was burned in 1805 and almost 300 American naval personnel captured. Following prolonged negotiations and the eventual release of the captives, the Americans maintained their ambition to gain a foothold in the Regency. The following decade, in 1817, the Admiralty Office had received intelligence that the Americans were attempting to occupy Derna and the port of Bomba in Barqa.[56] In a report to Thomas Jefferson, the US minister to Paris, the US government outlined its ambitions to sign peace treaties with the states of Algiers, Tunis and Tripoli in order to establish American trade in the region:

> The United States should use every means to obtain a peace with the Barbary states, although it would cost vast sums, for until all obstacles are removed that prevent commerce we cannot expect to be a commercial nation ... They [Algiers] seem well inclined to a peace with us. The English, French, Dutch, Danes & Swedes and I may say all nations are tributary to them ... Money is the God of Algiers & Mahomet their prophet.[57]

Yusuf Qaramanli's declaration of war against the United States in May 1801 signalled to the world that the Pasha could, and would, successfully defend the Regency's commercial interests and territorial integrity against foreign incursion. The war with the Americans also highlighted, once again, the strategic importance of Tripoli on the North African coast. From 1810 to 1817, the Pasha had undertaken an expansive and costly programme to consolidate his power across the Regency. Within his own family, Yusuf Qaramanli declared war on his eldest son Mohamed, causing him to flee to Egypt in 1817.[58] By 1826, despite a number of military expeditions to Benghazi and Fezzan, Yusuf Qaramanli had failed to address the long-term economic woes of his government, and Tripoli's 1818 treaties with a number of European states to establish commercial trade did not achieve the necessary income for the treasury. In turn, the power and stability of the Qaramanli government finally began to falter in the eyes of the foreign consuls in Tripoli.[59] Against a backdrop of economic decline and rising levels of social unrest, a row was developing within the castle walls over who was the rightful heir to the throne. The succession dispute was between Ali Qaramanli, the son and recognized heir of the Pasha of Tripoli, and Mohamed Qaramanli, grandson of Yusuf Qaramanli. This feud continued for more than a decade until 1833, caused a prolonged civil war and was one of the contributing factors to the destabilization of the entire Regency, the downfall of the Qaramanli dynasty and the disruption of British commercial interests and ambitions in the region.[60] In fact, in 1828, because of the growing instability, the Maltese population of Tripoli requested that the British consul charter a vessel in order that they could leave the Regency and return to Malta.[61]

Throughout the reign of Yusuf Qaramanli, the Regency was affected by periodic outbreaks of famine, disease and civil unrest. In 1794 Consul Lucas despaired of the 'wretchedness' of his residence in Tripoli because of the war that was being waged by Yusuf and his elder brother to reclaim the throne from Ali Borghul.[62] Not only was the city effectively cut off from the rest of the Regency, but food provisions and other 'necessaries of life' were extremely difficult to find and prohibitively expensive to obtain. Following severe drought in 1802, Acting Consul McDonogh pleaded for pecuniary assistance from British government. The lack of rain, he wrote, had 'reduced the inhabitants to the greatest misery and … all the cattle [had] died for want of Pasture'.[63] These concerns and worries for the welfare of their families frequently preoccupied the consuls at Tripoli.[64] Widespread social discontent as a result of demands for tribute by the Pasha, his sons and his officials, went hand-in-hand with rebellions in the territories of Barqa and Fezzan. These insurrections primarily sought to challenge the authority of Yusuf Qaramanli through a refusal to pay the annual tribute to Tripoli.[65] In consequence, the Pasha periodically dispatched military expeditions to quell the revolts of Arab tribes and to extract their pecuniary token of allegiance to him and his Regency. By 1832, however, events had reached a turning point: the level of insurrection had enabled Abd' al-Jalil Saif al-Nasser to win the support of the rest of the Regency in challenging the authority of the Pasha. Warrington observed that

> [Abd' al-Jalil] is in possession of the whole country from Beneleed [Bani Waleed] to Mourzook, and not even the Hostages [Abd' al-Jalil Saif al-Nasser's wife and children] in Tripoli (In Irons and starving) will prevent Tarhoona, the Gharian & Gibel joining ab Gelleel. From Bengazi to Egypt is in a state of Revolt having refused to pay the usual Tribute.[66]

While the battle to subjugate Abd' al-Jalil Saif al-Nasser and the Awlad Suliman tribal confederacy had been waged since the reign of Yusuf Qaramanli's grandfather Ahmad, the Pasha's military expedition to impose his own governor at Murzuq displaced the established ruling elite of the Suliman over the territories of Fezzan. The new governor installed by force in 1811–12 was Mohamed al-Mukni.[67] The conflict with the Awlad Suliman gradually escalated over the years of the Pasha's reign. Al-Mukni was replaced by Mohamed al-Ahmar in 1820. While a succession dispute in the Qaramanli family continued in Tripoli, the Saif al-Nasser tribe, led by Abd' al-Jalil, once again challenged the authority of Yusuf Qaramanli in Fezzan in the summer of 1831.[68]

Yusuf Qaramanli's reign, however, came at a time of political and economic turbulence on a regional and global scale. The Revolutionary and Napoleonic Wars between Britain and France had spread over the Mediterranean and into North Africa. Over the course of more than thirty years, manoeuvres and counter-manoeuvres were made in Alexandria, and, by 1830, France had taken Algiers while making a powerful impression in Morocco.[69] As the 'European wars' ended, the Holy Alliance of 1815 had created turbulence for Tripoli, Tunis and Algiers. This was because Britain, along with the Ottoman Porte, declined to be signatories to the new European peace. The Alliance had given a renewed momentum to British activity, as the British government was concerned about the growth in Russian influence in the eastern Mediterranean and was anxious to maintain Ottoman territorial integrity as a bulwark against both Russian and French regional ambitions. Meanwhile, the Congress of Vienna issued a declaration against the trade in slaves to and from the ports of Africa.[70] For Tripoli, Tunis and Algiers, this new European policy was re-emphasised by the Exmouth Treaty of 1816. This treaty, signed on 29 April, was specifically aimed at addressing the issue of White (Christian) slavery on the North African coast.

Simultaneously, anti-corsairing vessels and a strong British naval presence in the Mediterranean further reduced the traditional sources of income for Tripoli and its neighbours. On 7 September 1815, the secretary of state wrote to Consul Warrington in Tripoli, as well as the consuls in Tunis and Algiers, to inform them that the British government would prohibit the sale of 'warlike stores' to 'any of the Barbary powers'.[71] These developments, beyond the shores of Tripoli and outside of the influence of the Pasha, resulted in profound political and economic change in the region as well as the Regency of Tripoli.

The government of Tripoli under Yusuf Qaramanli had reached the height of its power by 1818. The Pasha had repeatedly attempted to establish new commercial relations with a number of European states, including Tuscany, Naples and the Papal States.[72] With a view to broadening Tripoli's sources of revenue and in an effort to modernize the economy, the Pasha signed treaties with those powers in 1818. Over the following decade, much to the anger of Yusuf Qaramnali, only Tuscany followed up on its agreement and entered into commerce with Tripoli.[73] In the meantime, while the future minister for foreign affairs, Hassuna D'Ghies (1792–1836 or 1837), was already discussing the development of the agricultural sector as a means of strengthening the Regency's resources and economic resilience, the Pasha faced substantial debts, owed to his neighbours as well as to European powers.

From 1809, Tripoli's government had also attempted unsuccessfully to develop a cotton industry in the Regency, and, following a prolonged period of drought, to increase its agricultural output to meet the needs of its population.[74] Tripoli's economic woes continued, however, and in 1822 Mohamed Ali sent an emissary,

Mohamed Dorby, to Tripoli to collect the repayment of a loan totalling $250,000.[75] Yusuf Qaramanli, however, was not in a position to repay, and declined Dorby's proposal to cede Benghazi, Derna and Ougila (Awjila) for a period of twelve years to Egypt.[76] Consul Warrington wrote to Undersecretary of State Wilmot Horton shortly afterwards, to explain the reason for the Pasha's refusal to accept this compromise: 'His Highness … views an army of occupation for that period little better than a permanent conquest' and that such a settlement would leave Yusuf Qaramanli's reign in serious jeopardy, because the Pasha would lose 'the best part of His Territory'.[77] As an alternative, Dorby offered 'to take 2000 male slaves, to be delivered on the coast for the sum of 200,000$ being 100$ per Head and the other 50,000$ to be paid in Merchandise'.[78] In the end, according to the consul,

> His Highness has resorted to a New measure to liquidate part of [the debt], and which has not added to His Popularity. He required of all His subjects to advance one Black Slave (if Possessing) at the same time promising that He would send an Expedition to capture others to repay the Debt.[79]

While the Pasha was forced to take measures to meet the demands of Mohamed Ali, his relationship with Britain suffered. Warrington believed that the Pasha, in order to continue to meet the debt repayment to Egypt, would 'monopolize the entire Trade & to exclude all Christian Traffic unless they pay whatever Duty His Caprice may levy'.[80] This was in direct contravention of the treaty of peace with Britain, and the consul voiced his wider concerns about British commercial interests, particularly at a time when the provision of cattle, wool, corn and other produce from the port of Benghazi to Malta had increased.[81] To return to the peace treaties signed by Yusuf Qaramanli in 1818, these agreements were successfully concluded with the mediation of the British consul and the British government, and the Pasha believed that the British government had a responsibility to call the other signatories to account. The British consul disagreed, however, and the Pasha, frustrated and disconsolate in his inability to diversify the Regency's economy and broaden its revenue base, finally declared war on those states in 1826. In the same year Brazil had attempted to establish a 'friendly intercourse' with Tripoli, inevitably for the export of slaves, and proposed to send a Brazilian consul to the city. The Brazilian minister Plenipotentiary in Lisbon, Baron d'Itabayana (d.1846), wrote to Consul Warrington to ask him to communicate the same, on Brazil's behalf, to Yusuf Qaramanli.[82] The consul refused on the grounds that he had to receive such a request with the approbation of the Colonial Department, and as he had not done so, declined to fulfil the Brazilian minister's request.[83]

In the case of the United States, the war with Tripoli marked the beginning and end of the drive to establish a significant commercial presence in the region. As President Franklin D. Roosevelt observed over 100 years later,

> Diplomacy, unsupported by any semblance of a Navy, failed woefully to prevent the capture of our trading ships and even the enslavement of their crews … Following the adoption of the Constitution and in the continued absence of

a Navy, our Government was persuaded to follow a long-standing policy of European countries and pay tribute to the Barbary Powers in the hope of thus gaining security for our commercial shipping. Even such an unhappy and sorry compromise failed to stem the growing depredations upon our commerce, or to prevent actual declarations of war against us for no reason other than the smallness of our payments.[84]

When the United States Navy failed to establish itself in a suitable Mediterranean port such as Derna, it also failed in its attempt to gain a serious commercial footing in the region. Britain on the other hand, along with France, continued to develop their expansive political and trading interests in North Africa.[85] This was because Britain could, and frequently did, reinforce its treaty agreements with the threat of force. As Consul Warrington reminded Undersecretary of State Wilmot Horton, in June 1822:

When Fear ceases Respect will also cease towards our Great Nation by this Petty Barbary Power, and it has always been my first study to cultivate the latter upon the soil of the Former & I trust my successful Exertions have been approved by His Lordship.[86]

Tripoli offered an attractive base for political and commercial pursuits for both the Old and the New Worlds. The Regency had fired the imagination of the British consul and provided fuel to British imperial ambitions in the region. Apart from financial incentive, Warrington came to believe that the threat of force was the only way to bring a contested matter to a satisfactory end for Britain. This was a far cry from when the consul had written of his hopes for Tripoli vis-à-vis the Vienna Congress, only a year after taking up his first appointment as consul general to the Regency. He had written to His Excellency Bartholomäus von Stürmer (1787–1863), His Imperial Royal Apostolic Majesty's Internuncio on 15 February 1815: 'I must own I think the European Powers have always acted towards the Barbary States, in the most pusillanimous way, and that I trust in God that subject may not be considered as too insignificant to meet the Eye of Congress now assembled at Vienna.'[87] The relationship between Yusuf Qaramanli and the British government was, however, a tortuous one in which internal developments in Tripoli and external events negatively affected both the longevity of the Qaramanli dynasty and the future course of British enterprise from Tripoli into Africa. The city acted as a gateway to the resources of Central Africa and offered a direct means of making contact with the sovereigns of the interior. The consul aimed to open the road for British manufactures and other commerce. The ancient caravan route from Tripoli offered, as Warrington noted, 'the shortest way to the Niger' as the city connected to the Great Sudan via the towns of Ghadames and Murzuq. These towns were strategically important for Yusuf Qaramanli and, in part because of the lack of tribute payments, the Pasha ordered both to be subjugated and tribute extracted. Unsurprisingly, insurrections by the local tribes of Fezzan continued and contributed to the destabilization of the dynasty. A succession dispute, debts owed to foreign powers and dwindling sources of revenue to address these issues also severely undermined the authority of Yusuf Qaramanli.

Despite the Pasha's repeated efforts, only Tuscany honoured its agreement to enter into commerce with Tripoli. In this case, the British government failed to take the hand of friendship extended by Yusuf Qaramanli. The British consul then refused to assist the Pasha in reminding those states of their 1818 agreements, despite the fact that Consul Warrington had personally acted as mediator in the negotiation of those treaties. As previously mentioned, the consul also refused to present Brazilian proposals to establish a commercial trade with Tripoli in 1826. Throughout the Regency, periodic drought, famine, civil insurrection and serious conflict with neighbours combined with British and European activity to undermine the Qaramanli government and the established order in Tripoli. While the city remained a point of geostrategic concern for Britain, and offered a useful point of intelligence cultivation, Warrington continued on his short-sighted path of refusing cooperation or threatening the Pasha with military intervention. British relations with Tripoli did not recover after 1826, and British activity on the coast and interior ultimately failed to realize its ambitions, despite the promising start and, as the consuls repeatedly emphasized, all the benefits Tripoli had to offer the British Empire.

Chapter 4

TRIPOLINE NOTABLES

In the early nineteenth century, Tripoli was a bustling city of labourers, merchants, foreign agents and an ambitious landed political elite. This local elite encompassed those in the service of Yusuf Qaramanli, and members of his inner circle or Diwan. The Qaramanli government itself was subject to shifting spheres of political influence amongst the local Tripoline notables and the major tribal confederacies from Ghadames to Fezzan.[1]

An elite here may be considered as 'a selected and small group of citizens ... that controls a large amount of power ... [b]ased on the social distinction with regard to other groups of lower strata'.[2] At a time when relations between the elite and local population could at best be described as ambivalent, it is important to consider the ways in which foreign agents enlisted the assistance or cooperation of members of the elite and other Tripoline subjects that were available to them. The notables of the Regency were composed of the landowning and merchant elite of Tripoli. Yusuf Qaramanli's government – the makhazaniyya – was chiefly composed of an inner circle of counsellors – some of whom also constituted the Pasha's Diwan.[3] These advisors were, in the majority, selected from the highest echelons of the local nobility. Other key areas of government included the administrative, fiscal (treasury), judicial and military divisions. The most important administrative and political roles in the government were those of the Bey, who was usually given Benghazi or Derna to govern (and by the end of the 1820s, both); the Agha, in charge of the janissary corps; the kahiya who acted as the Pasha's deputy, in charge of the civil administration as well as the navy (in coordination with the Rais al-Bahr – the Captain of the Marine); the Rais al-Bahr; the chief or prime minister; the khaznader who was in charge of the state treasury, the 'little' khaznader who managed the Pasha's personal treasury; and the Sheikh al-Bilad who was responsible for the administration and effective running of the city, except in the case of naval matters which remained strictly within the remit of the Rais al-Bahr. Most of these members also constituted the jama'a al-Bilad or the city assembly, responsible for the effective running of the city and for the affairs of the Regency. There were ten large families that composed the city assembly and were responsible for managing the affairs of Tripoli. These members belonged to some of the wealthiest landowning families, and although the roles were not hereditary, there were occasionally exceptions such as for Mohamed

D'Ghies's son, Hassuna, who was appointed the role of minister for foreign affairs in 1826. Otherwise, notables maintained their roles until their death or voluntary retirement. The jama'a al-Bilad was led by the Sheikh al-Bilad. While the Pasha was the supreme authority and the 'protector and governor' of Tripoli, the Sheikh al-Bilad was responsible for representing the interests of the citizens and crucially of the notables of the city.[4]

The nobility of the Regency defined themselves primarily by their familial background, their wealth accrued from land, property or commerce, their learning – including of the Qu'ran and jurisprudence – and crucially their connections to the ruling Pasha, whether directly or through marriage.[5] The chronicles of the merchant Hassan al-Faqih Hassan (b.1781) provide a contemporaneous account of the economic and political life of Tripoli in the early nineteenth century. Hassan maintained close connections to Yusuf Pasha Qaramanli throughout his career in the city.[6] Hassan noted that by the close of the 1820s, there were 88 notable families that held power and influence in the affairs of Tripoli.[7] As landowners and urban notables they acted as intermediaries between the rural hinterlands and the Pasha of Tripoli, as well as between foreign agents including the British consul.[8] Tracing the seams of interdependence between the nobility and the Arab tribes during the early nineteenth century is challenging, though archival material details the Pasha's hostility to the tribes of the Gharian, Ghadames and the Fezzan – in particular, his assassination of the head of the Haleefa tribe, Sheikh Mohamed, and the attempted murder of the Sheikh's younger brother Wooma in 1831, as well the kidnap and torture of the Sheikh Saif al-Nasser's wife and children in 1832. Hostage taking as a practice was not infrequently deployed to force the compliance of rebellious tribes.[9]

The unusual amount of information available in English and French sources about the D'Ghies family are because of the unique personages of Hassuna and his father, Mohamed. In the last decade of the eighteenth century, sometime between 1792 and 1800, Mohamed D'Ghies had moved his family to Marseilles where he then established his fortune as a merchant. Hassuna D'Ghies (1792–1836 or 1837), from his own accounts to Jeremy Bentham, was a boy at the time.[10] There, although it is unclear when he and his family returned to permanently reside in Tripoli, Hassuna D'Ghies and (presumably) his siblings, including his younger brother Mohamed, became fluent in French. Hassuna had later learnt some English, although he continued to prefer to communicate mainly in French on his overseas trips. Hassuna, by his own accounts, had close connections with the neighbouring ruling nobilities, including with Ibrahim Pasha of Egypt, Shehu al-Kanemi of Kanem-Bornu and the emissary in Tripoli of the Dey of Algiers, Hamdan Ben Othman Khoja.[11]

The D'Ghies family was highly respected and esteemed across northern Africa and originally descended from eastern Anatolia, where an ancestor of Hassuna was sent as an emissary of the Sublime Porte. In more recent times, D'Ghies's descendants had settled in Gharian or the wider Jebel Nafusa range, which are to the southwest of Tripoli. Hassuna had at least two younger brothers, Mohamed and Saed, as well as two sisters, Khadija and Fatima, who married the Pasha's sons, Ali and Mustafa Qaramanli. Hassuna's father and family gave their time and assistance to a succession of British explorers in the early nineteenth century.[12] Hassuna in particular was learned, well-liked and respected by foreign consuls and the Tripoline nobility alike. He particularly took an interest in Tripoli's future and in its relations with European states, much as his great-grandfather and father had done. In late 1832 or early 1833, in a letter to Viscount Goderich, Secretary of State for the Colonies, D'Ghies explained his illustrious background:

> I am the sixth in lineal descent from an officer, who was selected by the Sublime Porte about one hundred and fifty years ago, from a family of Erzeroum in Asia [Erzurum in Eastern Anatolia], to be the Viceroy of Tripoli. The descendants of this person have occupied an eminent station in the province ever since that period. It was one of my ancestors who signed the first treaty ever made by Tripoli with Great Britain. Another [Mahmud Agas?] was Plenipotentiary at Stockholm and Copenhagen. One of my uncles concluded a treaty with the Republic of Venice, and my father [Mohamed D'Ghies] made and preserved peace with Denmark, Sweden, America, and Portugal.[13]

In the 1820s, shortly before he took the place of his deceased father as Tripoli's new minister for foreign relations, he actively sought to engage European consuls in Tripoli, philanthropic society in London, as well as Jeremy Bentham in addressing the economic concerns of Tripoli and the need for internal reform. D'Ghies's efforts at publicly engaging in the discussion of abolition is a case in point. During his time as emissary in London, and after discussions with D'Ghies, Jeremy Bentham (1748–1832) developed a new constitution for the Regency that proposed nothing less than radical reform. One of the goals was to improve the plight, in D'Ghies's view, of the 'ignorant' masses.[14]

With few exceptions, there has been little discussion of notables or members of Yusuf Qaramanli's Diwan.[15] There are also no studies to date that focus on Tripoline (or Tunisian or Algerine) elite lives and viewpoints on the vital economic, social and political issues of the day. This is perhaps because of the scarcity of material from such notables, but also because it was highly unusual for individuals, such as Hassuna D'Ghies, to write and contribute to extensive written records like those of Jeremy Bentham or of the Colonial Office. Bentham himself used the information D'Ghies provided to write a 'Constitutional and Civil Code' for Tripoli, while simultaneously undertaking the same for Greece.[16] D'Ghies was minister of foreign affairs to Yusuf Qaramanli from 1826 to 1828 and Hajj Mohamed Bait-al-Mal (b. c.1793) was chief to the Pasha's treasury. D'Ghies and Bait-al-Mal were also approximately the same age – D'Ghies was 31 in 1823 and Bait-al-Mal was 'about 30' in 1824.[17] The views of these notables shed light on British activity and the calamitous political developments in Tripoli from 1825 to 1832. The ways in which the British consul affected the future course of local notables' careers reveals the layers of influence possessed by Consul Warrington in the Regency.[18]

The Government of Tripoli

While the city as a Mediterranean port maintained a cosmopolitan identity, constituents of the nobility were made up of a mix of Arab, Anatolian and other 'Ottoman' ethnicities, as well as the occasional European. The latter were originally renegades or former slaves and were able to rise to senior positions, such as the Kahiya Mohamed, formerly a Russian renegade and who held his post for a substantial portion of Yusuf Qaramanli's reign.[19] Another renegade, Murad Rais, formerly known as Peter Lyle, was appointed Rais al-Bahr or Captain of the Marine in the 1820s, and Mustafa Gurji (or Georgia), a Georgian and son-in-law to Yusuf Qaramanli who was a Captain of the Marine in 1824.[20] There were many more notables in the other areas of the government, particularly in the judiciary. The local elite maintained the Ottoman patrician system in the Regency, in similarity to the neighbouring provinces.[21] While the Qadi was the religious magistrate, the provincial Qa'ids (or amils) were, in their respective subdivisions, responsible for individual districts. The Mufti was in charge of the marabouts and religious direction.[22] The marabouts, as clerics, were represented along the expanse of the trans-Saharan trade routes and were deeply respected by the local Muslim populations.

It is through the role of the kahiya, the work of the judiciary and the jama'a al-Bilad that the notables' connections to the wider populace can be traced. While the kahiya would sit at the city gates and dispense justice, so would those responsible for the administration of shari'a laws in the judiciary and religious direction in public, the latter being the work of the Head Marabout in the city. The provincial administration of the Qa'ids – as local chiefs – in particular led them to work alongside the Sheikhs of the Arab tribes within the Pasha's territories.[23] Other parts of the population, such as the Berbers, were recruited into the ranks of the army. Other notables of the Diwan, however, apart from commercial activities, land purchases and construction projects, were usually removed from the masses and their interaction was usually limited to each other, notables and leaders of the interior, such as Mohamed al-Amin al-Kanemi (1776–1837), Shehu (leader) of Kanem-Bornou and with the European consuls in the Regency. To the south of the Regency, in the region of the 'Great Sudan' or Sahelo-Sudan, scholars were esteemed as the 'religio-learned elites', and al-Kanemi was one of many more influential scholars and political leaders in the region. Yusuf Qaramanli as Pasha of Tripoli maintained good relations with Sultan Muhammad Bello (1781–1837), the third Sultan of the Sokoto Caliphate (modern-day Hausaland in northern Nigeria), Sheikh al-Mukhtar al-Saghir (d.1847) of the Qadiriyya order and Kunta confederation in the Western Sahara, and al-Kanemi of Kanem-Bornou.[24] In 1823, D'Ghies wrote about Sheikh al-Mukhtar in particular and explained:

> Of all persons in Africa ... he [Mukhtar] derives most power and consequence from a high reputation ... patriarch of a vast and nomadic tribe, inhabiting the extensive country to the north and north-east of Timbuctoo; he is beloved and

reverenced by his numerous adherents, not for his wealth and power alone, but for his sanctity, honour, and magnanimity ... He is incomparably the greatest Arab Power in Africa, hardly excepting the Chief, commonly called in Europe, the Emperor of Morocco, who would scarcely venture to insult him.[25]

The resident population of the city itself was segregated into a number of quarters according to religion, and the port quarter was the one area where the foreign consuls were housed, along with both Muslims and Maltese tradespeople.[26] The primary language of business, much as for consular and diplomatic business, was Italian, though merchants usually spoke two or three languages. Due to the flows of trade at time, brokers for the Pasha such as Gaetano Schembri as well as for the European merchants including one Joseph Coen were of a Jewish Maltese background. Unfortunately, even as resident landowners, Jewish families were the first in line to be persecuted, from demands by the Pasha that they vacate their properties to house hostages from Arab tribes sent to Tripoli, to being burnt at the stake for suspected collusion in political schemes.[27]

The slave markets of the Regency, as well as the influx of annual Hajj pilgrims, brought large numbers of caravans from the interior as well as along the coast. It is estimated that there were approximately 200,000 pilgrims making their way to the Hijaz – Mecca and Medina – by the seventeenth century, though by the nineteenth century this flow had reduced in volume because of colonial conquests and the 'subsequent economic downturns in the Islamic world'.[28] Until then, the evidence suggests that the 'regional economy was far more important than links with the outside world' and that the modernization impulses of the early nineteenth century were primarily a response to foreign interventions in the region.[29] While the travels of the pilgrims are poorly documented, the ancient trade routes and religious pilgrimage together connected large expanses of territories and underscored the ties of religion from the northern coasts down into West and Central Africa.[30] Merchants along these routes relied on mutual ties of faith and trust in conducting trade and those placed at strategic points along the routes were the brokers between the northern port cities such as Tripoli and the commercial centres of the interior, such as Kano.[31] By the nineteenth century, pilgrims were mainly scholars, merchants and rulers.[32] Depending on their means, pilgrims could take years to make the pilgrimage to Mecca and Medina. The overland route through Egypt to the Hijaz could be made easier by joining caravans at Cairo to travel on to Suez or al-Qusayr (Quseer) and sail across the Red Sea to Jeddah.[33] This, however, was an option only for the wealthiest, the majority continued for a further forty days overland in order to reach their destination. In the Pasha's inner circle, not all undertook the pilgrimage and this is perhaps telling of the levels of religious observance that notables felt incumbent upon them. Certainly there is little to indicate that the D'Ghies family were particularly religious in day-to-day terms. Hassuna D'Ghies's contemporary, Mohamed Bait-al-Mal, undertook the Hajj, but there is no indication that Hassuna ever did before his death. Religious observance, however, was not a factor that secured a notable's place in the Diwan. Wealth and connections to the Pasha determined a notable's role in the political life of the city.

In 1824, the dispensation of justice in Tripoli was undertaken by the Kahiya Mohamed; public business by the Sheikh al-Bilad, Hajj Mohamed Mahsen; private affairs by the Qadi; and public religious direction by the Head Marabout Buttabel. Mustafa Gurji, a landed and wealthy notable in the Pasha's council also expended huge sums in the construction of a mosque, and purchase of lands to support it. Gurji Mosque, completed in 1834, still stands in Tripoli today. Gurji's investment projects are significant in demonstrating how local notables deployed their wealth in the city and how they created 'vertical linkages' with different parts of society in Tripoli.[34] Despite these linkages, however, representation and ownership (of wealth and property) were inextricably linked in nineteenth-century Tripoline politics.

The Relationship between Agents and Notables

What motivated the British consul and local notables to cooperate with one another? Britain wanted trade and favourable access to the interior of Africa from Tripoli; and Tripoli equally desired trade and favourable access to the markets of Europe. In the case of the British consul, contact with the political elite of the Regency began in earnest with the commencement of a series of exploratory missions in 1817 by Joseph Ritchie (1788–1819) and George Francis Lyon (1796–1832).[35] These missions were then followed in 1821 by those of Dixon Denham (1786–1828), Walter Oudney (1790–1824) and Hugh Clapperton (1788–1827).[36] The arrival of these explorers and the launch of exploratory missions from Tripoli acted as a catalyst in the development of communication and cooperation with the notables of Tripoli, and the sovereigns of the Sudan. Relationships and indeed friendships were struck between the consul, the missions' 'travellers', and the local notables – such as in the case of Ritchie, Lyon and Mohamed D'Ghies, then minister for foreign affairs to Yusuf Qaramanli, and later his son Hassuna.[37] Executing the logistics and goals of the exploratory missions were the primary reason for the assistance offered by various Tripoline figures. This favourable situation was because Hassuna D'Ghies had facilitated a warm reception and assistance to Denham and his party with the people of Ghadames and the 'Arabs of the mountains [Gharian]'.[38] Relations between the north and the interior of Africa became difficult by late 1825 because of the disruptive effect of the Fulani jihads, particularly during the war between Bello and al-Kanemi. Nevertheless, the following year, in March 1826, Hassuna D'Ghies still attempted to facilitate the work of the exploratory missions by writing to al-Kanemi.[39] The British consul tended to speak just as positively of a few other notables he met during the course of his work, at least in the first months – most notably Bait-al-Mal and Abubakr Bu Khalloum.[40] Bu Khalloum was a highly respected merchant and was employed to assist the travellers and to provide a means of introduction at key points along the travellers' route into the interior.[41] Warrington fostered relationships with individuals in the Pasha's Diwan only in so far as the service they could render him or the explorers. In Bait-al-Mal's case, in August 1823, Warrington explained to the Under Secretary that he continued to remain indebted to the treasurer for his sustained assistance to the consul on matters unspecified. In particular, Warrington recommended that a sum of $500 be 'quietly' given to Bait-al-Mal to ensure his continued expressions of friendship to Britain.[42] The consul emphasized that this was in agreement with Bait-al-Mal.[43] The repeated references to the consul's indebtedness to Bait-al-Mal appear to have been for the good favour consequently bestowed, following Bait-al-Mal's intervention, by the Pasha for a planned mission south to Kanem-Bornu. In fact, Bait-al-Mal was so successful with Yusuf Qaramanli that the Pasha, on 8 July 1823, personally wrote a letter to al-Kanemi recommending the British travellers to the Sheikh's favour:

> Thank God for your kindness & for the Information you have given us … as regarding our son Bobaker Bukaloom that He is safe arrived with you … also the English Travellers Our friends & that you have received them with such warm friendship & that you were pleased to see them there & that you have Shewn all Particulars of your Dominions both by Land & water & to their great satisfaction.[44]

In fact, Yusuf Qaramanli went further and asked al-Kanemi to enable the explorers of the mission to go beyond the boundaries of Bornu to the territories of the Great Sudan, and requested al-Kanemi to solicit the cooperation of the 'shiek's of those countries' or even to use force to progress the course of the missions.[45] Less than two years later, in May 1825, Warrington drew attention to the 'special' powers bestowed on him by the Colonial Office in a letter to Earl Bathurst to secure further assistance from Bait-al-Mal and, in turn, Yusuf Qaramanli. He wrote that those instructions, dated 3 October 1823, gave him the power 'to promise at a future period a small Equipment of Artillery, & also a Present to Haggi Mohamed Bethelmal [sic]'.[46] Warrington also recommended that further presents be made, in addition to the arms and $10,000 already promised for continued cooperation and the safe return of Major Alexander Gordon Laing (1794–1826) as well as to act as a reward for the release of Greek slaves by the Pasha in 1825.[47] As the consular correspondence indicates, gifts, or the promise of them, appear to have solicited a considerable amount of assistance to both the consul and the numerous British exploratory missions to the interior. The offer of pecuniary incentive was a policy long-established in relations with Yusuf Qaramanli, although Consul Warrington felt that pecuniary tokens to members of the Diwan facilitated a greater level of aid and 'friendship' than could ever be secured personally from the Pasha. In the latter case, the British consul as the most senior agent took a limited engagement with the Pasha of Tripoli on the subject.

This unequal footing between the two powers was primarily due to Britain's position of influence and military strength in the Mediterranean after the Napoleonic wars. It was unfortunate for both sides, however, that British and Tripoline ambitions were affected by short-term interests. Consul Warrington was motivated by the hope of gaining a safe passage for an exploratory mission or in securing peace for a friendly nation, while the Pasha had come under increasing pressure to generate revenue. Yusuf Qaramanli repeatedly attempted to shirk the responsibility of protecting the travellers on their expedition from Tripoli, or in ensuring their safe return. Despite being paid an agreed sum of £2,000 to defray the costs of providing a safe escort, in the end Yusuf Qaramanli would permit the explorers to leave Tripoli only if accompanied by a military escort of 200 cavalry. Warrington's efforts to secure assistance through the provision of 'pecuniary tokens' had backfired. The travellers feared they would receive a hostile reception as they would arrive not with a small escort as originally agreed, but instead with an armed force. It is unclear whether this force was simply intended as a display of his military strength, or as a threat of aggression towards the Pasha's powerful neighbours to the south of the Regency.

Local merchants and officers of Yusuf Qaramanli, both Maltese and Tripoline, had frequent and regular contact with the British consulate for the purposes of obtaining passes for ships and cargo, as well as for settling disputes between themselves or with the Pasha's naval officers. Contact and interaction with Qaramanli's ministers and other political figures within the Regency usually took place with the sanction of the Pasha and with a specific purpose in mind. There is little evidence to suggest that the consul showed any friendship to persons outside the foreign consular families and his own network of vice-consuls. Otherwise, the houses of the consular agents in the city were clustered together in one designated quarter and they and their families were isolated from opportunities for contact with the local elite, except at the invitation of Yusuf Qaramanli, or of one of his wives to the women of the consular households.[48]

Before being appointed a minister in the Qaramanli government in 1826, Hassuna D'Ghies had also acted as foreign emissary for Yusuf when in Europe, and during one of his longer visits to England in 1821 had presented his credentials as ambassador to London.[49] D'Ghies would have presented himself in much the same way as his predecessors had done during the reign of the Qaramanlis.

To a limited extent, and in exceptional circumstances, the Pasha did attempt to present his interests directly to British ministers in London through the dispatch of an ambassador, and by letters to King George III.[50] While consul in Tripoli, Warrington appeared to be unaware of Hassuna D'Ghies's activities and growing connections in Europe, and his unannounced dispatch to London. The deployment of a Tripoline emissary is insightful in what it reveals about the changing position of the British consul in Tripoli, rather than any influence an ambassador from the Regency could exert in London. Warrington's animosity towards D'Ghies appears to have begun in earnest when D'Ghies arrived in England in 1821 and was received as the accredited Tripoline ambassador to London. In particular, the consul viewed this step by the Pasha as a means to bypass him as British representative in order to conduct business directly with British ministers of state. In May 1822, the consul wrote to Oudney and Denham:

> If D'Ghies has been received as the actual & accredited Tripoline Ambassador depend on it you will suffer, as The Bashaw [sic] will resort to His Old Trick of

Humbug excuse the Term a Game that He may successfully play at a distance when a Bystander would immediately detect His object.

While the consul was taken by surprise, his underlying objection to D'Ghies's mission was that he believed he would be 'unpleasantly situated' in Tripoli – excluded from communications between Tripoli and London because one of his primary functions as intermediary would be effectively suspended. Following D'Ghies's arrival in London, the Pasha reneged on the original agreement with the consul to ensure the safety of the African Association's expeditions for £2,000 and demanded further sums from Warrington. In June 1822 Warrington once again wrote to Oudney and Denham to complain about the Pasha's treatment of him following D'Ghies's arrival in London:

> It having been intimated to me that Mr D'Ghies had been received as Tripoline Ambassador to the British Court, I expressed my surprise that His Highness has not mentioned it. He unblushingly said that He had told me of it. I replied that ... He laboured under [a] Mistake – He answered 'that you now know it & that is sufficient'. Such an Expression addressed to me in my Public capacity or as an individual must naturally awaken every sensation of displeasure. Therefore with a dignified look I made my bow and wished Him Good Morning.

Warrington also expressed shock at the acceptance of D'Ghies's credentials because past government practice was to not receive resident ambassadors from Tripoli or from other foreign powers without prior application and approval by the relevant minister of state. This had been the case in 1811 with Hajj Mahsen when General Oakes had communicated to Consul Langford that Mahsen would not be received as an official emissary of Yusuf Qaramanli to London. D'Ghies's accreditation and eventual arrival in London in June 1821, however, should have come as no surprise as the consul had been involved in an attempt to postpone the arrival of an ambassador from Tripoli as early as August 1819. Nevertheless, despite the recognition of D'Ghies as Tripoline ambassador in the summer of 1821, Warrington continued to complain about the perceived breach of diplomatic protocol by Yusuf Qaramanli, and the Pasha's subsequent treatment of him, to the Colonial Office. The purpose of D'Ghies's visit was officially to move the British government to revise the imposed debt settlement of 1 October 1813 that had been negotiated by à Court on behalf of Spain.[51] This was because the settlement was not in Yusuf Qaramanli's favour and only sought to repay the monies owed by the late Spanish consul in Tripoli from 1796 to 1814, Don Gerardo José de Souza, to (amongst others) Hassuna D'Ghies's father Mohamed, and other brokers and merchants in Tripoli. In May 1822, à Court wrote to the undersecretary of state, Wilmot Horton, and detailed that, of the 57,776 debt, 13,049 was owed to 'Turks' – and of this 5,039 to Mohamed D'Ghies. A further 19,632 was owed to 'Christians' and 25,095 to 'Jews'.[52] D'Ghies also made his case to Bathurst that his father had not received the promised repayment of de Souza's debt from the Spanish government. In any case, the agreement concluded by the British ambassador had explicitly laid aside the claims of the Pasha in full, as à Court subsequently explained:

> The Convention, I am ready to admit, was a disadvantageous one to the Bashaw [sic], but it was one the nature of which he certainly never misunderstood for a single instant ... it was of the highest importance that the Spanish resources should be as little diminished as possible, & her commerce unmolested & their considerations alone induced England to interpose between Her & the Barbary Powers.[53]

D'Ghies's mission was underscored by the intimate ties of marriage between the Qaramanli and D'Ghies families. Ali Qaramanli was 27 in 1822 and was married with children to Khadija D'Ghies. Mustafa was 18 in that same year and married to Hassuna's second sister, Fatima.[54] Ali was heir to his father's throne, on account of the eldest Mohamed having been exiled to Egypt, and Ahmad, the second eldest being 'infirm' of mind.

Warrington continued to maintain a cooperative relationship with Bait-al-Mal for several years, from the consul's first recommendation of him in July 1823 to at least March 1828.[55] This relationship was in contrast to many others in the Pasha's council, including Sidi Hamet, Yusuf Qaramanli's prime minister (Figure 6). The prime minister, by 1824, was seventy-seven years of age and was married to a sister of Yusuf Qaramanli, and only by virtue of this connection did he maintain political office, otherwise, in the consul's opinion, he was 'useless' and 'unworthy of confidence'.[56] In July 1823, Warrington wrote to Wilmot Horton about the unusual level of influence, in his view, that Bait-al-Mal held with the Pasha. Further, Warrington strongly recommended the treasurer to the Colonial Office for the services which he had rendered to the British consul:

> I am particularly indebted of late to Haggi Mohamed Bethelman [sic]. He has unbounded Influence, & in some measure is to the Bashaw [sic] what the Shaik of Bornou is to the Sultan. His Highness told me that He even loved Him more than His own Eye Sight. His is a superior man & a determined character and with His good offices (which I now have) I can accomplish anything. I beg leave strongly to recommend Him as a fit Person for His Majesty's favour, as any mark of Favor or however trifling would be equal in Result to 20,000$ given His Highness.[57]

The following year, in October 1825, Bait-al-Mal interposed with the Pasha, on behalf of Consul Warrington, in the case of a Sardinian vessel sailing under the protection of the British flag.[58] Two years later, the treasurer once again intervened to assist the British consul, when he advised Warrington to detain a British ship of war, the *Isis*, to ensure the Pasha would provide protection to Clapperton. Bait-al-Mal reassured the consul that he would take whatever steps were necessary to ensure the return of Laing's papers.[59] How Bait-al-Mal negotiated his relationship with foreign agents such as the British consul is unclear, though Warrington wrote

Figure 6 A. Earle, *Prime Minister to the Bay of Tripoli*, 1815–17 [watercolour and black pencil]. This was, in fact, 'Sidi Hamet', prime minister to the Pasha, Yusuf Qaramanli. National Gallery of Australia, Canberra.

that, as late as August 1830, the treasurer had continued to remain a 'valued' member of Yusuf Qaramanli's Diwan.[60]

The Qaramanli succession dispute that began in 1822 and continued to flare up intermittently until at least 1832 also brought the British consul into communication and professed friendship with notables of Fezzan and the Kingdom of Kanem-Bornu. Intermittent wars on the fringes of Tripoli – in the Central Sudan – and recurrent civil conflict within the Regency also affected the formation of new alliances and caused the rupture of existing friendships between the consul and members of the local political elite. The threat of a wide-scale civil war became a particular preoccupation of D'Ghies, who was earnest in his attempts to prevent political instability in Tripoli. In January 1823, while in London, D'Ghies wrote that, as a result of the coming disputed succession in the Qaramanli family, a serious danger was posed to both the safety of his own family and to the established order in Tripoli.[61] His position was made significantly worse because of the British consul's claims to the Pasha that Hassuna D'Ghies was complicit in the murder of the explorer and his son-in-law, Alexander Gordon Laing. D'Ghies had anticipated the political upheaval that the coming decade would bring to the Regency, and he was sincere in his ambitions to improve the system of governance, both for the survival of the current political elite in Tripoli and for the general populace. D'Ghies was keenly aware of the privileged position he held, and the work of his father in establishing both the wealth and status of the D'Ghies family.[62]

A Tripoline Perspective

The years 1822–5 represented the height of the ambassador's political activities overseas. D'Ghies's publication 'A Letter Addressed to James Scarlett' provides a welcome departure from the Eurocentric perspective and public rhetoric on the slave trade, in order to attempt to open a dialogue on the intimate connections between the traffic and the issues of economic and political reform in the North African provinces. This publication was an explicit departure from the official rhetoric of the Qaramanli government, and some of the statements contained therein were dangerous for a Tripoline notable and soon-to-be Qaramanli minister.[63] It may have been that the ambassador neither envisioned a political career within Yusuf's Diwan nor was concerned that such a document would reach the attention of the Pasha. In any case, in 1822, in an address to a meeting of the African Association, D'Ghies explained the reliance of Tripoli and its neighbours on the slave trade:

> Gentlemen, that the *land trade of negroes* is a *principal branch* of the commerce of Morocco, Algiers, Tunis, Tripoli, and Egypt, and that thousands of negroes, intended for sale, supply their public markets. Indeed, at a certain time of the year, they are like your bank notes, which circulate from hand to hand for want of specie. Yes, you must certainly make the Northern coasts enter into the same views as the African Institution, as a preliminary towards the absolute abolition of the slave trade.[64]

The time spent by Hassuna D'Ghies in Europe over the course of eight successive years allowed him to develop an expansive set of contacts, and importantly, to articulate his ideas about the reform of the government in Tripoli and on measures to curtail the slave trade.[65] He envisioned permanent change through the introduction of a constitution that sought to redress the autocratic and absolute powers of the Pasha in Tripoli. He believed that he could do this through slow but purposeful reform, and with Yusuf Qaramanli's consent. He also had faith in his close ties to the Pasha, and as a last resort, the ability of his sisters Khadija and Fatima to help persuade Yusuf's sons of the credibility of his political ideas.

The other major preoccupation of D'Ghies was the evil of the slave trade. He strongly felt that European attempts, including those of the African Association, to abolish the trade in slaves were misconstrued and were not viable long-term solutions in ending the capture and export of slaves from the African interior. In the early 1820s, both of these contentious but popular topics drew Hassuna into the philanthropic and political circles of London during his residence in the City of Westminster.

On receiving an invitation to attend a meeting of the African Association in 1822, Hassuna D'Ghies wrote to his friend Sir James Scarlett, M.P. (1769–1844) about the Association's intention to abolish slavery in Africa. D'Ghies felt that 'neither religion, nor country' was an obstacle, as distance was surmountable and religion 'a necessary restraint, rather than a rampart which tends to separate society'.[66] In his correspondence with Scarlett, Bentham and other friends in England, he expressed his frustration that the evil of slavery and the abolition of the traffic were not being addressed within a broader framework of political and economic reform. D'Ghies observed that African states 'mutually make war on each other, in order to obtain from victory, those resources which they know not how to draw from a state of peace'.[67] He further emphasized that, on the West African coast, there remained a great demand for slaves in the states of North Africa, and that captives were additionally sent to Persia through Abyssinia and the Red Sea, as well as to Izmir (Smyrna) and Istanbul. D'Ghies went on to explain to Scarlett the futility, in his view, of the superficial attempt to bring about full abolition, adding that

> the cause of wars cannot be abolished either by the Congress of Vienna, or the Holy Alliance; and the number of *men-hunters* will always be the same. But although the slave trade ... is sufficiently profitable to the vendors and purchasers, to induce the first to continue to kill as formerly, and the last, advantageously to supply the markets of America.
>
> There cannot therefore result a reflux of captives in the markets of the interior, for the vendors might destroy, at less expense, towards the Western coasts, such of their *flocks* as remain a burden; and the purchasers will besides know how to find in the *monopoly* of this smuggling, sufficient to pay them for their trouble and risk, even though they were obliged now and then to throw their unhappy victims overboard in hogsheads, at the unexpected approach of some English ship of war in order that they might not themselves be subjected to punishment from the *new laws of humanity* ...
>
> Now, I do not know if it is not better that the negro captive should be sent to plant sugar and coffee in a foreign land, rather than suffer a certain and useless death from the sword of the conqueror, who cannot dispose of him.[68]

In 1823, Bentham described D'Ghies as his 'dear son'.[69] And Scarlett spoke in Parliament of the 'ancient and illustrious family' of the D'Ghies, that he was proud to be able to call Hassuna his friend, and that the British government owed a deep debt of gratitude to this family which, instead, it had repaid with 'ingratitude and neglect'.[70]

D'Ghies's friendships and his activity during his time in London also provide an insight into the diplomatic life of the city and offer an alternative view of politics and life in the Regency of Tripoli. The perspective of Hassuna D'Ghies and his political friends in London is important as it helps to balance the perspective of the British consul in Tripoli. The affection felt for D'Ghies extended beyond his professed anti-slavery sentiments and had in fact began with D'Ghies's provision of assistance to Lyon and Ritchie in their mission to explore the African interior.[71] Bentham's utilitarian proposals in his paper 'Securities against Misrule' provide a further indication of Hassuna D'Ghies's acquiescence in, if not explicit consent to, a vague plan to overthrow the government of Yusuf Qaramanli, in the event political reform could not be introduced through peaceful means.[72] The document is in fact a partial plan to supply equipment and arms to assist in a military offensive against Tripoli from Malta.[73] Indeed, it is also clear from both D'Ghies's published letter to Scarlett as well as his later petition to parliament that he had had help with the drafting of these documents.

The Influence of the British Consul

The decline of the Regency in the final years of Yusuf Qaramanli's reign created a political vacuum in which foreign agents could exercise an unusual level of influence, and, in this context, notables such as D'Ghies had to petition for foreign assistance in an attempt to re-secure their position and status in Tripoli. In 1836, while Consul Warrington was still the British representative in Tripoli, Scarlett provided the following summary to the House of Commons on the negative influence of the British consul general in the Regency:

> [Mr Scarlett] would content himself upon the present occasion with noticing the disastrous state to which the regency of Tripoli had been reduced by the indiscretion, he would not use a stronger term, of the British agent.[74]

At a time when the fortunes of the elite in Tripoli were fragile, D'Ghies's position and his family's estates were at risk of being lost as a direct result of the consul's influence with the Pasha. Meanwhile, in Tripoli, Warrington began to attack various members of the D'Ghies family, particularly two of D'Ghies's siblings, Mohamed and Khadjia (wife to the heir Ali Qaramanli). In the summer of 1822, in a bizarre case, Warrington accused Khadija D'Ghies of having faked a pregnancy and of an attempt to obtain the infant of the late Spanish consul's daughter.[75] D'Ghies's activities, and the friendships that grew from his time in London, lasted until at least 1834, when former acquaintances such as Scarlett had rallied around him in support of his petition over the wrongs committed against him and his family by the British consul in Tripoli. In his efforts to seek redress and to have Warrington's interventions curtailed by the British government, D'Ghies submitted a lengthy petition to Parliament in 1834. However, this appeal to the House of Commons came to little, and Warrington remained as consul general.

In Tripoli, Warrington was motivated to make the acquaintance of any knowledgeable locals who could be of service to British exploration of the interior of Africa and in particular the Kingdom of Kanem-Bornu. Individuals such as Abubakr Bu Khalloum had a good reputation, although he did not hold political office.[76] While it is unclear how Warrington obtained information on individuals with whom he did not usually have reason to come into contact, he nevertheless found opportunities to communicate directly with local Tripolines that went beyond officially sanctioned channels. This method of obtaining cooperation was particularly evident in the consul's enlistment of the assistance of Bu Khalloum. Bu Khalloum was 'well known and highly respected through the whole [of] northern Africa' and that the travellers' success 'would be certain if they have such a person with them'.[77] All went well until Consul Warrington and the explorers were provided with a greater level of assistance than the Pasha had originally sanctioned.[78] The Pasha then promptly ordered Bu Khalloum to return to Tripoli, and explicitly warned all parties that failure to do so would result in the termination of the protection extended to the travellers by his authority.[79] This incident goes some way to demonstrate how closely the Pasha guarded access to both the people and the territories around him. A friendly disposition towards foreign agents was promoted, but only in so far as it served to gain the Pasha's treasury valuable coin. Yusuf Qaramanli's frequent demands for money proved to be a source of enormous vexation for the consul. Warrington also disliked dealing with any but the most senior of the Pasha's Diwan, and Yusuf Qaramanli himself. The consul's scorn became at best indifference when dealing with the Captain of the Marine Murad Rais. This was in part because of Murad Rais' past as a Scottish renegade who had, during the consulship of Simon Lucas, allegedly embezzled British cargo and deserted ship in Tripoli.[80]

The formative years of Warrington's time as consul in Tripoli are important in considering the ways in which he began to ingratiate himself with Yusuf Qaramanli and members of his council. Initially, on his first encounters with the D'Ghies family, the consul wrote warmly of both Hassuna and his father, and of the 'friendly disposition' they showed towards the 'travellers' and to the British presence in the Regency.[81]

By February 1826, following D'Ghies's appointment as minister for foreign affairs, the relationship between the consul and D'Ghies had resumed its former friendlier footing, with D'Ghies having approached the consul to enquire about progress in England on the abolition of the slave trade.[82] In the same month, Consul Warrington had also written to the Danish consul, Andreas Peter Knudsen (1793–1865), to assure him that Hassuna D'Ghies had 'pledged His Honor' that Yusuf Qaramanli would not make a further demand for tribute for the renewal of treaties between Tripoli and Denmark, and that Consul Knudsen could 'depend on' the assurances of D'Ghies in the matter.[83] By November the following year, cooperation between the consul and the D'Ghies family continued, as Warrington wrote to Hay on 7 November 1827:

> I will recollect one Evening walking in the British House & conversing on different Topics with Mr. Hassuna D'Ghies, the Foreign Policy of this Government became the subject, when I remarked that Sweden and Denmark paid the Bashaw [sic] a large annual sum, that His Highness ought from Policy alone to respect those nations and evince every kindness and good will to those Representatives.[84]

In August 1828, however, the cooperative relationship between the minister and the consul was abruptly ended by Warrington. The consul had received confirmation in Tripoli that Laing had been murdered on 24 September 1826 on his return from a successful mission to Timbuktu.[85] Warrington subsequently accused Hassuna D'Ghies, Mohamed D'Ghies and the French consul, Baron Jean-Baptiste-Louis-Jacques-Joseph Rousseau (1780–1831), of having conspired together to orchestrate the assassination.[86] Warrington also believed, though again without any evidence, that Hassuna D'Ghies was continuing to interfere in affairs between him and the Pasha, and as a consequence, that he was once again at risk of losing his influential position in Tripoli. Warrington had caused the French consul to be recalled to Paris and attempted to bring about the imprisonment and execution of D'Ghies on his return to Tripoli. Like the cooling of the friendship between the British consul and Bait-al-Mal, deep hostility towards French activity in the Regency and in Egypt served to stoke the fires of suspicion that these Tripoline notables were actively colluding with French agents such as Rousseau to challenge British interests and activity in the region. On 29 August 1828, having received the news of the death of Laing, Warrington wrote a pained letter to the Secretary of State Sir George Murray (1772–1846):

> He died by murder three days beyond Timbuctoo ... In the first attack He received twenty four wounds Eighteen of which were of the most Serious nature which was merely a Preface to the most barefaced and diabolical murder thatever was committed, and I apprehend the Treacherous Proceedings which I always suspected will now be fully realized. His journals & Papers are yet to be had, & having this moment received the account my sorrow does not admit of Detail.[87]

In May 1829, only a few months after the confirmation of Laing's death, Consul Warrington stated his conviction that Consul Rousseau and Hassuna D'Ghies had orchestrated the murder of Laing and the theft of his papers.[88] While the investigation of the murder was ongoing, the consul and the Pasha offered a reward totalling $2,500 for the recovery of the explorer's papers. They were, however, both unsuccessful in inducing any person to come forward and cooperate, understandably so despite the Pasha's promise to pardon any persons involved in the affair.

It was no coincidence that, only a few weeks later, D'Ghies was confirmed as having lost his position as minister and was no longer regarded as a trusted member of Qaramanli's council.[89] According to D'Ghies, however, he had had no involvement in either the murder of Laing or in the theft of his papers. Moreover, he recounted the repeated assistance and cordiality extended to all the travellers by his family. D'Ghies's accounts of the events following the death of Laing were consequently rather different to the consul's and he continued to proclaim his innocence throughout the turbulent political years that followed. In 1834, D'Ghies submitted his petition to Parliament that was both a defence of his character and a condemnation of the British consul's behaviour in Tripoli. This petition was a request for redress and D'Ghies's attempt to secure his own, and his family's, welfare in the Regency. Eleven years previously, in January 1823, D'Ghies had told Bentham that the 'greatest fault' in Tripoli was insecurity of property.[90] It was no surprise therefore, that, following Warrington's intervention, the D'Ghies family's property had been sequestered.[91] The former minister had also stated to Parliament that Warrington had a direct hand in the civil unrest that had plagued Tripoli and that the consul was actively involved in activities 'to destroy the Petitioner's family and friends, including the present Pasha [Ali] his brother-in-law'.[92] Finally, D'Ghies believed that Warrington was attempting to 'set an Adventurer supported by some wild Arabs upon the Throne' and therefore force the landed political elite, including the D'Ghies, to abandon their properties and flee Tripoli.[93]

In the end, Warrington conflated external events and his deep-held suspicion of 'Mussulmen' to cause a permanent rupture in relations that had been fostered between him and Bait-al-Mal, D'Ghies and, ultimately, Yusuf Qaramanli himself. The mission to Timbuktu was limited in its success as Laing was murdered and his papers recording his endeavours had disappeared. Warrington had caused a protracted diplomatic row with both the French and American consuls, as the consul strongly believed that Laing's murder and the theft of his journals was on the behest of the French consul, and with the knowledge of the Pasha.[94] In August 1830, just two years after Bait-al-Mal had secretly assisted Warrington, the consul concluded – despite a lack of evidence – that Bait-al-Mal, like the D'Ghies family, had worked in the interest of the French and had conspired in the assassination of Laing, along with the chief protagonists Rousseau and D'Ghies. That same month, Warrington had further written to Murray about Bait-al-Mal's alleged continued complicity in the affair and that he had persuaded the Pasha to 'disavow all participation in the charge against Rousseau'.[95] The consul wrote that, following his questioning, Hassuna D'Ghies had prepared to flee, and that Bait-al-Mal had been kept 'out of the way' in Benghazi during the course of the investigation. The consul was also convinced that Bait-al-Mal knew the whereabouts of Laing's missing papers and became even more so following Bait-al-Mal's despatch to Paris as 'special envoy'.[96]

In 1828, when Warrington had received confirmation of Laing's death, the French consul requested a fresh declaration of the Pasha's respect for the neutrality of the Regency. Consul Warrington, however, had refused to support the French consul on the grounds that such a measure was unnecessary as it would supersede the existing treaty provisions between Britain and Tripoli. He added that he had also received no orders to seek a fresh declaration of Tripoli's neutrality. Moreover, that Yusuf Qaramanli would not accede to such a request 'as it would involve His

Highness in War with the Porte, which wishing to avoid He would naturally refuse such a formidable Document against Himself'.[97] He concluded that 'the Christians are thoroughly respected, & it appears of little consequence what may be the Policy, as long as His Highness observes the strictest Neutrality'.[98]

For Hassuna D'Ghies, he ultimately found no redress through appealing to the British government. On 19 April 1836, Scarlett summarized the political situation in the Regency, and D'Ghies's situation, thus:

> The Petitioner [D'Ghies] was therefore previously to the late revolution and rebellion in Tripoli in the situation of a man who for his honest endeavour to ameliorate the condition of his country by legal and honourable conduct was deprived of his situation in the service of his Sovereign compelled by an ignorant barbarous and corrupt Agent of the British Government to abandon his Country and his family with the loss of fortune and health and was reduced to solicit in vain the impartial attention of the Colonial Department, to his case.[99]

The relationships established between British agents and members of the political elite of Tripoli were few in number and volatile in 1822–31, during the height of British activity in the Regency. The need to provide the British explorers with logistical assistance, as well as a safe passage beyond the territories subject to the authority of the Pasha, necessitated that the British consul develop his acquaintances with notables of the Qaramanli Diwan, as well as with Yusuf Qaramanli himself and powers beyond the borders of the Regency, including Sultan Muhammad Bello. Warrington's professed friendships with the treasurer to the Pasha, Mohamed Bait-al-Mal, and the minister for foreign affairs, Hassuna D'Ghies, were short-lived because of the political instability within the Regency, as well as the tragic incidents outside the control of these individuals – including the murder of Major Laing in 1826. The relatively short lifespans of the exploratory missions combined with a lack of understanding about the regional affairs of the Regency, all exacerbated communication and cooperation between the two sides. The cumulative effect of these issues did not make for stable or lasting connections between Tripoline notables and British agents, including the consul.

Through successive roles as ambassador to London and later as Qaramanli's minister for foreign affairs, the exceptional life and career of Hassuna D'Ghies provides a unique and unexpected insight into the life of a privileged member of the elite in Tripoli, a notable's perspective on the political issues of the day in Britain, as well as the difficult relations that could be experienced with the British consul. Notables such as D'Ghies and Bait-al-Mal highlight the friendship and assistance extended to the consul's endeavours in the Regency, despite the perceived insolence and bullying behaviour of Warrington at the court in Tripoli. The accounts left by Hassuna D'Ghies and his friends in London reveal that he and his father were both keen to explore different ways to introduce political reform and greater representation throughout the Regency. Moreover, D'Ghies felt that to effectively reduce, and in turn abolish the slave trade, European powers needed to adopt a longer-term strategy to assist the governments of the North African states in diversifying their sources of revenue. This strategy might have included measures such as agricultural reform and a greater level of trade in manufactures with Britain, France and their European counterparts. Contrary to the views of the British consul, there was a desire within the Pasha's Diwan to quickly and peacefully resolve the succession dispute, and to avoid the outbreak of civil war across the Regency.

D'Ghies's testimony and Scarlett's representations to Parliament emphasize the highly contentious role of the British consul. Warrington repeatedly acted according to his own personal convictions, including in pursuing Consul Rousseau and Hassuna D'Ghies for collusion in the murder of Laing. The British consul did not follow official instructions to desist from interfering in the dynastic succession dispute that had plagued the Regency. The desperate pleas of D'Ghies to the British government in 1834 highlights just how far the consul's influence was able to extend in Tripoli. Hassuna, and his entire family – despite the position he and his father had held, and despite his sisters being married to the Pasha's sons, including the heir to throne – were at serious risk of permanently losing the reputation, respectability and property they had accrued in the Regency. Warrington's influence with Yusuf Qaramanli, aided by his sporadic threats of military aggression against the Pasha, had served to banish the Regency's treasurer to Benghazi, and had lost a minister his position, causing him to flee the Regency. Altogether, these relationships between Warrington and the notables of Tripoli in the years 1823–32 witnessed a calamitous end to Yusuf Qaramanli's rule. The activities of the consul had caused upheaval in the lives of a number of the local political elite, providing evidence of an unprecedented rise in the role and activity of the British consul at Tripoli.

Chapter 5

THE BRITISH CONSUL AT TRIPOLI

In Britain, while there were concerns over the British government's overseas spending, following the American War of Independence (1775–83), diplomatic and consular activity in the Mediterranean nevertheless reflected a British Empire in the ascendency.[1] British consuls were occupied in renewing formal treaties of 'friendship and commerce' with North African powers with the aim of securing strategic British garrisons across the Mediterranean, providing effective communication channels on political and military concerns, and exploring new opportunities for commercial enterprise. Meanwhile, the Regency of Tripoli occupied, and acted as a bridge between, two distinct political and social spheres – one firmly African-Ottoman and the other European-Mediterranean. Tripoli as a port city provided a meeting point for these two worlds – a place where Christians, Jews and Muslims intermingled and transacted for the purpose of profit.

This discussion proposes a more detailed and nuanced understanding of the role, professionalism and skillset of the consuls to North Africa, and in particular, to the Regency of Tripoli.[2] To what extent did the British consul at Tripoli act autonomously and exercise diplomatic privilege? The exercise of personal initiative also significantly expanded British representation through the fostering of a vice-consular network that branched out from Tripoli.[3]

A Competitive Field

The daily work of the British consul concerned the protection of British subjects and trade as well as the promotion of strategic British interests in the overlapping regions of North Africa, the Middle East and the Mediterranean. The consular caseload involved the registration of the births, deaths and marriages of British subjects, the registration and issue of passes to ships stopping at Tripoli and, in turn, the investigation of the maltreatment or murder of a British subject. Detailed accounts and reports of the state of geography, politics, trade and resources of the Regency and the surrounding provinces began to be undertaken in earnest with Consul Langford's arrival in Tripoli in June 1804, although Simon Lucas, prior to his appointment as consul, did undertake an exploratory account in the territories to the east of Tripoli in 1788–9.[4] As his successor,

Warrington continued the provision of regular communications and, following Captain Smyth's survey of the North African coast, the consul published his own account – *A Short Account of Tripoli in the West* – in 1844.[5] The consuls provided detailed, albeit rather subjective, reports on the history, politics, and commerce of the Regency, though they were not consistent in their coverage of subjects, nor did they provide these accounts on a regular basis.[6] The Colonial Office finally instituted standard reporting templates in an attempt to capture information systematically and to encourage the consuls to adhere to set guidelines for the submission of reports.

There were also other British agents who temporarily served between the permanent consulships of Lucas, Langford and Warrington. They included Bryan McDonogh, James Somerville, Pat Wilkie, Joseph Dupuis and J. Fraser – who was sent to Tripoli to 'assist' Warrington in his duties following serious allegations of misconduct against the consul. Figure 7 is a list of British agents at Tripoli from 1795 to 1832.

William Wass Langford arrived as consul general Tripoli on 26 June 1804 and remained in that post until his forced departure from Tripoli on 24 January 1812.[7] Previously, Langford had acted as secretary to Consul Lucas in Tripoli as early as August 1793.[8] Following Langford's recall, and until Warrington's arrival as the new consul general in November 1814, Bryan McDonogh served as the acting consul. He had been formerly employed as a surgeon at the British consulate.[9] Lucas and McDonogh had become close, and in his last will, Lucas had left the last of his material possessions to McDonogh as his 'adopted son'.[10] The vital role played by the consul as the most senior British agent to Tripoli was underscored by the untimely recall of Langford in 1811 and his eventual departure from the city in January 1812.[11]

His Majesty's Agents at Tripoli, 1795–1832			
Name	Position	From	To
Simon Lucas	Consul	24 July 1793	4 May 1801
Bryan McDonogh	Acting Consul	4 May 1801	end 1803
William Wass Langford	Consul	26 June 1804	24 Jan. 1812
Patrick (Pat) Wilkie	Proconsul	20 Jan. 1812	20 July 1813
James Somerville	Proconsul	20 July 1813	28 Nov. 1814
William à Court	Ambassador	after 1 Aug. 1813	end 1814
Hanmer Warrington	Consul	28 Nov. 1814	1846
Joseph Dupuis	Vice-Consul	10 Nov. 1826	to at least 17 Oct. 1831
J. Fraser	Vice-Consul	end Nov. 1830	-

Figure 7 A list of the agents officially appointed to Tripoli during the reign of Yusuf Qaramanli. ᵃNote that the vice-consuls stated in Figure 7 are not part of Warrington's effort to develop a vice-consular network in and beyond the Regency.

Consuls Lucas, Langford and Warrington varied in professional backgrounds, but not in their motivations for seeking a consulship. While most British consuls, including Warrington, had a military background, others such as Lucas and Langford had started their careers as secretaries and vice-consuls in the region.[12] Other British agents, including Ernest Toole, James Somerville and J. Fraser, also held military rank. In the exploratory missions, from which Toole was originally recruited, several members were also of officer background. This included Major Dixon Denham, Lieutenant Hugh Clapperton and Major Henry Beechey.[13] Ranks roughly corresponded with the seniority of individuals in their new appointments and the location of their posting – Colonel Warrington as consul general, Major Denham as head of the southern and southeastern missions, and Ensign Toole and Major Henry Beechey as vice-consuls, respectively, to Kuka and Benghazi.

At least two of the consuls, Langford and Warrington, also landed at the Regency with large debts and in serious financial difficulty. Lucas and Warrington had the additional responsibility of large families to support. Unfortunately, the correspondence reveals very little about what happened to Lucas's fourteen family members who had accompanied him to Tripoli. In 1798, Lucas did write, however, that his 'poor dear wife [was] no more', having died on 11 January 1790.[14] In May 1801, after Lucas's death, McDonogh provided some additional information on his predecessor. Despite having earlier described himself as Lucas's 'adopted son', he continued:

> [M]y worthy friend Mr Lucas in one of his frolicks got married to a Dame of easy virtue belonging to Barbary, but shortly after the happy union the Lady not content with the embraces of an old man, a mutual separation took place, and divorced by the same Clergyman that married them. The Lady as I am informed is to be married one of these days to a Frenchman under the Tree of liberty but not in Tripoli, as no Tree of that name (thank God) grows in the Bashaw's [*sic*] Dominions.[15]

Apart from bringing three servants and a governess for his young family with them to Tripoli, Warrington increased his family to ten children with his wife Jane and had an additional three children with his long-term mistress Clara Portelli in Tripoli.[16] Langford suffered the misfortune of losing all his worldly possessions while en route to Tripoli, in a fire on board the *Hindustan*. In February 1807, in reply to Secretary of State William Windham's request for further information about the losses he claimed to have suffered in the *Hindustan*, Langford complained:

> I know not how to express my disappointment that my Memorial for a compensation of my losses in the 'Hindustan' has not been attended to – the misery and inconvenience We have felt from that shipwreck, in a country like this, has been almost insupportable.[17]

Windham's reply, which had served to only increase Langford's despair, was decisive. The secretary of state questioned Langford's honesty and requested from him an impossible amount of evidence to submit in order that his appeal for compensation to be reconsidered:

> Your Claim for compensation for your losses by the wreck of the Hindustan has not been attended to … [I]t is indispensably necessary before you receive any compensation whatsoever, you should produce the strongest evidence the case admits of … What the nature of this Evidence can be, whether the Bills of the Tradesmen who supplied you with the Articles lost, and those Bills vouched by the Testament of the Tradesmen themselves, or whether by the Testament of Persons of Credibility who witnessed your having been in possession of those Articles you had lost, or whether by the Evidence of both, you are the best Judge.[18]

Langford's claim, on its own merits, was rather large at £3,890, and the Colonial Office correctly estimated this to be 'an amount equal to the outfit of an Ambassador to an European Court'.[19] Even by 1825, nineteen years after the consul's original claim for compensation, the cost of the 'outfit' of an ambassador to Turkey was £2,500, with Austria at £3,000, and Russia and France at £4,000 each. In the end, Langford could not provide the necessary proofs of ownership, and was never reimbursed for any part of the losses that he said he had sustained on his way to Tripoli.[20] In the end, the consul left Tripoli as he had arrived, with little to no official assistance and with his continued deep impoverishment ignored.[21] Like his predecessor Lucas and his successor Warrington, Langford appeared unable to gain any assistance following an unfavourable end to his consular career in Tripoli. Ultimately, Langford could not secure the necessary patronage at home that would have eased his anguish and financial difficulties in both Tripoli and, following his recall, in England.[22]

The consular salary itself was modest and was traditionally supplemented by the trade and commercial enterprise of individual agents. Following the reorganization of the management of the consuls to Algiers, Tunis and Tripoli, mercantile and trading pursuits were no longer permitted. On 28 November 1814, Warrington received a salary of £800 on his arrival in Tripoli with no trading or mercantile pursuits permitted, and he was provided with an additional allowance of £150 for a secretary.[23] By the end of his career as British consul to the Regency, his salary had doubled to £1,600 per annum, and this was the pay granted to his successor, Consul George Crowe.[24] The situation for the consuls was altered for the worse, however, following the reforms of 1822 and 1835, which aimed to reduce their remuneration and to prohibit any commercial activity by British officials overseas.[25] Warrington's career finally ended following his consulship at Tripoli, while Lucas died at his post, and Langford a couple of years after his departure from Tripoli. Consul Langford had, in his dispatches, described himself as the 'longest serving' consul in the Mediterranean, and Warrington, by 1832, had been stationed as consul general at Tripoli for eighteen years, and this would increase to a total of thirty-two years on his retirement in 1846.[26] When Warrington was appointed consul general and landed at Tripoli in November 1814, he actively supplemented his income by acting as chargé d'affaires, until at least 1826, for Holland, Portugal, Naples and

Tuscany.²⁷ By June 1826, the British consul had earned $5,600 from these additional duties.²⁸ Indeed, Warrington (see Figure 8) established himself as a charismatic and ambitious man in Tripoli, and he made a strong impression on those whom he met. In 1830, Lord Richard Grosvenor wrote of his meeting Warrington following his arrival at Tripoli, and his impressions thereon:

> The consul, his son, and the vice consul, were there to receive us. Uniformity of costume is not the characteristic of our Levantine consuls. The east is the region of fancy, and it is remarkably exemplified in the dresses of these distinguished individuals. They seem determined to represent their master in every function, civil and military. The hat of a field marshall, the coat of an ambassador, the epaulettes of an admiral, the trowsers, boots and spurs of a hussar, present a model of united service, which could only have been produced by the ingenuity of an Oriental imagination.²⁹

According to this description, as well as a faint image of the consul in his 'English Garden' in Tripoli, the standing figure depicted in Lyon's account of his time in the city (see Figure 8), is probably also of Consul Warrington.³⁰

Figure 8 G. F. Lyon, *Triumphal Arch: Tripoli* [sketch]. Lyon, *A Narrative of Travels in Northern Africa* (London: John Murray, 1821), 19.

In the case of Simon Lucas, he had begun his consular career in 1768 when he had been appointed vice-consul under Joseph Popham, consul general to Morocco.[31] Lucas continued to act as vice-consular agent successively in Tetuan and then Tangier in 1772 under Consuls James Sampson and Charles Logie. He also operated at a time when commercial activities were not explicitly prohibited by the government, and, combined with 'some trifling emoluments of office', he had managed to support himself during his postings.[32] In 1777, while Consul Logie was in England, Lucas was additionally charged with the dispatches of Rear-Admiral Robert Man (c.1748–1813) to the emperor of Morocco relative to a British vessel belonging to Young & Green of Poole that had been taken by one of the emperor's cruisers.[33] Lucas succeeded in the restoration of the vessel, cargo and crew. However, despite his constancy in fulfilling his duties, he still had not received an official wage from the secretary of state for his loyal services of 'near ten years'.[34] Prior to securing the consulship at Tripoli in 1793, Lucas had invoked precedent to repeatedly call on the government for remuneration for his earlier services as vice-consul. By 1790 he had succeeded and obtained £250 from the Lords Commissioners. He did so by drawing on General Cornwallis's warrant of 1772 and a salary of £100 that had been previously paid by the government to 'a Jew Vice Consul named Jacob Benidér' in 1767.[35]

From February 1784 until the writing of his memorial in August 1790, Lucas had occupied the vacant position of 'Oriental Interpreter' in His Majesty's government. The role is explained concisely by one Dr John Gilchrist in a letter to Lord Castlereagh in June 1805:

> The oriental interpreter to the king may be considered a subordinate branch of the secretary's office for foreign affairs, or in the board of controul; and, were the memorialist honoured with the appointment, and encouragement commensurate to the utility and exertions which might be expected of an office of that description under him, he would hazard credit as an Orientalist, that the British metropolis would, in a reasonable time, produce a number of gentleman, adepts and proficients in all the oriental tongues … no person can hold any office in this department without appropriate qualifications for the duties required.[36]

Consuls Lucas and Langford were fluent in the languages of the Qaramanli court, including Arabic and Italian – languages used by both the ordinary populace in Tripoli (both Tripoline and foreign) and the political elite of the city. Lucas also claimed fluency in Spanish and French and could clearly demonstrate his loyalty and dedicated service to the Crown. As oriental interpreter in London, he remained close to the political and diplomatic life of the court. This role may well have played a part in securing him the position of a consulship to Tripoli and he duly arrived in the city on 24 July 1793.[37] His successor, Langford, had also held the position of oriental interpreter in London following his return from Tripoli in May 1812.[38] There is little information on Langford's background, but in Lucas's case, and according to the available records, he had spent at least eighteen years working for the British consular service, though he displayed the ability to utilize and translate correspondence in Arabic from Tripoli to London, and his skills as a linguist were further confirmed by his appointment to the government as official interpreter of the 'Oriental languages'. In contrast, Consul Warrington did not possess any experience in the consular profession though he did, in his military capacity, briefly serve in Spain in 1812. In order to develop his communication with the government of Tripoli, Warrington used his children as interpreters – his son Frederick for Arabic and Italian, and his daughter Emma for French.[39] In 1830, Lord Grosvenor added that the consul's younger daughters, Louisa and Jane Warrington, also spoke Arabic 'perfectly'.[40] With the development of the vice-consular network, Warrington also utilized the local knowledge and language skills of the Rofsonis, Caravanas and Regiginianis and later, the Gagliuffis.[41] Even after decades in Tripoli, Warrington continued to rely on others. Following an injury to his chief dragoman, Mustafa (see Figure 9), Warrington had consequently found himself unable to present matters of import to the Pasha.[42] He told Bathurst in June 1826 that 'not being able to have audience of the Bashaw in consequence of Sidi Mustapha being dangerously ill … I waited on His Highness's Minister & demanded the Restitution of the Louisan schooner of Hamburgh'.[43] The consul's ambition and personal qualities had triumphed over his linguistic shortcomings, though in some cases had been reprimanded for sending inadequate translations of correspondence.[44] Abraham V. Salamé, the official interpreter in London during a large portion of Warrington's consulship, undertook the translation and correction of translations forwarded by Warrington.[45]

In Tripoli, Consul Warrington not only conveyed the dispatches of the explorers and of his vice-consular agents on to London, but he had also usually acted as the conduit for official communication between the Pasha of Tripoli and the British government. The evidence further suggests that the consul frequently provided substantially different accounts of the representations he had made to the Pasha and his subsequent activities in his official capacity as consular agent. In May 1818, Yusuf Qaramanli had employed an agent, one Mr Gueddalla, to transmit a letter via the emperor of Morocco. The Pasha's address to King George III contained serious allegations against Warrington, including the regular extraction of 'sums of money at interest' by the consul. In this letter, the Pasha wrote that Warrington had demanded the punishment of a Tripoline Rais that had captured a Hanoverian prize. However, once the Rais had been hung from the mast of his own vessel, the consul then demanded $8,500 for the loss of the ships voyage 'which sum was much above the value of both ship and cargo'.[46] Yusuf Qaramanli detailed several other complaints about the consul, and added his disappointment that despite having previously raised the issue of the consul's conduct with both à Court and Pellew, that neither had responded to any of the charges that had been laid against Warrington.[47] Like D'Ghies's later complaints about the same consul in 1834, the Colonial Office took no action over the allegations and there is no record to indicate that a reply was ever provided, merely that an official, likely to have been the undersecretary of state, had noted on the back of the letter; 'This does not appear to require any answer'.[48]

Figure 9 A. Earle, *not titled (Mustopha, Head Dragoman to the Consul of Tripoli)*, 1815–17 [watercolour, black pencil and pen and ink]. National Gallery of Australia, Canberra.

Warrington's lack of trustworthiness and dishonesty about his actions while consul has been detailed by both Tripoline and British agents, including D'Ghies and Dixon Denham. In May 1818, Yusuf Qaramanli utilized an alternative means, like Denham would later do in 1822, to circumvent the British consul in order to transmit correspondence to England.[49]

While there may have been substance to the consuls' often poor financial state, particularly following their arrival at Tripoli, the Orders in Council of 1822 and the later drive to alter the way in which the consular service operated suggest a government that was concerned less with the professional capacity of its agents, than with a desire to curtail overseas expenditure.⁵⁰ In part, the Colonial Office was responding to a demand at home to save money and to reduce 'unnecessary' overseas spending, primarily in the form of salaries and expenses.

It is also clear that patronage was an important factor in the appointment to, and service of, public office for at least Lucas and Warrington. Lucas and Warrington enjoyed influential friends in England, and all three benefitted from connections in the government in order to gain their appointments.⁵¹ In Lucas' case, he bemoaned the case of Consul Logie, who, following his forced departure from Morocco, was able to secure the position of British consul general at Algiers, and that he, Lucas:

> never had an opportunity of forming connexions or procuring Friends at home who might be serviceable to him, owing to the many years he resided abroad … was consequently deprived of Patronage and Protection sufficient to recommend his hard case to His Majesty's humane consideration.⁵²

This claim is hard to believe when Lucas cited in his memorial no fewer than five respected figures who had been involved in recommending his case for both pecuniary recompense and for his capability if granted a consulship in any of the Regencies of Algiers, Tunis or Tripoli.⁵³

The Exercise of Autonomy and Diplomatic Privilege

Since the seventeenth century the Levant Company was responsible for the management of consuls and diplomats to Istanbul and the 'Barbary States', as well as other agents stationed throughout the Levant. Following Napoleon's invasion of Egypt in 1798, the management of British consuls to Algiers, Tunis and Tripoli underwent a series of changes, because of governmental reorganization and reform at home as well as political and economic developments in the Mediterranean. The supervision of these consuls now fell under the purview of the Colonial Office. The decline in the fortunes of British merchants in trading centres such as Aleppo and Izmir (Smyrna) contributed to the end of the monopoly of the Levant Company in the Eastern Mediterranean. Despite this change, the consuls appointed to North African posts continued, until at least 1835, to exercise a level of autonomy and diplomatic privilege in the service of British imperial interests.

On arriving at their destination, Consuls Lucas, Langford and Warrington all encountered challenging political and social conditions that tested their capabilities to the full. With an often unstable or threatening political climate, Lucas and Langford repeatedly appealed to London for assistance, though without success. Indeed, in 1794, shortly after his arrival in Tripoli, Consul Lucas wrote to his friend, the Home Office Undersecretary John King (1759–1830):

> I hope my conduct on this occasion will be approved of by the Secretary of State, and my Friends in the office, and that some steps will be taken for my relief; for should this new Bashaw [sic] for whom they style an usurper go on in the

manner he has done hitherto we have nothing better to expect, than Famine, Plague and Wars. My poor wife joins me in best Respects to your good Lady.[54]

In June 1804 Langford wrote of his arrival in Tripoli to take up his responsibilities as British consul.[55] Like Lucas before him, and Warrington in the decades to come, Langford collected information that would be of interest to the government, namely in the political and commercial spheres. In December 1804, the consul reported on an excursion beyond Tripoli to the south for:

> the purpose chiefly of remarking on the state of the country from the coast to the foot of the mountains. The Land is remarkably fine but not one quarter of it is cultivated. Malta however … might be well and reasonably supplied with grains and live-stock; and with great pleasure I am able to assure you that the Bashaw [sic] is well inclined to furnish such supplies.[56]

Following the departure of Langford in 1812, with a new permanent consul not due to arrive in Tripoli until 1814, and Spanish commerce in the Mediterranean subject to depredation, an ambassador in the person of William à Court was appointed on an extraordinary mission to the Regencies of Tripoli, Tunis and Algiers in 1813–14. À Court was appointed to settle outstanding debts owed by the Spanish government and to renew treaties of peace and commerce between Spain and the Regencies. À Court succeeded in averting declarations of war against Spain and procured a resolution from Yusuf Qaramanli overwhelmingly in favour of British and Spanish interests.[57] The appointment of an ambassador on this exceptional occasion emphasizes the importance of the post of the consul general to Tripoli and the highly political role the agents had to play.

The exercise of political influence enabled all the consuls to Tunis, Algiers, and Tripoli to enjoy privileges that would normally be the reserve of an officially appointed 'Ambassador Extraordinary and Plenipotentiary'.[58] This exceptionalism had its origins in the historical autonomy permitted to 'Barbary' consuls by the Levant Company, as Lucas wrote to the Duke of Portland on 30 June 1795, he had been employed by His Majesty's government 'in the Diplomatick line'.[59] Despite the fact that the consuls to Algiers, Tunis and Tripoli had been placed under the authority of Maitland as governor of Malta in 1815, Warrington did not change the way he exercised his duties after eleven years in post and, by 1826, had become a highly influential figure in the politics and life of Tripoli.[60] In fact, Warrington viewed his relationship with Maitland as one of mutual assistance, whereby, working together, the consul and the governor could address some of the most pressing issues of the day, including the slave trade.[61] Furthermore, Consul Warrington had received the acquiescence of the secretary of state, as Earl Bathurst felt that the consul's degree of influence with the Pasha, despite complaints about Warrington's behaviour, was to be commended. The correspondence of Lucas, Langford and Warrington attests to their use of political powers. Beyond the maintenance of friendly relations with the Pasha, the British consul's responsibilities included the negotiation and renewal of treaties, as well as the enforcement of preferential terms for British trade with the Regency.

In the context of continuing imperial rivalry between Britain and France, the correspondence reveals the importance attached by the British consul to the practice of diplomatic protocol and ceremony in all encounters with the Pasha. Langford and Warrington accorded a great deal of significance to existing treaty provisions that stipulated that Britain and its agents be accorded 'most favoured nation' status. In contrast to the dogmatic consular resolution process and the stiffness with which procedure could be applied and decisions made, the consul took a more flexible approach to diplomatic matters. This flexibility was not least because consular issues were often between 'low class' Maltese subjects, local Tripolines and occasionally Jewish merchants (who were either British or Tripoline subjects), while diplomatic matters were between the court of Yusuf Qaramanli and Britain or with senior British figures such as Pellew or Maitland.[62] As a result of the Napoleonic wars, the number of subjects in Tripoli falling under British protection continued to grow, including with the 1817 'Maitland Constitution' that created a federation of Ionian Islands and placed those islands under British administration.[63]

When controversial or protracted cases arose for the consul to investigate, negotiate and resolve, these normally followed a well-defined arbitration process whereby the final judgement and resolution was usually down to the personal opinion of the consul. This process remained surprisingly unaltered, even when exceptional circumstances warranted extraordinary measures, such as in the case of John Watson, who placed his case in a memorial before the Colonial Office and pleaded that his property – the ship *La Fortuna* that had been sequestered and sold by the British consul – be restored.[64] This case had come to the attention of the Colonial Office because Watson had petitioned Earl Bathurst and claimed that the consul had to indemnify him as the claimant for the losses he had sustained as a result of the consul having 'illegally' sold *La Fortuna*.[55] Watson requested the assistance of the secretary of state because he could not begin any legal proceedings as the consul possessed legal immunity. In addition, as the property had already been sold to another party by the consul, the undersecretary of state took the unusual step of seeking legal advice, and it was recommended that Consul Warrington place aside his immunity from prosecution and make himself available, in what was essentially a dispute over private rights, to the jurisdiction of the courts of Malta. As counsel to Earl Bathurst, Evan Nepean (1752–after May 1823) wrote to the secretary of state on the subject on 2 May 1823:

> I have to suggest to you, for Lord Bathurst's consideration, whether it is not just and reasonable that the Consul should give his opponent an opportunity of bringing the question between them to trial? and whether, for that purpose, he should not be required to do such acts as may be necessary for rendering himself amenable to the jurisdiction of the Courts of Malta? as that is the part of His Majesty's dominions most contiguous to the place in which the dispute arose, it is therefore the jurisdiction within which the facts of the case would be

ascertained with the least expense or delay. If Lord Bathurst should conceive it right that the controversy should be thus decided, his Lordship has it of course in his power to require the Consul to do whatever may be necessary on his part for that purpose.[66]

Notwithstanding this recommendation that Warrington place himself before a legal tribunal at Malta, Warrington disagreed, and despite repeated requests to settle the ongoing dispute, it was not until 1831 that the consul summarily announced that the matter had been 'resolved' to the satisfaction of all parties.[67]

The diplomatic privileges of the consuls, in combination with often lengthy postings, encouraged them to act independently and in a more reactionary manner than perhaps they would have done if they had followed standard procedure and advice from their superiors in Malta or London. Warrington had seized the initiative and palpably enhanced the standing, influence and role of the person and imperial bridgehead at Tripoli, by acting as a mediator between Tripoli and European states, the Pasha and Arab tribes, including in the conflict between the Pasha of Tripoli and the powerful tribal confederacy of the Awlad Suliman of Fezzan.[68]

The vice-consular recruitment process itself was rather haphazard and the successful candidates owed their positions largely to the personal patronage extended to them by the British consul. This method of appointment was a continuation of a system of patronage that at least both Consuls Lucas and Warrington had relied upon to secure their own positions in Tripoli. With the possible exception of the vice-consuls to Murzuq and Kuka who were recruited directly from the exploratory missions, the majority of vice-consuls appointed to Tripoli, Benghazi and Derna were Italian-speaking British subjects who were on intimate and friendly relations with the Warrington family. The British consul wrote in favourable terms of Benedetto Regiginiani whom he had appointed to Derna. The consul wrote similarly of Giacomo Rofsoni, vice-consul to Benghazi. Though the consular correspondence does not provide an indication of any existing relationship between Warrington and Rofsoni's successor to the post at Benghazi, Thomas Wood, the two nevertheless became close as Wood married Warrington's widowed daughter, Emma Laing, and after her death, her sister Jane.[69] Warrington had also named his youngest child Walter Bornou, in memory of his friend, Dr Oudney. Walter Bornou Warrington was born in late 1823 or the first days of 1824, after the death of the explorer at Murzuq.[70]

Consuls Langford and Warrington also both attempted to secure posts for their own family members. Warrington failed in his attempt to install his son George as permanent vice-consul in Benghazi from 1826 to 1831, though he was able to retain another of his sons, Frederick, as the official translator for his office at Tripoli. From 1826 to 1828, Warrington encountered further difficulties when he tried to gain commissions for one George Dalzel, 'son of the late Governor to cape coast castle', as well as for his own eldest son Charles Thornhill Warrington.[71] In the case of George Dalzel, his father the 'late Governor' was the well-known slave trader Archibald Dalzel (1740–1818), father-in-law to Warrington's close friend in Tripoli, naval surgeon Dr John Dickson.[72] Despite the memorials and the consuls' letters of appeal for themselves and their choices of vice-consuls, they were informed by the secretary of state that their requests could not be accommodated because of the overwhelming number of candidates seeking the very same posts.[73] In an unusual move, Langford in earlier years had taken extraordinary steps to block the attempt of his brother-in-law, Sandford Peacocke, to obtain a consular position in Africa.[74] Following Vice-Consul Woods's brief retreat from Benghazi to Europe in 1831 because of ill-health, Warrington was quick to appoint his son George Warrington to act as temporary vice-consul.[75]

With regard to the joint government and African Association missions into the interior of Africa, the consul reviewed and forwarded their correspondence, determined the amount of money and provisions supplied to the travellers and kept an account of the missions' expenditure at the consulate. The success of British enterprise in Africa depended on the consul being able to not only exercise influence over Yusuf Qaramanli but also reach amicable agreements with local Sheikhs outside the Qaramanli sphere of control. The Pasha's authority, despite the official rhetoric, was also tenuous beyond the borders of the Regency, with loyalty to Tripoli in question as close as Ghadames. For the British consul, imperial ambitions for the establishment of a regular profitable commerce with the Sokoto Caliphate and the Kingdom of Kanem-Bornu, and wider strategic concerns about the protection of the existing Empire, naturally manifested themselves in the political agenda regarding the Regency of Tripoli.

The British consul general in Tripoli – at least from 1795 – began to acquire a more elaborate system of office and representation. As British acting consul, Bryan McDonogh also acted as proconsul following the death of Consul Lucas on 4 May 1801.[76] Lucas's successor Consul Langford likewise benefitted from having a vice-consul to assist him in his duties. Warrington took the vice-consular establishment to a new level and fostered a network of agents in Kuka, Murzuq, Benghazi and Derna, while maintaining a vice-consul and a full consular staff at Tripoli. The connections between these individuals and the relationships they fostered were decisive in setting forth a series of events that created instability and weakened the authority of Yusuf Qaramanli in his own Regency.[77]

It appears, however, that personal and professional connections did not always work in the consul's interest. This was especially so in the case of John Tyrwhitt, vice-consul to Kuka. Tyrwhitt was appointed directly to the position because of Warrington's patronage. While Warrington strongly advocated, and succeeded in obtaining, Tyrwhitt's appointment, the vice-consul's recruitment was for altogether different reasons. Warrington was, as the Chancery Court records in 1807 and 1810 detail, in a financial bind following the loss of an inheritance from his wife's family. One of his debtors was a relative of Tyrwhitt, and in lieu of payment of the debt, Warrington took on responsibility for Tyrwhitt and on 12 December 1821 nominated the young man to a post in the interior.[78] In support of his nomination, Warrington wrote enthusiastically to Earl Bathurst in December 1821:

> I trust the nomination of Mr. John Tyrwhitt to that situation will meet with your approbation. He is cousin to Sir. Thomas Tyrwhitt … and a Gentlemanly Quiet young man & by not Trading in any shape He is not likely to excite suspicion or jealousy. I mention Mr. Tyrwhitt's Pedigree my Lord from a thorough conviction that the higher a man's connections are, the less He thinks of dangers and difficulties and can endure Privations better than other Men.[79]

Consul Warrington, in his letter of support for Tyrwhitt's appointment, emphasizes the important role played by both personal connections and 'gentlemanly' status in making a candidate suitable for a position in the consular service. These 'requirements' provide further evidence that the procurement of a position in North Africa, even as vice-consul, had also become highly competitive.

In his continued attempts to assert his own preferences for the vice-consular posts, Warrington recalled the historical precedent of the relative autonomy of the consul general. On 25 June 1826, the consul wrote to Secretary of State Bathurst to request he be exempted from the new consular recruitment instructions and, indeed, if he might be permitted to appoint his own choice of vice-consul.[80]

Warrington did not hesitate to transfer powers conferred at the start of his consulship to any situation where he felt that the exercise of those privileges was warrantable. This flexibility was important as it conveyed a position of significant autonomy. In turn, the consul's ability to serve an ultimatum on Yusuf Qaramanli palpably enhanced the influence of the British bridgehead at Tripoli and enabled the consul to exercise a considerable level of diplomatic privilege in Tripoli.[81] On 18 August 1830, Warrington wrote to Murray following his threatening of the Pasha with the force of the Royal Navy:

> My Language [to the Pasha] was Intimidating and surely the admiral [Edward Codrington] intended it should be. N.3 [enclosed document] is full authority to justify the Threat and although it was in support and particularly alluding to a Mercantile claim I trust you will not censure the transfer in favour of the Travellers, as the affair to which it referred had been previously settled. The Intimidation has afforded entire Protection.[82]

In this despatch to the secretary of state, Consul Warrington attempted to justify his expansive use of diplomatic privilege by explaining that he felt it appropriate, in an effort to secure the success of the exploratory missions, to use a previous sanction of military threat against the Pasha. Leaving Warrington in post for such a long duration, and largely without reprimand, reconfirms the government's primary concern for its agents to maintain an influential British presence in Tripoli. Warrington went above and beyond his duties by actively expanding British representation in the region. Throughout Warrington's consulship, he had responded to threats against himself and his family and had also proved himself able to navigate the waves of political upheaval. Following a temporary recall to Malta, the consul returned to his post in 1831, whereafter he maintained the British bridgehead for another fifteen years. During this time, Yusuf Qaramanli was succeeded by his son Ali, despite the frequent challenges by his grandson Mohamed. The reign of Ali Qaramanli as Pasha, however, was cut short by the Ottoman Porte with the order that the city be once again placed under direct Ottoman administration.

Personal Connections and Influence in Tripoli

In 1804, Consul Langford had experienced the most challenging case of his career at Tripoli – and which came from within the small world of the foreign consular families – when a British subject, Mr Church, was murdered apparently on the orders of one Giacomina Fornelles, the wife of the Spanish Master Shipwright to Yusuf Qaramanli.[83] This case is important as it highlights the cooperation that could exist between the Pasha and the British consul, as well as the lack of assistance that could be encountered with a foreign consular counterpart if a matter involved one of their own subjects. Mr Church was residing at Tripoli as a merchant, although Langford noted still on the half pay of the 40th Regiment, with his family. After having dined with the Spanish Master Shipwright on 19 August 1804, Mr Church returned home that evening and was stabbed to death on his doorstep by two servants from the Fornelles's household.[84] Yusuf Qaramanli provided manpower in the hunt, as well as a financial reward for the capture of the assassins. On their detention, the younger man confessed that he had been promised $50 by Giacomina Fornelles to kill Mr Church. The motives of Fornelles remain unclear, and no record survives of either her interrogation or that of the two convicted locals. As a result of their capture and the execution of one less than a week after the murder, Langford wrote to the secretary of state:

> On the 26th the Murderer was put to death in a most brutal manner, and then laid at the door of Giacomina Fornelles during that night, and on the following morning was buried among some ruins of the city, and without their rites of sepulchre – the youth, the Bashaw says, He shall immediately banish.
>
> I have since called on the Spanish Consul, who declines arresting Giacomina Fornelles, or taking any steps in the affair until he has heard from his court.
>
> I think it is more than probable a ship may be ordered here immediately; by which time farther particulars of this transaction may have transpired.[85]

In the same dispatch Langford also communicated, alongside the murder of Mr Church, areas of agreement with the Pasha on the export of cattle to Malta as well as demonstrations he (Langford) had made against French interests in the Regency. In consequence, despite a great deal of cooperation and assistance offered to the British consul in his work, including compensation given by the Pasha to a number of Maltese plundered at Zuwara by Tripoline subjects, the consul still requested that a ship of war be sent to Tripoli to threaten the Pasha. Following this request for naval reinforcements, the consul received a reproving reply from the British government that it was vital that he have a 'proper understanding' of the necessity of preserving friendly relations with the Pasha. The secretary of state for war and the colonies added, that while his observance of Qaramanli's ministers as 'you think are in the French interest, [is] perfectly proper', he was absolutely not to interfere in, or attempt to influence 'matters connected with the administration of his government, in which the interests of this country are not decidedly concerned'.[86]

Despite his repeated letters of entreaty to Earl Bathurst, and his assurances that no misunderstandings existed between him and Yusuf Qaramanli, the consul was forced to return to London after almost eight years as consul in Tripoli.[87] While there is little to indicate that animosity existed with Yusuf Qaramanli and his Diwan, there is evidence to suggest that Langford was occasionally overzealous in his representations. A letter from Yusuf Qaramanli to London, supported by various statements, including from Saverio Naudi (the Pasha's official broker), had moved the British government to take the unusual step of ordering the consul to relinquish his duties with immediate effect. Despite his best efforts, Langford could secure passage for himself and family from Malta to England only on board the *Malabar* storeship. The entire voyage home from Tripoli to London was at his own expense and he was forced to leave all his possessions in Tripoli.[88] His subsequent letters and petitions to the secretary of state went unanswered.

The bonds between the British agents in and around the Regency of Tripoli involved complex layers of interests that were often personal, commercial and professional. The consuls could show patronage and favour and likewise withhold and withdraw support if their own ambitions were not being served. Following the death of Vice-Consul Toole, Warrington wrote to London on 18 August 1824 to recommend a commission for Toole's brother and expressed his hope that the undersecretary of state, Wilmot Horton, would bring it under the consideration of Earl Bathurst.[89] The relationships developed by the consuls were cultivated over a period of time that was interrupted only by outbreaks of drought, disease and, occasionally, bad luck. In 1832, Warrington authorized a Maltese resident of Tripoli, Pietro Caravana and his brother-in-law Mr Casalaina, to travel to Derna to 'protect' British commercial interests, as well as permitting Caravana to pursue his own commercial activities. Leaving behind a heavily pregnant wife and extended family, Caravana and company reached their destination only to have four barrels of gunpowder they were transporting with them explode, killing Caravana, his brother-in-law, and at least five other locals that had been travelling with them.[90] Pietro Caravana was also the brother-in-law to the late American consul, Mr Coxe.

The vice-consular network that Consul Warrington fostered and expanded throughout the 1820s and 1830s was a testament to the vision and ambition of the consul general for a permanent and active British presence in the territories of Fezzan and the African interior as far as Kuka. Following the cessation of hostilities with France, the British government did not oppose Warrington's efforts to develop a network of British agents from the Regency of Tripoli. This network, in professional terms, expanded the scope and political (as well as consular) representation of British interests from Tripoli eastward to the borders of Egypt, and south down the trans-Saharan caravan routes past Murzuq. These agents enabled the regular communication of intelligence on various matters that interested the consul and the Colonial Office. Reports from the vice-consular offices were always addressed to the consulate in Tripoli and sometimes extracts were copied or forwarded by the consul to London.

Though the vice-consular office at Kuka did not appear to relay much useful information because of the premature death of John Tyrwhitt, his appointment in the first instance demonstrates how status and connections could directly assist in the attainment of a consular appointment. Indeed, Tyrwhitt's complaints to his father, shortly before his death, led to his uncle, Sir Thomas Tyrwhitt writing, in June 1825, directly to the secretary of state.[91] The vice-consul's grievances included the lack of financial support provided by Warrington and the impoverished state in which he was being forced to live while dependent on the consul. Though Warrington vehemently denied the charges, Tyrwhitt's unhappy state and tragic death in turn forced Warrington to account for a number of large debts that he owed to creditors in England, including to Tyrwhitt's father.[92] As he wrote to Undersecretary Hay on 15 April 1826,

> I believe my just acquaintance with Mr T. Sen. was in the year 1798 – I had the pleasure to renew that acquaintance in the year 1813, under circumstance probably not so flourishing ... In the year 1806 a dear Friend & Relation died & left myself & Mrs Warrington about sixty thousand pounds with various other Property. A caveat was lodged against the will, & as quickly withdrawn, but which so alarmed the Executor Mr Templeman that He filed a Bill under the Term amicable & a most unfriendly act it was, as from that circumstance I date my Financial Ruin, as the torture of a chancery Court plunged me ... into that awful abyss from which I have never yet been able to extricate myself ... in times of need He [John Tyrwhitt Snr] acted towards me as kind and as handsome a part, as man could do – & I believe I owe Him about 500£.[93]

The relationships maintained by the consul and his family with the rest of the European consular families in Tripoli were usually close-knit because of their official functions and their personal identities. The consular ties were strengthened by occasions of mutual cooperation and, when required, in acting as a united lobby before the Qaramanli government. In May 1826, a serious and dangerous controversy arose that threatened the well-being of the British and Swedish consular presence in the Regency. Two months previously, in March 1826, Warrington had agreed to help the Swedish consul Jacob Gråberg (1776–1847) to hide and remove 'three large boxes' of Bibles. The Swedish consul was 'in the greatest state of alarm' and appealed to the British consul for help. Although Warrington assured the undersecretary of state that he 'should never think of circulating anything of the sort without orders' he nevertheless acted on his own initiative when he decided to assist Gråberg by hiding the Bibles. The British consul later asked the permission of the government to send the Bibles on to the British Bible Society.[94] Warrington explained that the matter involving the Bibles was not about the observation of the rules laid down by the Qaramanli government, but in fact was an attempt by Yusuf Qaramanli to exact a higher tribute from the Swedish government.[95] Warrington summarized the matter to the undersecretary as one in which he had successfully 'defeated the Intrigues of Xavier [Saverio] Naudi [agent to Yusuf Qaramanli] & saved the Swedish consulate [from] being searched'.[96] Towards the end of July 1826, Warrington was able to write to John Thornton at the Bible Society and, between them, they arranged for the boxes to be sent to Reverend W. Jowett in Malta, where the Society's committee then arranged for their subsequent distribution elsewhere.[97] However, in neighbouring Egypt, the role of the church and its missionaries had not been quite so confined. In December 1827, sixteen months after this incident in Tripoli, the Church Missionary Society in Alexandria (under the leadership of one Mr Gobat) played host to two Abyssinian emissaries, who wanted to convey an important letter to King George III. This communication was from Sapergâdes (or Sapergâder), the 'Ras of Tegree' (Tigré) – one of the 'four Provinces into which Abyssinia is now divided'.[98] The Ras wrote that he was 'desirous to open a communication with the British Government', and his emissaries entrusted one William Coffin, who was connected to the British consulate at Alexandria, to convey the letter to England. The capital of Abyssinia was initially at Axum in Tigré and it is therefore significant that Ras Sapergâdes was attempting to open up 'a communication' with the British government via the bridgehead at Tripoli.[99]

Almost three years later, on 28 September 1830, following the death of American Consul Coxe, Warrington wrote a private letter to Hay protesting that the 'head of the catholic church' had refused an application to permit the (American) consul's body to be buried in the Catholic cemetery of Tripoli.[100] Both the Catholic and Greek populations of Tripoli had maintained places of worship and cemeteries in the city during the reign of Yusuf Qaramanli. Unfortunately, there is very little documentation in the consular correspondence about the role of these establishments in the Regency, and the relationship between the consuls and their faith, beyond their duty to protect Christian subjects and to free Christian slaves.[101] Proconsul Pat Wilkie did, however, note in 1813 that there had been a Franciscan convent consisting of 'three Fathers', though the Greek Church had had no priest in attendance 'for some time past' and that it was under British protection.[102] The letters also detail that, by 1822, relations between the consul and Dixon Denham had deteriorated to such a degree that Denham would not entrust his dispatches to Warrington, and so sent some of his letters to London not through the consulate, but through the medium of the Franciscan Fathers in Tripoli.[103]

There are also numerous instances of the consuls intervening to free enslaved Europeans brought to Tripoli; and there was one notable case of a major diplomatic incident between Britain and the Regency that involved allegations of the Maltese population deliberately burning an effigy of a Turkish saint – instead of one of Judas Iscariot – during the Easter Sunday ceremony in 1807.[104] This incident also highlights the discord between the consuls in Tripoli, as Langford alleged that his foreign colleagues were behind this intrigue. On returning to Tripoli in 1830, Warrington informed the British government that the Protestant consuls had met on 28 September 1830 to discuss what action to take to address the lack of a

Protestant cemetery in the Regency. Warrington continued to complain about the lack of cooperation from the Catholic Church in Tripoli at the time:

> I am at a loss to assign a just reason for the non compliance, as I should suppose the greatest Fanatic could not imagine Pollution or contamination when the spirit has fled … The Protestant consuls were shocked to see the Catholic Gate closed against their colleague and to see His Body consigned to that Earth which as the Moors observed would have received a Dog.[105]

Together, following the meeting, the consuls agreed that they would act together to obtain a portion of land to erect a wall around and have consecrated for future burials.[106] This cemetery was established, and at least one of Consul Warrington's children by Clara Portelli, Julia Warrington, was later buried there. Inevitably, however, because of the close relationships between the consuls, and also in part due to the consuls' lengthy residence in Tripoli, relations between them also broke down from time to time. The most protracted of these incidents followed the murder of Laing in 1826. The British consul's dispatches on the murder and his investigations thereon fill volume upon volume in the consular archives and are a testament to Warrington's determination to see the French consul permanently recalled and replaced. In earlier years, relations had been on more amicable terms, and encounters between the two consular families had resulted in a relationship between Warrington's daughter Emma and the French consul's son. As Warrington later admitted, Emma (prior to her marriage to Laing) had become fond of Rousseau's son and Warrington was horrified to have a portrait of his daughter returned on the death of the young man on 1 December 1828.[107] The consul had not suspected that they had formed a close relationship and that the French consul's son had intended to propose to his daughter.[108]

In 1827, Warrington was officially reprimanded for his attack on the Neapolitan consul and his family. Warrington had publicly accused the Neapolitan consul's daughter of being in a state of 'open prostitution' for passing Maltese merchants.[109] Ten years previously, in 1817, the consul was similarly instructed to refrain from any further insults to the Sardinian consul.[110] These attacks were personal and were completely unrelated either to the business of the British bridgehead at Tripoli or to Warrington's consular duties. Indeed, they served only to embarrass the government and to force Warrington to retract his accusations and to apologize.

Deeply disappointing for Warrington was the fact that there would be no return to the exploratory activities in the interior or an expansion of trade with the commercial hubs of the 'Great Sudan'. By 1830, events in the Regency had reached a crescendo of uncertainty and chaos. The fragility of Yusuf Qaramanli's government was exacerbated by the succession challenge, and the Pasha's resources overstretched by military reprisals against the Arab tribes of Barqa and Fezzan because of a perceived lack of loyalty to his rule.[111] For the British government, the unstable political and social environment inevitably had a negative effect upon the resources and connections on which its agents could draw, and on the range of their activities.

Against this background, the activities of foreign agents in the Regency came under closer scrutiny by the Pasha's government and none more so than the conduct of the British consul general. In the service of his own interests, Warrington secretly, and against the orders of the British government, supported the cause of Mohamed Qaramanli and continued to maintain parallel alliances with key political leaders in Murzuq and Kanem-Bornu. These relationships highlight the near-fatal level of suspicion that was aroused by the British consul's intimate involvement in the political upheavals that gripped Tripoli. On 5 November 1830, Warrington wrote to Murray of the 'threat or attempt to assassinate my two children & myself' and placed the Pasha at the centre of the plot.[112] The previous week, on Thursday 28 October, Warrington had been riding nearby his house in the Menshia district with one of his daughters and his youngest son Walter when they were rounded on by two 'Turks', one of whom had threatened them with a stiletto.[113] The consul wrote that, to afford his children time to escape into the nearby 'English Garden', he had confronted the horsemen head on, and despite his being unarmed, both men had subsequently retreated.[114] While this fateful year had temporarily halted the activities and influence of the British consul and the British bridgehead as a whole, the unfolding events of 1830 also reveal just how powerful the person and position of the British consul had become in the Regency during the final decade of Yusuf Qaramanli's rule. Only the following month, on 5 November 1830, Warrington reflected on his position in Tripoli to the secretary of state:

> The Language of this Govt. is 'that the murder of Major Laing would never have been inquired into, had it not been for the British Consul. That the British Govt. never would have compelled us to pay British subjects if it had not been for the British Consul'. In raising their Tribute from the poor Arab – it is now 'for the English Consul'. In carrying some old silver through the streets to have weighed, 'that was also for the English Consul' … With great deference founded on years experience, I say that to demand justice from this Government is to have it, on every point.[115]

In making the claim for an influential British presence in the Regency of Tripoli in the early nineteenth century, contrary to accepted historiography, the consuls posted to the three states of Algiers, Tunis and Tripoli – as well as Morocco and Egypt – were usually highly skilled and experienced imperial agents. Furthermore, the consular posting was a desirable position and was not unduly affected by the cutbacks of 1822.[116] Significantly, the consuls to North Africa also held unique diplomatic privileges, in contrast to their counterparts at other Mediterranean consulates, and they regularly exercised these privileges in the service of British interests.

The powerful British presence at Tripoli was built on the person of the British consul and on the close networks that he fostered around him. Moreover, the evidence attests to the frequent exercise of diplomatic privilege by the consul at Tripoli and to the considerable influence he was able to hold over Yusuf Qaramanli by the early 1820s. While there were some differences in the consuls' respective career progression, their motivation and skillset saw Consuls Lucas, Langford and Warrington rise to the top of a highly competitive field. Alongside professional capabilities, the impact of individual personalities played a singular and significant role in defining the bridgehead's activities. While the House of Commons Committee papers and instructions from the secretary of state reveal how the government resolved the issue of recruitment, the attempt to professionalize the consular service also inadvertently highlights how influential the British consul at Tripoli had become at home as well as at his North African post.

Chapter 6

AN IMPERIAL BRIDGEHEAD

An imperial bridgehead is defined by the set of interconnected networks, be they intelligence, commercial, missionary and so on, that are established and developed at a particular site.[1] The concept of a 'bridgehead' at Tripoli is significant for understanding British strategic interests and activities as they unfolded in North Africa and the Middle East. The British bridgehead in the Regency constituted an essentially protected imperial space and presence in a precolonial territory in the early nineteenth century, and which preceded the formulation of imperial strategy by the West African bridgehead by more than two decades.[2]

Since the late eighteenth century, the British bridgehead in Tripoli came to represent an evolving body of commercial and scientific enterprise, as well as a rapidly expanding range of strategic priorities in the Mediterranean. These formal and informal British initiatives coincided with three important developments: the launch, in the 1820s, of a series of exploratory missions from Tripoli into the African interior;[3] the expansion of a vice-consular network into new territories; and the increase in the individual enterprise of the consuls themselves. These activities came at a time of a growing anti-slavery movement at home, a determination to reduce agents' overseas expenses, and an increasingly fragile political, social and economic climate in and beyond the Regency of Tripoli. Since at least the early modern period, Tripoli had acted as a gateway to the caravan routes to the commercial and trading centres of the kingdoms and territories of Fezzan, Kanem-Bornu and the 'Great Sudan' of Sultan Bello (see Figure 12). Following the French invasion of Egypt in 1798, Britain formally occupied Alexandria in 1801 and again in 1807, while France in 1830 conquered new territory to the west, from Bône (Annaba) across to Oran in present-day Algeria. This military action was justified on the pretext of ending piracy.[4]

After the Napoleonic Wars, the bridgehead at Tripoli served three main purposes: it acted as a vital link in a communication network along a strategically important region for the British Empire; it maintained the supply of provisions to British naval garrisons; and it provided British agents with a favourable base from which to access the most desirable trading routes into the interior. These functions of the consular establishment were complementary – they increased knowledge about the kingdoms, people and commerce extending southwest to Timbuktu, east as far as 'Grand Cairo' and southeast to the Kingdom of Darfur and Kordofan. Though agents' ideas and initiatives were often formulated on a reactive basis at their respective postings, policymakers in London nevertheless did propose and support enterprises on a case-by-case basis – Bathurst's sanction of the exploratory missions from Tripoli, Consul Warrington's interventions on behalf of British subjects throughout the 1820s and Palmerston's support of Beecroft's imperial scheme in the Bight of Benin from 1849.[5] As the 'men on the spot', these agents directly shaped governmental policy at the frontiers of empire – through sheer force of personality as well as through an influential bridgehead.[6] In turn, the consuls in Tripoli came to make decisions about a growing portfolio of strategic and commercial interests that directly affected the strength of the British naval presence in the Mediterranean. While the British government never held a coherent imperial strategy regarding overseas territories (formal or otherwise), local agents were often in a position to affect both the course of local politics, British influence and policy formulation in the region.[7]

The explicit recognition by the British government of the intimate connections between the British economy, the slave trade and the need for allies in Africa in order to successfully establish British trade with the African interior are also important factors. As the most senior British agent in Tripoli, the British consul played a vital part in the promotion of political alliances and a series of more expansive networks into the interior.[8] Within the last decade, studies have come together to shed further light on our understanding of the British Empire and of British imperial activity in North Africa and the Middle East – as well as in other pre- or non-colonial states across the world.[9]

With this in mind, theories on 'informal empire' still do not sufficiently account for the range of British interests and activities, as represented by consular agents in North and West Africa (and Latin America) during and after the Napoleonic era. In addition, the consular correspondence strongly indicates that the rhetoric of free trade and the prospect of commercial trading opportunities had constituted important 'motivating factors' for the British Empire in both North Africa and the Latin American republics of La Plata.[10] Importantly, studies of networks of exchange remain empirically driven and enable a detailed analysis of the role of 'informal empire' and how cooperation between British and local agents developed during a time of deep social and economic change.[11] In this light, the case that North Africa was of little political or strategic importance from the seventeenth to the nineteenth centuries simply does not stand up to scrutiny. The creation of a bridgehead at Tripoli and the ensuing imperial endeavours were manifestations of a powerful British presence in the Regency, a protected presence that has been neglected in both imperial and Maghrebi historiography.

A Bridgehead at Tripoli

The idea and practice of the bridgehead goes beyond one of a simple 'outpost' and adds weight to the influence and effectiveness of the consul as the 'man on the spot'. As a theoretical and practical construction, it allows for a more detailed understanding of the complex layers of personal and professional relationships developed for the purposes of intelligence-gathering, profit and, in some cases, friendship.[12] And, while there is a substantial literature on individual consuls as well as on the consular and diplomatic service, much less has been written on the significance and meaning of a consular or diplomatic bridgehead as an imperial point of influence and activity.[13] This issue is addressed directly by utilizing the returns of British trade to and from the Regency, which were submitted to the Colonial Office by the British consul in Tripoli.[14] The bridgehead tells us much more about the scale and operation of agents' activities, as well as how their relationship with London was defined and directed. The alliances between the British consular bridgehead in Tripoli and the enterprising missions of the British government were unique, as together they brought the work of the African Association into the interior of Africa, with the individual initiatives of the consul in the city.

The bridgehead at Tripoli may also be viewed as an imperial space wherein British agents represented British commercial and strategic interests and enforced treaty agreements between Tripoli and Britain. The networks which the three successive consuls developed and maintained may also be better understood in terms of their levels of interaction and nodal points of contact.[15] These points of interaction are vital in answering some of the key questions that are raised, and which have also been previously highlighted in the dialogue between the new imperial and diplomatic histories.[16] Did the bridgehead at Tripoli and its associated networks, whether social or intelligence-gathering focused, enable the exercise of British influence in the political and commercial spheres? For the British government, a fundamental objective of a consular representative was to exercise influence over the local power structure, in this case the notables and the Pasha of the Regency of Tripoli, Yusuf Qaramanli. Importantly for a bridgehead, 'how effectively could it lobby for military, financial or diplomatic assistance?'[17] The bridgehead created a means of communication and cooperation between the consuls and the local polity, as well as fulfilling its primary objective of providing British representation in a North African port of strategic importance. It provides an effective framework with which to understand the ways in which British interests developed in Africa and in the Mediterranean. It also encapsulated a series of imperial networks that radiated from Tripoli and that was developed largely by the British consul in the city. These networks, or formal connections and interactions, were composed of representatives of the diplomatic, consular, naval and merchant professions, as well as of the local elite and ordinary populace of Tripoli – Muslim, Christian and Jew.

A number of the main commercial centres of the interior converged around Lake Chad, and, combined with the powerful belief, in both local narratives and foreign accounts, that the waters of the Nile originated in the river Niger, a strong incentive was provided for agents aiming to prove themselves and make their name in England.[18] For Europe, Tripoli also provided a valuable satellite point between Algiers, Alexandria and Cairo – and vitally – the overland route to the Levant and Asia. The British consul, augmented by his vice-consular network in and around the Regency of Tripoli, reported information on French movements, plans and apparent schemes during the Napoleonic and post-Napoleonic era. For the operation of the bridgehead, the Regency occupied, and acted as a bridge between, several influential political and commercial spheres, which included the African, Ottoman and European arenas. The Regency was both a gateway to the interior of Africa and a vital link in the supply and communication network of the British Empire.

Following the French successive occupations of Alexandria in 1798 and 1807, and the continued threat posed by Napoleon's troops to Britain's trade and empire, Britain launched a series of expeditions to remove the French presence in Egypt. The Royal Navy also attempted to deter the capture and enslavement of Christians by local powers, particularly with Lord Exmouth's 1816 expedition against Algiers.[19] Despite the success of British influence in Tripoli and Kanem-Bornu during this period, particularly with Shehu al-Kanemi of Kanem-Bornu from 1823 to 1825 and Sheikh Abd' al-Jalil Saif al-Nasser of Fezzan from 1831 to 1832, the British consul's interventions had a deleterious effect on the stability of the Regency and the surrounding provinces. All the while, France remained active in the region and continued to expand its own interests. In 1830, because of threats posed to the remaining Ottoman territories in North Africa, the Porte once again directed that Tripoli be formally reoccupied by Ottoman forces, which brought an end to the rule of the Qaramanli family and so temporarily resecured the Regency as a loyal province of the Ottoman Empire.

The consul's day-to-day formal despatches included correspondence with the secretary and undersecretary of state at the Colonial Office and the British governor of Malta. The consul also corresponded with other British consuls and ministers throughout the Mediterranean. In the protection of British subjects and the favourable terms of the treaty provisions with the Regency of Tripoli, including only 3 per cent duty on imported goods, the consul often utilized the support of the Admiralty and the British fleet stationed in the Mediterranean.[20]

The threat to British Empire in India was amplified with the successive French occupations of Egypt that had commenced in 1798 and continued into the early nineteenth century. Following the French invasion of Egypt in 1798, the British government feared that Napoleon's troops would advance to challenge empire in India. In June 1798, Secretary of State Lord Melville (1742–1811), in an effort to counter any possible French moves, despatched 'a naval squadron to the Red Sea and 5,000 reinforcements to India'.[21] In order to remove the French from Egypt, Melville, with the backing of the government, sent there 'the biggest expedition after 1796, 15,000 men from the Mediterranean and 6,000 from India'.[22] In 1801, Britain had succeeded in expelling French troops from Egypt.

British strategy, both military and diplomatic, was, however, not limited to countering French imperial ambitions but also to direct the preservation of relations with imperial Spain and the control of strategic interests in the Aegean. The October 1813 peace between Spain and Tripoli was negotiated by Britain and averted the repayment of the full amount of debts owed to Tripoli, as well as a war that Spain could ill-afford.[23] À Court's intervention also reflected the concern of the British government to maintain the resources and troops of the Spanish government, as well as to maintain the supply of provisions from Tripoli to the British-led army stationed in Spain.[24] Unusually, this settlement was negotiated by à Court as Envoy Extraordinary to the Qaramanli court in September 1813, because there was no consul general in Tripoli at the time. Although the consuls in 'Barbary' usually exercised diplomatic powers in such circumstances, the bridgehead at Tripoli had suffered a temporary but serious setback because Consul Langford had been recalled to London. The following two consular agents, Proconsuls Wilkie and Somerville, held no diplomatic privileges, and the next permanent consul general, in the person of Hanmer Warrington, would not arrive at the Regency until 28 November 1814.[25] In addition, it was not until 1826 that Bathurst, as secretary of state for colonial affairs, instructed the British consul in Tripoli to give up his extra-consular duties for other European powers.[26]

The provision of British garrisons in the Mediterranean and the maintenance of favourable treaty terms with Yusuf Qaramanli was a priority for the consul. The British presence in Tripoli had to maintain and encourage a continuous supply of livestock and stores that included horses for the cavalry, bullocks and sheep, and timber for the naval bases in the Mediterranean. As treaty ties and commercial relations greatly varied between European states and the Regency of Tripoli, such as Genoa's and Sweden's, the foreign consuls worked to uphold the principle of neutrality and were often united in opposition against any real or perceived threats.[27] These threats included treaty infringements by the Qaramanli government, in particular, by the Pasha's officers against Christian subjects in Tripoli.[28] Aside from this 'brotherhood' of foreign cooperation in Tripoli through initiatives such as the Board of Health, the British bridgehead maintained close and regular contact with its agents in the region.[29] During Warrington's consulship, this network was extended to include the growing vice-consular network built partially from the missions of the African Association. These vice-consuls acted as British representatives in Derna, Benghazi, Tripoli, Murzuq and Kuka and so covered Tripolitania, Barqa, Fezzan and Kanem-Bornu. Beechey was assigned the vice-consulship of Benghazi, Oudney to Murzuq, Tyrwhitt and Toole to Kuka and Clapperton 'as consul' to Bornu.[30] This vice-consular network was never more numerous and active than during Warrington's consulship. His promotion of local Christian subjects to the office of vice-consul in Benghazi and Derna was followed, however unplanned, by the launch of the Southern, Southwestern and Eastern Missions.

Despite the 'enclosed' nature of the foreign consular corps at Tripoli, the consul's networks also intertwined with the pre-existing political and commercial networks in the city and throughout the wider Regency. Such networks could encompass relationships with merchants in the interior as well as with the limited European merchant houses in Tripoli, such as the House of Concenza and Beaussier & Company.[31] Indeed, Consul Warrington lamented the 'extensive nature' of profitable French commercial dealings and actively tried to develop the network of British agents at Tripoli as early as 1820, with the aim of expanding British commercial interests in and beyond the Regency. The proposal he made to the British government in March 1821 was for the urgent institution of a British merchant house in Tripoli, and for the presence of British merchants, as well as the establishment of a regular vessel for trade between Tripoli and Malta. In a letter to Undersecretary Wilmot Horton on 31 March 1820, Warrington reiterated his ambition that Britain should be the primary beneficiary of trade to and from the Regency:

> The Preponderating Influence of the British Flag at the present period, affords that security to commercial Pursuits, the Benefit of which She ought to derive, instead of other Flags.[32]

Prospects for Trade

At a time when British commercial interests predated the 'imperialism of free-trade', British consular and diplomatic agents were active in the promotion of British interests at the frontiers of empire.[33] The Mediterranean was certainly no exception, and the Ottoman provinces of North Africa played a vital role as gatekeepers to the African interior and to the lucrative trading routes from Central Africa to the Levant and beyond. The vice-consular network augmented the work of the consul general and, vitally, embodied the physical representation and expansion of British interests east towards Egypt, reaching as far as Derna, the largest trading settlement to the east of the Regency, and the contested Bay of Bomba.[34] The increasing multitude of interests expressed by British diplomatic, naval, commercial and consular agents can most usefully be understood in terms of a network of professional relationships and allegiances shaped by a changing imperial Britain. The explorers of the African Association, whether intentionally or otherwise, provided a recruiting ground for future vice-consuls in the newly explored territories of Murzuq and Kuka. These included the appointments of Beechey, Tyrwhitt, Toole, Oudney and Clapperton to vice-consular positions.[35] There was a noticeable shift, in the consular and vice-consular recruitment process, from 'British' to 'British-born' subjects after 1825. 'British-born' excluded all colonial subjects and the other European subjects that resided in Tripoli and that, from time to time, came under British protection and were therefore designated 'British subjects'. These included Maltese, Greeks and Tuscans. The ties of British agents became much closer to London than to the bridgehead at Tripoli and the towns in which agents were stationed.[36] However, the loyalties and connections of agents such as Toole and Oudney may well have developed entirely differently had they not died at their posts so soon after appointment. The vice-consular network was also meant to support an increasing number of travellers into the interior. As Warrington wrote to Earl Bathurst in February 1825:

> I trust in God that this Research may yet establish an Epoch in the Reign of His Majesty little Inferior to the Colombian Discovery, as altho' the Maritime Parts of this great continent are unknown, still the geography of the Interior, customs, manners, civilization, commerce and in short everything were as little known

even at this enlightened period as the surface and production of those Heavenly Bodies on which we daily gaze with admiration & wonder.[37]

The very prospect of economic gain and trading opportunities provided His Majesty's agents with one of their primary tasks, alongside the protection of existing British commercial interests in the Mediterranean.[38] These responsibilities went hand in hand with providing an effective intelligence network to challenge French ambitions in the region, and to prevent Egypt from being used as a hostile military base. Merchants and traders from Britain and closer neighbours on the Mediterranean coast contributed to the identification of Tripoli, Algiers, Tunis and other port cites as 'cosmopolitan' in make-up and affiliation.[39] The heady atmosphere of European power-rivalry served only to increase the geostrategic significance of Tripoli and its neighbours in the aftermath of the Napoleonic Wars.

It was the prospect of trade and access to the wealth of the interior that provided the incentive for the establishment of an active consular and vice-consular network that extended from Tripoli to the African kingdoms in the south.[40] In February 1802, despite his initial reservations, Acting Consul McDonogh expressed his belief in the potential for extensive trade between Britain, the Regency of Tripoli and the African interior. In the years to come, Consul Warrington's despatches unequivocally alluded to the instructions of the British government to the explorers in opening trade with the interior. In fact, in December 1802, McDonogh detailed the opportunities for trade in senna, madder root, gold dust and other goods, including manufactures, with Benghazi and Tripoli. The correspondence, unlike that of his successor Warrington in the 1820s, suggests that any official thoughts on 'commercial intercourse' with the Kingdoms of Kanem-Bornu and Bagirmi were not yet mature. In 1802, McDonogh reported:

> The wool of Tripoli would not answer exportation but the Wool of Benghazi ... being a finer quality, the French and Venetians before the war carried on a lucrative trade in that article; and I'm informed the French mean to renew the same trade again, having already sent two vessels to load wool at that place. The importation of broad cloths, and every other article of Woollen goods in small quantities in the beginning would answer this market well; the Turks consume a vast quantity besides what they send to Fezzan, and what is sold to the pilgrims that annually pass this way from Mecca in caravans to the number of 12 or 15,000 men.[41]

Consul Warrington would, however, take exception to activities by other British agents acting without his direct sanction to establish commercial relations with the kingdoms of the interior. This was the case with Major Denham when, on the mission to Bornu, the displeasure of the Pasha was incurred upon rumours of Denham having involved himself in mercantile pursuits.[42] Nevertheless, by 1818, the consul had eagerly observed the trade, quantities and value of goods from the interior, and was determined that Britain should benefit from this commerce, in exchange for British manufactures. On 17 April 1818, he wrote to Bathurst:

the Trade of this Place is very considerably encreased of late ... I cannot avoid expressing my regret that there is not a direct Commercial Intercourse between this and Great Britain, which altho' at the present time, would certainly be very limit'd, still it would open the avenue to a more extensive Trade.[43]

Later the same year, Warrington reported on the arrival into Tripoli of the governor of Fezzan, with '30 Camels of Senna, 3 Camels of Gold Dust, 3 Camels of Ivory, 8 Camels of Ostrich Feathers, and 100 Camels of Dates' as well as 1,300 Black slaves. The total value of these 'articles' was $293,480. While the consul believed that the slave trade had impeded British geographic and economic enterprise in Central Africa, he felt that British merchants and Britain should take the initiative in exploiting the strength of the regional economy and the desirable produce of the African interior.[44] The commercial benefit was so great, that such articles generally produced a profit of '50 to 100 per cent' for any British merchant or agent.[45] The produce that was exported from Tripoli also included live cattle, salt, dates, wheat, barley, oil, wool, saffron, saltpetre, madder root ('not known in England'), senna, natron ('better than that from Egypt'), tanned skins and hides ('altho' much Inferior to Buenos Ayres'). The consul was keen to bring to the attention of the government that saltpetre was in the interior in the 'greatest abundance' but that this was not generally known in Europe, and that madder root was shipped in 'great Quantity' to Marseilles and Trieste, and that this 'Barbary root' was preferred to that of Cyprus or Izmir (Smyrna).[46] Madder root produced a dye that was used in the British textile industry known as 'Turkey red' while senna was used for medicinal purposes.[47] These explanations are important as they highlight the potential for the expansion and diversification of trade for British merchants, as well as for the British government and its naval garrisons in the Mediterranean.

In 1824, the British consul's enthusiasm was further fired by a report from a local Sheikh on the trade between Britain and Timbuktu. Although British agents were already familiar with the West African coast, Warrington saw this information as a re-emphasis of the continued opportunity to expand British trade into Africa by reconnecting, for British merchants, places such as Benin and Timbuktu along the established and ancient trade routes. Three of the four principal trade routes connected the commercial hubs of the interior to Tripoli via Murzuq and Ghadames, while the other connected to Benghazi via Wadai and Kufra (Figure 12).[48] In a letter to Wilmot Horton on 24 July 1825, Warrington wrote that he had learned of

an extensive commerce at Tombuctoo, of English and other European manufacture, that it is brought from the Sea in large Boats, which navigate regularly. That Mouckta [Chief of Timbuktu] can with safety pass Major Laing by water to the sea which we have now reason to believe [is the Bight of] Benin.[49]

In considering the state of trade between Britain and Tripoli, two charts are presented on page 85, covering the period from 1823 to 1831. These charts (see Figures 10 and 11) have been composed using the data provided by the consul

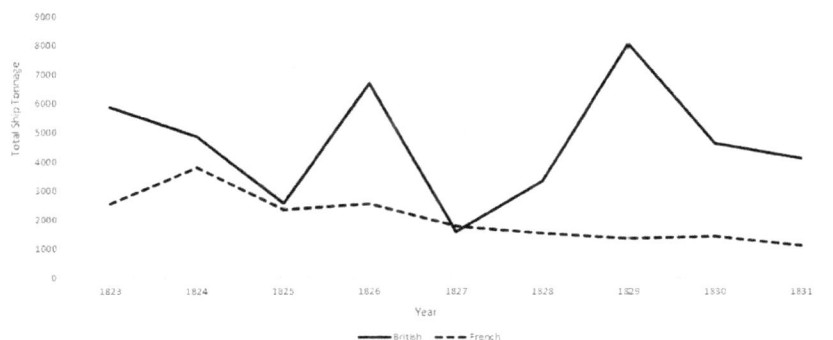

Figure 10 Tonnage of cargo arriving and departing at the ports of Tripoli and Benghazi for the purpose of British trade, 1823–31.

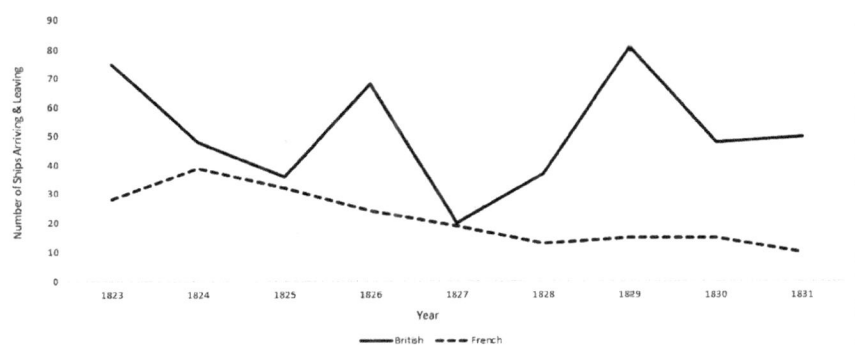

Figure 11 Quantity of vessels arriving and departing at the ports of Tripoli and Benghazi for the purpose of British trade, 1823–31.

at Tripoli and, later, also by the vice-consul at Benghazi.[50] In previous years, the consular correspondence indicates that Consuls Lucas, Langford and Warrington included information on an ad hoc and occasional basis, with details that were not uniform, consistent or complete.[51]

According to the data provided by the British consul at Tripoli and by the vice-consul at Benghazi, based on both the number of vessels and tonnage, trade had largely remained steady between 1823 and 1829, in stark contrast to the declining trade between France and the Regency. The figures for 1825 and 1827 appear lower than they should due to political instability and missing data. British trade arriving and departing from the Regency of Tripoli began to peak following the successive exploratory missions into the interior and the accompanying rise in the influence of Consul Warrington in Tripoli. Trade noticeably declined in 1830 for a number of reasons, including the growing internal insecurity in the Regency due to a succession dispute between the Pasha's son, Ali, and grandson, Mohamed, as well as the temporary cessation of diplomatic relations between Tripoli and Britain.[52] Yusuf Qaramanli was also deeply frustrated by the externally driven restrictions on corsairing activity and on the Regency's trade in slaves. The Pasha had failed to realize his commercial ambitions to secure trade with individual European states, in part because the British consul, who negotiated the majority of the original treaties in 1818, failed to mediate again to remind those states of their treaty obligations. In turn, British trade also suffered. These data are significant as they highlight the growing interest and strength of British trade with Tripoli from 1823 to 1831.

The returns of British trade also show the shift in the goods traded to and from the ports of the Regency. Taking the years 1823 and 1829–31 as a sample, there is a clear move to more trade in colonial goods by 1831 – including coffee, sugar and cotton – from an earlier trade that was largely made up of nails, boards, wine, earthen pots, drugs, cochineal, logwood and 'English' manufactures.[53]

In terms of strategic and political priorities, the consular dispatches emphasize continuing concern with the security of British garrisons in the Mediterranean, including the entrepôts of Gibraltar, Minorca and Malta, and with the Egypt of Ali Bey and Mohamed Ali. In combination with the supply of grains and further livestock from Tunis and Egypt, the provision of goods required to maintain British naval strength in the Mediterranean was thus secured. Unlike Egypt, Tripoli did not suffer for a want of timber – another commodity that was in short supply for the British garrison at Valletta.[54] Consul Warrington, following reports from his vice-consul at Benghazi, wrote to the Secretary of State Bathurst in March 1821 to inform him that there was an abundance of timber from the Jebel Akhdar (Green Mountain) range in the east (near Benghazi) to meet the Royal Navy's needs in Malta. In typical fashion, prior to writing to Bathurst, Consul Warrington had already approached Yusuf Qaramanli and had obtained the Pasha's permission for the future extraction of this timber.[55] It is unclear whether this intelligence was acted upon, and, if so, what quantity of timber was shipped to the naval dockyard at Malta. The consul, in fact, wrote twice to Earl Bathurst in early 1821 on this discovery and on his successful exertions in securing the forest for the benefit of the Mediterranean fleet:

> A short time since I found it necessary to send a Vice Consul to Derna. I gave him strict orders to visit every part of the Cyrene & report … the nature of that extensive Forest which I have at various periods visited & which has excited a most zealous Interest, as I consider it might render an Important benefit to the British navy in the Mediterranean.
>
> My Vice Consul informs me the Timber is equal to the Building of the largest ships, situated near the sea, & one thousand ship loads might without difficulty be embarked. In the commencement of this object I secured this Forest from the Bashaw provided the British Govt. wished to extract Timber from that Quarter.[56]

The consular records indicate that Proconsul Pat Wilkie had a trading background. In 1804, eight years before becoming the British proconsul to Tripoli, Wilkie had been contracted to supply 'wine' and 'fresh beef' to the Royal Navy, and had received the direct approval of Rear Admiral Horatio Nelson to do so.[57] Bonaventure Beaussier (1749–1814), the French consul in Tripoli, wrote to Wilkie in March 1812, at a time when Britain and France were at war, to enquire further about his connections to Marseilles:

> I've known in Marseille, fourty or fifty years ago, an opulent house of trade under the name of Sollicoffre brothers & Wilkie. Was you their partner or some of your relations? I desire to be excused for that indiscreet question.[58]

This letter was written at a time when the British government preferred that its agents not participate in commercial pursuits while acting as official representatives of the Crown. By 1822, this view was made explicit in an Order of Council, followed by the formal regulations of 1835 that were issued to further reform the consular services.[59] In fact, Beaussier himself recognized that his enquiry was an 'indiscreet' one and, for this reason, there is no reply recorded in the consular archives. Nothing further is currently known about the relations between the House of Sollicoffre Brothers and Wilkie in Marseilles.

Despite the resolution among European powers at the Congress of Vienna to abolish the trade in slaves and the Exmouth Treaty of 29 April 1816, outlawing Christian, White slavery, raids along the northern Mediterranean shores remained a political and humanitarian issue. These attacks also posed a continued obstacle to the development of British trade in the African interior, particularly around the territories of Lake Chad. Indeed, the British consul continued to protest strongly against the capture and enslavement of both African and European subjects almost a decade after the conclusion of the Exmouth Treaty. Nevertheless, despite these serious challenges, the consul had gained increasing confidence in the abilities of British agents to gain access to the interior's wealth and to establish commerce with those kingdoms. As Warrington wrote to Alexander Gordon Laing in 1825,

> The Road by way of Benin is yet untried & probably many obstacles will in effort arise as Government have to conciliate the King of Benin & His Royal Neighbour ... We ought (or it appears to me we ought) to keep this Road open to the Interior, & which would certainly establish its Geography & make us acquainted with the Inhabitants, altho' that could not by the medium promote a direct Trade but in the end the Niger will be opened to the Navigation of English Manufacture.
>
> To me this appears a most extensive, & a most Important Subject, as it embraces the abolition of Slavery, the civilization of Northern Africa, it opens a most extensive Trade, makes us acquainted with the Geographical Positions, Introduces us to unknown cities & even Kingdoms, affording us a knowledge of the Inhabitants, their manners, customs & in this will certainly be an Honor to England & will be appreciated by after Ages.

> Clapperton & Pearce ... have two Doctors with them one for Bello I presume, the other for the Sheikh of Bornou. Pearce goes to the latter place, & as the whole country of the Beghirme is now open to the Sheikh, there will be no difficulty to go round the Shad [Lake Chad] & pursue its Evacuation into the Nile ... I think you would do more Important Service to your Country to return to Tombuctoo & to establish a Permanent Relationship with that People in Commercial Pursuits & get the name of their agent at Benin or the mouth of the Niger, so that English manufacture might be consigned to Him, having ascertained the most saleable articles.
>
> I wish you had a Person to leave as Agent, Doctor or Consul, as having got a footing it ought not to be lost. Many a Merchant will with avidity try the Experiment.[60]

The British consul also acted on behalf of other European states that, for various pragmatic and political reasons, solicited his intervention and legal representation. The treaties and agreements concluded between Britain and Tripoli emphasize the paramount importance of the maintenance of favourable terms of trade and the protection of British interests and subjects in the Regency. Some of the smaller European powers, such as the Hanseatic towns, formed an alliance among themselves, and Warrington offered his assistance in concluding a favourable treaty on behalf of Hamburg, rather like the treaties the consul had negotiated in 1818 on behalf of several other European powers such as Naples and the Papal States.[61]

In terms of real and perceived strategic priorities, however, one of the most serious was the threat which Bonaparte's forces posed to the British Empire in India, through the utilization of an overland route through Egypt and the Levant.[62] Indeed, in 1797, King George III wrote on the subject to Yusuf Qaramanli:

> You may judge with what reluctance it is we feel ourself under the necessity of declining to comply with any desire of yours, particularly your request of sending an English Ship to Tripoli, but at this time, it is totally out of our power so to do. The multiplicity of the Enemies, with whom We have to contend, making it necessary for Us to collect Our whole Force, to counteract their designs, and protect the Property of our subjects. We hope you will be convinced that nothing but this necessity prevent our complying with your wishes, and that on all occasions, We are most anxious to shew Our true Regard and friendship for you, as a token of which we send you a Present of some things of the manufacture of our Dominions, particularly some Fire arms, which we have been informed you have expressed a desire to have. We therefore hope you will accept them as the Gift of a friend, who is sincerely interested in promoting your satisfaction. Your loving friend.[63]

The African Association Missions

At the turn of the nineteenth century, companies competed for the limited but prized commercial opportunities along the North African shores, including in coral fishery.⁶⁴ The Coral Company was reported to be active in the region as early as 1810, although the role of this enterprise is little documented.⁶⁵ The ensuing activities of the African Association are, however, better documented, and they chimed closely with the ambitions of both the Colonial Office and the wider British government.⁶⁶ The African Association was founded in 1788 and was originally called 'The Association for Promoting the Discovery of the Interior Parts of Africa'. The Association was also called the 'African Society' and as previously highlighted, it was not only motivated by scientific research, but it also became a strong anti-slavery voice in Britain in the early nineteenth century. Cooperation between the Colonial Office and the African Association resulted in the funding of the Eastern Mission to Barqa, and of the Southern and the Southwestern Missions to the Niger and Timbuktu with the assistance of the Lords Commissioners of the Treasury. This series of expeditions launched from the bridgehead at Tripoli since 1817 included notable personalities such as George Lyon, Dixon Denham, Hugh Clapperton, Walter Oudney, Henry Beechey and Alexander Gordon Laing. There were, of course, many more men involved in these missions, including Ernest Toole, John Tyrwhitt and William Hillman (a relative of Oudney), as well as three men who died with Ritchie's earlier ill-fated mission, two of whom remain nameless in the dispatches of the British consul in Tripoli.⁶⁷ The consul general also played a direct role in the exploratory missions of the government and African Association, and had a clear influence on their progress. As the chief intermediary between London and the missions, he determined the amount of supplies and monies sent on to the travellers, and, crucially, he also influenced how they and their individual endeavours were perceived back in Britain.

The progress of the African Association expeditions was also adversely affected by local politics, clashes among party members, financial shortages, disease and bad luck.⁶⁸ Though perhaps not officially intended, there was a positive correlation between the expansion of British consular representation and the increase in exploratory activity into the interior.⁶⁹ The recruitment of vice-consular personnel to Fezzan and Bornu from 1817 to at least 1823 came directly from the ranks of the Southern and Southeastern missions, and included Oudney, who was charged with setting up a vice-consular office in Kanem-Bornu.⁷⁰ According to the *Caledonian Mercury*:

> [In] letters from Major Denham, who commands the expedition into the interior of Africa ... It was proposed that the expedition should depart for Fezzan in February last [1822], and a competent escort was provided by his Highness to convey them considerably beyond Bornu, at which place the learned Professor, Dr Oudenay [*sic*], is to remain as British Vice-Consul.⁷¹

This network of consular agents tied in closely with the missions of the African Association, providing logistical and practical support to the explorers, and acting as intermediaries with local tribes and notables. Unfortunately, because of the remoteness of their posts, Tyrwhitt and Toole did not last long and fell prey to local maladies such as 'cholera morbus' and 'hemma' (malaria). Oudney also died early in the mission, but, contrary to Warrington's account to the Colonial Office that Oudney was in the best of health on his departure from Tripoli, Oudney was in fact already 'consumptive before he left England'.[72]

Unfortunately for the missions, serious differences also arose between the members and with the consul general at Tripoli.[73] Such conflicts had a negative impact on the cohesion of the missions and on both their ability and willingness to send reports on their progress and findings. The missions, however, gradually became fragmented and members refused to work together, as was the case for the Southern Mission when Major Denham would not be part of any team that included Lieutenant Clapperton. This was because of allegations of homosexuality and gross misconduct against Clapperton while on official duty.[74] Major Denham wrote to Clapperton in April 1823, after they had parted ways:

> I should neglect my duty were I any longer to delay setting before you in the strongest light I am able the continued extreme impropriety of your conduct both public and private which I regret to say is no less discreditable to the mission and the country than to your self as an officer and at the same time injurious in the highest degree to our Interests at the present moment.[75]

The consul unsuccessfully attempted to mediate and to reunite the missions with their original objectives.[76] Crucially, he also encouraged members to send their dispatches to him to forward to London. Unfortunately, disputes between rival parties had become irreconcilable. Despite the limited achievements of the missions, Warrington continued to attempt to establish commercial intercourse with the prosperous territories to the south of Tripoli. The vice-consular network in itself signified the growth in the influence and role of Britain in the Mediterranean, and in particular in the Regency of Tripoli during the first decades of the nineteenth century. British agents worked successfully to gain access to the caliphates and kingdoms south of Tripoli, to promote the researches of the African Association, and to further the ambitions of the British government for a greater trading relationship with the powers of the African interior. British naval personnel had also become involved as another point in the transmission of information on the exploration of opportunities in the region.[77]

On the suggestion of Hassuna D'Ghies, Warrington wrote to Earl Bathurst in 1826, proposing a new initiative be joined to a proposal to abolish the slave trade. This initiative was an explicit recognition that, commercially, abolition needed to go hand in hand with the promotion of 'legitimate trade'. Warrington wrote that he was hoping 'His Highness [Yusuf Qaramanli] will use His Influence in the Interior to get the Native chiefs to abolish slavery & to open a channel for Trade the Bashaw [sic] deriving the advantage of what is carried on by this Regency ... [and will] use His best offices and Exertions, for a certain Number of British Agents to be received and respected in the Interior'.[78] While the determination of the British government to abolish slavery gained momentum, the consul recognized that in consequence of the great loss of Revenue ... His Highness to receive thirty thousand Dollars per Annum & if the contract is broken by England the Engagement absolved; In the first Instance the Term to be for Ten years ... if your Lordship would wish the Question not to be agitated you have only to cast this Letter into the fire, & with me the subject will be as Irrevocably consumed as the Paper on which I write. But should the subject be thought worthy of consideration I trust in God it may lead to the final Abolition of Slavery & various other great and most Important Events.[79]

A Board of Health at Tripoli

In a 37-year period, from 1794 to 1831, the consuls officially reported no fewer than thirteen occurrences of famine and disease, including the plague and cholera, that directly affected the Regency of Tripoli and the surrounding territories. Such devastating outbreaks affected the health of the consulates and during that time reduced the daily preoccupation of the consuls to keeping their families and themselves from ill health, as well as from malnourishment due to the prohibitive cost of provisions. All the European consuls were united in times of hardship provoked by famine or civil unrest, when they and their families suffered alike.[80] As Consul Lucas wrote to Dundas in September 1794,

> Our Markets [are] once more tolerably well supplied with Provisions, just at a time when the Spanish Consul and myself had determined to send our Families away to Malta, and Mrs Lucas's Baggage and servants has been actually shipt on Board a Spanish vessel which we had Freighted for that purpose, as the scurvey has began to make a rapid progress amongst us, and my wifes life despaired of.[81]

Experiences with food shortages and recurrent epidemics could also contribute to agents actively working together in cases of mutual interest. Since Lucas's consulship, waves of epidemics periodically besieged the Regency with the plague, cholera, malaria and other pestilential diseases. These outbreaks had terrible consequences for the local population, while droughts could result in crippling food shortages and deep civil unrest. Lucas reported in June 1794:

> The Mortality amongst the Poorer sort of the Inhabitants has been very great within these 8 months past, for want of food – particularly, vegetables and fruits which formerly constituted the principle part of their Nutriment upwards of 600 of these poor wretches have died within that time, merely of a scurbutic complaint attended with a total debility, but thank God we have hitherto escaped the Plague; myself and the greatest part of my Family, have been slightly attacked with that complaint and a Fever, but by my Surgeons skills, and proper Medicures we are again restored to health, tho very weak for want of proper Nutriment.[82]

By 1831, in response to years of continual famine and disease, Consul Warrington worked – in cooperation with the consul general of France and with the support of 'two respectable French merchants, one Imperial and two Doctors being British subjects' – to establish a Board of Health in Tripoli for the 'superintendence of the health of the place'.[83] This included John Dickson, British naval surgeon, physician to Yusuf Qaramanli and superintendent of health in Tripoli. Warrington was earnest in his desire to effectively tackle and limit the devastating impact of epidemics on the lives of the local population. On 30 September 1831 the consul wrote to Viscount Goderich (1782–1859): 'If we only succeed in stopping the march of such a horrid Enemy', he continued, 'we may preserve the Health of the whole Coast, & prevent the Disease being imported in to the South of Europe'.[84] The consul, in an effort to gain the support of the British government, appealed to the need to maintain British shipping and the health of the British garrisons in the region. Warrington understood that such wide-scale outbreaks of disease also undermined hopes for the development of British commerce with Tripoli, or for a British settlement in the Regency.

The initiative to establish a Board of Health went hand in hand with an earlier initiative that had begun in 1816 – to undertake a comprehensive vaccination programme of the population of the Regency and to introduce through Tripoli, the 'Lymph' (smallpox) vaccine to 'the greatest part of Africa'.[85] Warrington planned to carry out this inoculation drive with the assistance of Dr John Dickson. Dickson was a naval surgeon, described by Lord Grosvenor on his visit to Tripoli in 1830 as 'an Irish doctor'.[86] In 1816, approximately one year after arriving in Tripoli, Dickson succeeded one Pietro Crocillo as the Pasha's personal physician. In January 1832, when Dickson had been a Royal Naval surgeon for 25 years, Consul Warrington wrote to Viscount Goderich to ask that Dickson's half-pay not be withdrawn on the basis of Dickson's former employment by Yusuf Qaramanli from 1815 to 1826.[87] Having obtained the sanction of the Pasha, Consul Warrington wrote to the First Lord Commissioner of the Admiralty, Viscount Melville (1771–1851), to make an application, on behalf of the government of Tripoli, for a regular supply of the smallpox vaccine.[88] On 5 August 1816, the consul wrote to Melville that he was convinced of the vaccine's 'full efficacy' not only in eradicating smallpox but also

> [in] the probability of its exterminating very considerably the Effects of the most dreadful Maladies [including] the Plague, if not proving in many Instances a Preventative.[89]

This plan for a vaccination programme, the enlistment of the Pasha's support and the formation of a Board of Health emphasize the scale and ambition of Consul Warrington for the British bridgehead in Tripoli. Following an epidemic of cholera in 1831, the same year that Consul Warrington established the Board of Health in Tripoli, a French doctor, 'Clot Bey', similarly founded a board of health and a quarantine service in Egypt in an effort to undertake a 'wide-ranging' vaccination and public health reform programme.[90] Unfortunately, in Tripoli, the British- and French-led Board of Health was short-lived, because the British consul could not secure the secretary of state's approval to continue with the endeavour, and, although Warrington did not provide the reason why, it was likely that this lack of approbation signified a lack of financial support for the fledgling Board. The British consul, at least until after the reinstitution of an Ottoman governor, Mustafa Negib Pasha, in 1835, did not attempt to revive either of these initiatives. Nevertheless, these new consular activities at the frontiers of empire may be viewed alongside the Colonial Office's efforts to engage in a more systematic relationship with Tripoli, and to exploit the markets and commercial resources of Central and West Africa.

As these examples show, the British consul was connected not only to his peers and colleagues in his official capacity but also to other European governments, as well as to the British government agencies – namely the political, naval and philanthropic. In Tripoli, the British consulate was connected to those of France, Spain, Imperial Austria, the Netherlands, Denmark and Norway, Sweden, the United States of America, as well as the long-established Venetian, Neapolitan, Tuscan and Roman powers, and their naval forces. These agents, communicating with and working among each other on a regular basis, constituted one of the essential parts of the British consul's professional network.

'A Stupendous Piece of Policy It Would Ill Become Me to Argue On'

Over the course of Yusuf Qaramanli's reign, from 1795 to 1832, the British imperial bridgehead at Tripoli witnessed an unprecedented rise in its presence and influence as a direct result of the British consul's activities in the Regency.[91] In the 1820s, the vice-consular network under Consul Warrington was significantly expanded and this, in turn, extended British representation beyond the boundaries of the Regency, to Murzuq and territories south of Fezzan (see Figure 12). This expansion was enhanced by the launch of the missions of the African Association, which provided a recruiting ground for vice-consular personnel. The attempts to reform the consular services did not affect the activities of the bridgehead at Tripoli, primarily because the consul, as the 'man on the spot', continued to act on his own initiative. British representation was subsequently established in the territories beyond the Regency of Tripoli, in Murzuq and as far south as Kuka and Bornu. Looking across the Mediterranean, despite the fluctuating volume of supplies and provisions from Tripoli to British garrisons in Minorca, Malta and Sicily, British trade to and from Tripoli had remained steady, and the Regency emphasized the potential for British trade in manufactures and in the export of desirable produce from Tripoli and the interior of Africa. Throughout this period, the bridgehead at Tripoli maintained close communication with other neighbouring British consulates as well as with the Admiralty and the Colonial Office in London.[92]

The bridgehead developed by Consul Warrington, and the networks he continuously cultivated, embodied the success of British agents in enhancing British representation and reputation in new territories. The vice-consular network, along with the consul general in Tripoli, navigated the complex political landscape in order to gain access to and pursue commercial ambitions in the interior, engaging with powerful leaders such as the Sheikh of Fezzan, the Shehu of Kanem-Bornu and Sultan Bello of the 'Great Sudan'. The consul himself exercised a unique level of influence and intervention between Yusuf Qaramanli and the powerful tribal confederacy of the Awlad Suliman throughout the 1820s.[93] This 'mediation', as Warrington preferred to term his actions, was unique, as the consul extended British influence in lands which were, strictly speaking, outside both the political and moral authority of the Pasha of Tripoli.

The British presence was also strengthened in a pragmatic sense, as the bridgehead organized and channelled intelligence reports from all the British agents posted in the hinterlands of Tripoli. These agents acted as intermediaries between British subjects and the Qaramanli dynasty and they explicitly represented British ambitions on the frontiers of empire. Ultimately, the bridgehead at Tripoli during the reign of Yusuf Qaramanli conveyed the multiple and complex layers of British interests – commercial, consular and diplomatic – that emanated simultaneously from the 'man on the spot' and the bridgehead at Tripoli, as well as from the government in London.

Chapter 7

SURVEYING NEW FRONTIERS: INTELLIGENCE-GATHERING AND INTERVENTION

> The last accounts we had for Egypt, were, that Buonaparte had preceded from Grand Cairo to Syria with about 45,000 men, and fixed his head quarters at St John d'Akkra ... I shall not fail to communicate your grace by the earliest opportunity every other intelligence worth your notice.
> – Consul Lucas to Duke of Portland, 4 Sept. 1799.[1]

Intelligence cultivation by British agents in Tripoli during the reign of Yusuf Qaramanli suggests an unprecedented level of activity by the British bridgehead in the Regency, including through the expansion of a network of vice-consular agents. Tripoli played a role in wider British concerns over French manoeuvring, Egypt and the protection of Greek territories and British subjects. In July 1823, Consul Warrington summarized what he believed to be Britain's primary objectives in Africa:

> I have been consul to Tripoli Ten years last month ... During my consular Residence more Political Events of Importance have taken Place then ever occur'd from the Earliest period of time. The noble act of abolishing Slavery, the happy Prospect of an opening into the Interior & the Progress towards civilization which daily encreases will be an everlasting Honour to the British Nation and to His Present Majestys Ministers.[2]

For Britain, the Ochakov Affair of 1791, and the treaties of Amiens (1802) and Tilsit (1807) underscored the government's political concerns in the Mediterranean and on the future security of its empire. As a capitulatory and as an emerging imperial power in the Mediterranean, Britain was motivated to contain French ambitions and Russian incursions into Ottoman lands. The Admiralty was also concerned over access to the Arabian seas by the maritime route around the Cape of Good Hope, the (mostly) overland trade route from Egypt to Arabia, and the overland route to the Levant. In both practical and symbolic senses, Tripoli transcended the Mediterranean, African and Ottoman spheres of political and commercial interest. Though Tripoli lay beyond the boundaries of formal empire, a succession of British agents had worked tirelessly to expand the interests of Britain both on the coast and into the interior of Africa.

The British government's ability to foresee the future was challenged by the competing demands on its economic and military resources during a period of global upheaval.[3] While directly confronting French manoeuvres in Egypt, Britain found itself enlisting collaborators in territories as yet unoccupied by European states. This was undertaken in order to respond to the immediate strategic and economic concerns arising from a number of quarters – including the safeguarding of the empire in India. Fierce competition with France remained one of the most significant factors that helped to define Britain's overseas ambitions and its military ascendency in the Mediterranean.

The beginnings of the Eastern Question could be detected in the provinces of the Ottoman Empire as early as 1770 with local revolts against Turkish rule in the Morea.[4] The rebellion of the Pashas was underway, from Tripoli in 1793, across the Balkans in the first decades of the nineteenth century, and in Egypt and then Algiers up 1830. This crisis – or series of political upheavals – questioned the central authority of the Ottoman Porte through an age of violent revolution that also swept Europe, and which questioned the global balance of power. The successive naval defeats suffered by the Porte opened the gate to British, French and Russian ambitions in the Mediterranean, the Black Sea and beyond.

Britain's primary concern was the very real threat posed by French ambitions to gain access to the sea and land routes to the Middle East and India. The British government's military-strategic priorities therefore logically converged on Egypt and France's repeated attempts to establish French influence in North Africa. Britain's defensive response to the French invasion of Egypt in 1807 provoked an additional increase in hostilities with Russia. The question over the future of Greece and its demands for independence in the 1820s also contributed to British concerns over the political stability of the Mediterranean region. In addition to the increasing concern over Russian ambitions that culminated in the treaty of Hünkâr İskelesi (1833), Bonaparte's Eastern expedition and ambitions via Egypt and the Levant also continued to hold the attention of the British government and its naval fleet in the Mediterranean.

Within the context of the Eastern Question, there is a plethora of work on Greece and Egypt during and after the Napoleonic era.[5] There is also scholarship on the work of consuls and diplomats, and growing studies on the value and utility of these agents' official correspondence. The roles of both distance and patronage are critical in shaping our understanding of the world in which British agents operated at the time. As a direct result of patronage extended from London, consuls' opinions and advice carried weight with the local power structures.[6] The 'remote' location of the consular post at Tripoli also influenced its role as a bridgehead. It was often impossible to request and wait for official direction when political matters on the ground often required an immediate response.[7]

Despite differences in opinion over the motivating factors behind British activities in North Africa and the Mediterranean, British concerns, primarily over the empire, nevertheless generated 'efforts to secure military, political and social information'.[8] The relationship between successful intelligence-gathering strategies and British activity and intervention in a non-colonial territory is crucial. While Britain never possessed territory in the Regency of Tripoli, it did develop a successful imperial bridgehead that emphasized the imperial ambitions of both the British government and the consul general at Tripoli. The intelligence collection process was a central component of both the bridgehead and the consuls' longevity at Tripoli. The view of the intelligence-gathering network as a means to influence and conquer is a useful guide to understanding the ways in which imperial agents could interact with the local polity as a non-colonial domain.[9]

Scholarship on go-betweens and cross-cultural encounters illuminates how the consul mediated in a variety of issues, because of official and personal interests, with the government of Tripoli, and how an effective intelligence network was developed from the consul's station at Tripoli.[10] This is significant as the British consul was never able to acquire patrimonial or affective knowledge in the Regency.[11] Information provided by go-betweens or 'social communicators' proved valuable to the consul and he filled his dispatches accordingly with records of interviews that he had conducted, supplemented by details of local developments that had been relayed to him from the interior.

The role of the British consul as a component of a wider imperial network in the Mediterranean is paramount. These connections reveal much about the 'processes of knowledge movement, translation, transmission, and the ways in which people, practices and places are linked and assembled into knowledge spaces [that] are often hard to discern and bring into visibility'.[12]

Correspondence

Consular dispatches provide details of the intelligence-gathering process and the local intelligence network. These official dispatches to and from the bridgehead also provide evidence of an unexpected level of intervention in the affairs of the Regency. Here the consul played a key role in gathering and coordinating information, and in developing a network of contacts alongside his vice-consuls that were reliable, local sources of information. The information communicated by the British consul at Tripoli most often focused on the routine consular and occasional diplomatic duties, but it also contained information on financial, military and political developments of interest to ministers in London. The correspondence, furthermore, provides a detailed insight into the life and career of the British consul at Tripoli, into the relationships he fostered with others, including superior officers, and into the network of agents he developed in the service of the empire. Crucially, these accounts also assist in understanding the motives and priorities that pressed at any one time on a consular agent.[13]

In providing a detailed, everyday account of a consul's responsibilities and their career trajectory, the dispatches constitute evidence of the frequency and quantity of each consul's official reports to the Colonial Department. The volume and content of a consul's correspondence also reveals much about the position and perception of responsibilities by consuls at their posts, as well as the changing commercial and political interests at home and overseas. The correspondence of the three resident consuls from Tripoli – Lucas, Langford and Warrington – varied considerably in volume and quality during their postings. The forms of communication utilized by the consuls and their distance from London undoubtedly affected the intelligence-gathering process as well as the consul's ability to make decisions. In a similar vein to works focusing on the official correspondence – rather than the private papers – of British imperial representatives, Sabine Freitag and Peter Wende write:

> It can be argued that more 'authentic' or more 'relevant' information is found in the informal, private correspondence which every Secretary of State for Foreign Affairs maintained with envoys, especially those to whom he was personally close … [However] [t]he really important information was never delivered only in private letters, but had to appear first in the official correspondence.[14]

In terms of the local affairs of Tripoli, the correspondence is limited in what it does not reveal about the Regency's relations with its southern neighbours, because the British consul did not provide detailed reports on political relations and economic ties between Tripoli and its neighbours. With the exception of Egypt, Fezzan and Wadai, the consular reports did not appear to pay much attention to political events beyond the boundaries of the Regency. Details in the consular dispatches may have been limited for a number of reasons, including the consul's preoccupation with reporting on 'Mediterranean' events, especially developments in Egypt. Another possibility was that the consul did not consider that the 'regional' politics of the interior had a significant bearing on future British enterprise in Ottoman North Africa, nor how British ambitions were intimately tied to the interests of the Tripoline government. Although this leaves an unsatisfactory gap in our knowledge and understanding of the political and economic connections of Tripoli, the focus nevertheless is on the utility of Tripoli in the service of British interests. In this respect, beyond the words of the British consul, 'all is conjecture'.[15]

Meanwhile, the British government was preoccupied with the protection of British Empire in the East, and the maintenance of the political status quo in the eastern Mediterranean in order to counter French and Russian ambitions in the region. While these priorities were not necessarily contradictory, they did signify the responsibility of the consul to draw the government's attention to British interests in Tripoli and the surrounding territories. In an indication of how communications between London and Tripoli could sometimes be delayed or go amiss, there were also rare instances where the British consul received intelligence of his own government's actions from the Pasha of Tripoli. On 28 February 1807, Consul Langford had received news of Britain 'acting with Russia to declare war on the Sublime Porte'.[16] The uncomfortable situation Langford subsequently found himself in was probably because the dispatch to the consul containing the news went missing on its way to Tripoli. This scenario was a distinct possibility as the consular correspondence details that, from time to time, either the consul or Colonial Department had not received a particular letter or report. After a meeting with Yusuf Qaramanli in February 1807, Langford immediately wrote to Lord Collingwood, Sidney Smith and the governors of Malta and Gibraltar to clarify Tripoli's position in the conflict. Langford explained that the Pasha had

> communicated to me His intention of writing a letter to His Majesty, and in which He should state His determination to remain neutral. As His Highness requested me to make publick these His sentiments, I have written to that effect.[17]

Tripoli's desire to remain neutral in the increasingly unstable political environment of the Mediterranean was later adjusted in 1828 into a refusal by the Pasha to provide a further declaration of the Regency's position. Although Tripoli was relatively independent of the Porte, Yusuf Qaramanli did not want to provoke Istanbul into a confrontation following its naval defeats in the eastern Mediterranean and the tense atmosphere over the future of Greece.

The consul needed to be able to exert influence over the reigning Pasha and reach amicable agreements with local tribal leaders outside the Qaramanli sphere of control. For the British consul, imperial interests concerning commerce, politics and the security of the empire all went hand in hand and manifested themselves in the political agenda with Yusuf Qaramanli. Influential Tripoline notables such as the minister for foreign affairs, Hassuna D'Ghies, and the treasurer, Mohamed Bait-al-Mal, all provide an insight into how the British and French consuls worked to exercise influence with Qaramanli's advisors.

Egypt

> If one looks at the events of the late eighteenth century; and any attempt to assess the influence of the possession of India upon the formulation of British foreign policy in the nineteenth century must take account of fears of France as well as Russia.[18]

British concerns on the future security of its empire were justified. By 1798, France had planned an invasion of Egypt in order to 'threaten an essential component of British economic power, its trade with India, and to compel Britain to divert resources that would otherwise be used to support its continental allies'.[19] Alongside French ambitions, the wider issues represented by the Eastern Question – the future role of Russia and the stability of the Ottoman Empire – also played a significant role in British policy formulation and activity in Tripoli. There was an increase in reporting on any and all developments in Tripoli's relations with the Porte and Egypt, as well as intelligence-gathering on strategic interests in the southern and eastern Mediterranean.

In addition, the rise of Mohamed Ali to predominance in Egypt was significant for broader British political and strategic concerns in the eastern Mediterranean. This was because Mohamed Ali challenged the status quo in the region, as represented by the Ottoman Porte. Ali desired the territory and trade of the Levant, Syria and

North Africa down to the 'Great Sudan' of central Africa. The Pasha of Egypt also challenged the European consensus that sought to abolish the slave trade, and British political interests in the Aegean. As Mohamed Dorby's mission to Tripoli in 1822 evidenced, Egypt (and Tripoli) still used slaves as valuable currency. The exploitation of the trade in slaves remained a point of disagreement, and measures to reduce and abolish the trade had a negative effect on the revenues of North African states. Meanwhile, Egypt's military ascendency did not go unnoticed by her neighbours. While Yusuf Qaramanli refused to cede vital territories in the east of the Regency to Mohamed Ali, Bernardino Drovetti, the French proconsul in Egypt, suggested in 1829 that Mohamed Ali take the opportunity to annexe the Regencies of Tripoli, Tunis and Algiers.[20]

Meanwhile, the consular correspondence also indicated that Britain continued to concern itself with political developments that affected the integrity of the Ottoman Empire. As early as 1810, the intelligence reported by Consul Langford underscored how this interest went beyond the eastern Mediterranean and into Arabia. The consul wrote of intelligence received that Abd' al-Wahhab of Nedsjed (Najd), the 'Grandson of "abd-el Warhab" the Reformer of "Mahometanism"', had been driven from key territories of the Hijaz, including Mecca, Medina and 'adjacent territories'.[21] Langford added that the removal of al-Wahhab was a consequence of Ibrahim Pasha of the 'highlands of Yemen' on behalf of the Ottoman Porte. This war was followed by military incursions in 1811 by Mohamed Ali and a war between Egypt and the Ottoman Empire that lasted until 1818.[22] The dispatch from Langford in February 1810 highlights the close connections and communication between British imperial agents in North Africa, because the intelligence was relayed from Alexandria to the British consul in Tripoli.[23]

To protect Britain's existing imperial possessions, and to counter French influence in the Mediterranean, British naval commanders and the governor of Malta prioritized the security and provision of Britain's military garrisons in the Mediterranean – including in Spain, Gibraltar, Minorca and Malta. Along with Tunis and Egypt, Tripoli provided a regular export of livestock, grain and other provisions to these naval bases. According to the consular accounts, from 1806 to 1810, at a time of relative prosperity, Tripoli more than doubled its supply of livestock to the British garrisons to over 3,000 bullocks and sheep.[24] The consul worked assiduously to maintain these export agreements with Yusuf Qaramanli, and thus helped to secure British naval strength and capacity in the Mediterranean region as whole, despite the occasional threats of the Pasha:

> His Highness [Yusuf Qaramanli] ... would fair have us to believe that 'Malta' is of no use to His wants, but that the Island is and ever must be necessitated for cattle from 'Tripoli', in the hope that We may, under such idea, permit Him to act as He pleases towards Us by Sea and Land.[25]

By 1821, when Warrington reported on the timber resources of the Jebel Akhdar in the east of the Regency, the Admiralty had commissioned Captain Smyth to undertake a detailed coastal survey of North Africa.[26] Smyth's survey of the southern Mediterranean shores eastward from Tripoli came at a critical time, when Mohamed Ali was believed to be 'busily employed in Erecting various Forts &c to command the Entrance into the Harbour of Toubrook, situated near Bomba on the confines of [the] Regency [of Tripoli]'.[27] Consul Warrington further wrote that no fewer than two thousand men were reported to be working on the fortifications, along with 'several French articifers'.[28] Warrington continued:

> I conceive it is my duty to Inform you of the circumstance … as from the retired Locality, Forts, and even a Town might be Built without His Majesty's Government knowing one word of it.[29]

Smyth's survey, and the assistance provided by the consul, ushered in a closer working relationship with the Admiralty, beyond the usual consular endeavours to seek assistance for actual or perceived breaches of treaty articles. Following the arrival of Smyth in Tripoli, John Wilson Croker of the Admiralty Office wrote to Undersecretary Henry Goulburn (1784–1856) with an update on Smyth's removal of antiquities from Leptis Magna, and Consul Warrington's ambitions for research into the interior.[30] Meanwhile, while still in Tripoli, Smyth had published his well-received survey of Sicily and nearby islands.[31] On 2 February 1818, Croker wrote:

> I am commanded by the Lords Commissioners of the admiralty to transmit to you for the information of Earl Bathurst, a copy of a letter from Rear Admiral Sir Charles Penrose, dated the 21st of November; accompanied by an Extract of a report from Captain Smyth, relative to the embarkation of some of the Ruins discovered at Lebida [Leptis Magna], on board His Majesty's store ship the *Weymouth*; and an extract of a Letter addressed to the Rear Admiral by Mr. Consul Warrington, on the subject of prosecuting researches into the interior of Africa by the way of Tripoli.[32]

At the time of this increase in intelligence reporting on the coast, the consul was also occupied in transmitting details of Mohamed Ali's military incursions into the interior, and the possible motives behind them. The consul was also keen to continue to extend the hand of friendship towards the Mamluks who had travelled into the Regency of Tripoli to escape Mohamed Ali's troops.[33] These Mamluks had been living in a state of insecurity and exile since the massacre at the Cairo Citadel in 1811.[34] While opinion is divided over the reasons for the arrival of Mohamed Ali's troops, whether to capture Wadai, slaves or the surviving Mamluks – or whether they were Ali's troops at all – the Mamluks hastily departed Sennar (south of Khartoum) and arrived in Murzuq by October 1822. According to Major Denham, Mohamed Ali's troops had not arrived in the Kingdom of Wadai, but rather the 'runaway Mamelukes' had sought refuge in that place.[35] The consul had been informed of the movements of the Mamluks prior to their arrival in Tripoli. On 17 September 1822, Oudney wrote to Warrington:

> A Remnant of the unfortunate Mamluks of Egypt have arrived here [Murzuq] – they have been moving about for several years in Kordofan and Wady [Wadai]. They left the latter country twenty in number, but fifteen were killed in Bergherme ... [a] trifling dispute having risen between them and the natives. They will soon be in Tripoli and I beg you will look out that no ill befalls them.[36]

According to Warrington, the Mamluks that had arrived in Tripoli had left Egypt fifteen years before, and that they had resided at Dongola for eight years followed by a 'desirable time' near Sennar – at Kordofan, Darfur, and finally 'Borgoo and Wadey'.[37] A month later, on 19 October 1822, Warrington wrote to Wilmot Horton to assure the British government that he would extend his 'best offices' to the remaining five Mamluks, who were on their way to Tripoli. The consul also believed that both he and Oudney would be able to obtain the 'most valuable Information' from the Egyptian exiles. The consul undertook extensive preparation for their arrival and had gained the Pasha's permission to interview the surviving Mamluks. In a private letter, he assured the undersecretary of state, Wilmot Horton, that 'I shall take good care no consul here obtains any correct Information, as after the trouble & expense we have been at it ought to be exclusively Britain's'.[38]

As usual, Warrington's ambitions extended far beyond immediate temporal or geostrategic concerns. His vision of his own standing, and Britain's position in Africa, was a monumental one. The consul believed that Britain would be able to utilize a 'comprehensive' knowledge of the interior and extend its influence as far as Dongola, then south to Sennar, west to El Obeid (the centre of Kordofan before its division into three provinces), then to Darfur and as far west as Timbuktu (see Figure 12). Once again, the consul wrote to Wilmot Horton outlining his view of how the year, 1823, would progress:

> I trust the Ensuing year will lay down the Geography, East to West from Dongola, nearly approaching Tombuctoo & Southward fully as far as Darfoor – as well as gaining Information of the Resources of the unknown country, & I hope the friendly Relations will be so cultivated, [as] to leave a permanent Impression on those suffering People.[39]

After the arrival of explorers in Tripoli, Warrington argued with several members over their decision to travel in 'Turkish dress' and, in Clapperton and Denham's cases, for also adopting Arabic names.[40] The consul felt that these measures were unnecessary, that the explorers should travel as Englishmen because Fezzan was 'as safe as Bond Street'.[41] Warrington held a fixed view on how the missions should proceed, and he was determined to present an imperial and 'civilized' image of Britain and British agents.[42] The consul believed that the travellers would be protected by the authority of the British flag, as well as by the assurances of safety made by the Pasha and the 'Sheikhs' of the interior, including Abd' al-Jalil Saif al-Nasser. He simply could not understand the viewpoint of Denham, Clapperton or their contemporaries, let alone the sensitivities of the locals who repeatedly complained of the 'indecency of English trousers'.[43]

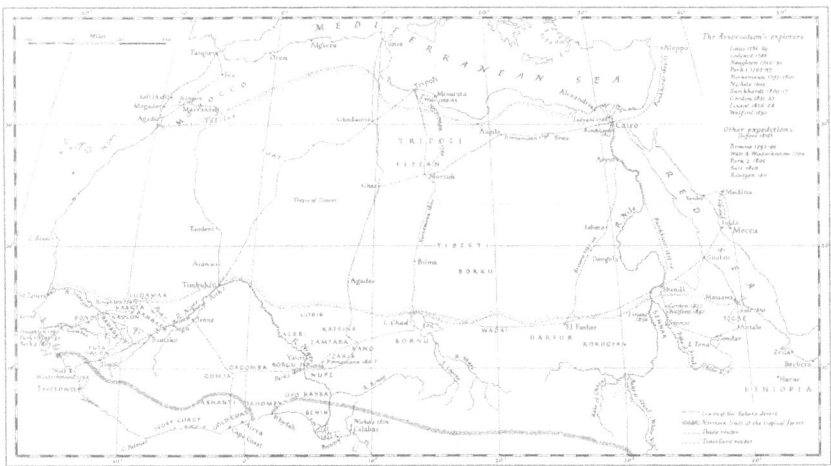

Figure 12 Robin Hallett, *Map of North and Central Africa, with Trade and Traveller Routes*. Hallett, *Records of the African Association, 1788–1831* (RGS: Edinburgh 1964), n.l. © Royal Geographical Society (with IBG).

In the same year, 1822, the surviving Egyptian Mamluks finally arrived in Tripoli and sought refuge in the city. Despite the earlier preparation and negotiations with Yusuf Qaramanli, Warrington was forced to interview them with the Pasha's officers present, and he noted how they were 'under restraint' during the course of the interview. The consul nevertheless remained optimistic that he could obtain valuable intelligence from them.[44] A full year later, the consul's network continued to report on the movements of the Mamluks and their families. Warrington's vice-consul to-be at Kuka, Ernest Toole, provided a rare insight into the lives of the Mamluks, particularly on why fifteen of them lost their lives and the reason the remainder were forced to travel on to Murzuq:

> There is here now a woman & child belonging to one of the Mamluks who came across from Dongola to Tripoli. She was purchased by them at Darfour – The account she gives of their route is that being driven by the Packá [sic] of Egypt out of Dongola they went to 'Sennar' from thence to Fur [Darfur] and there to Waadi where they way were civilly told they were not wished to remain they therefore quitted for Fezzan – at 'Bergoo' a Tibboo [Tibu] country about half way between this and Waadi or 20 Days from each Their slaves commenced plundering the Date Groves & would not desist though enticed to do so by presents. The Tibboo then took to arms & drove them away. The Mamluks thought it necessary to revenge this & attacked the Tibboo in turn who fled to one of their strong Holds on the top of a hill in the attack of which 14 Mamluks were killed & some wounded the rest made the best of their way here – as far as I can collect they met the utmost kindness everywhere & resided at Dongola many years.[45]

In the end, Warrington did not appear to gather much useful intelligence from the surviving Mamluks and concluded that they 'either affect to know little, or in reality but little know'.⁴⁶ Meanwhile, despite various attempts to influence the course of the missions and its members, Warrington could simply not direct British activities as closely as he wanted. While the mission of Denham, Clapperton and Oudney had been forced to travel with a heavy military escort, and the members had subsequently gone their separate ways, the newly appointed Vice-Consul Ernest Toole had been involuntarily drawn into local politics. In a letter to Warrington on 27 October 1823, shortly after his arrival in Qatrun in Fezzan, and on his way to Kuka in Bornu, Toole explained the difficult position in which he had been placed by a resident of Fezzan (and originally a native of Palermo) and that this in turn may reflect badly on the British presence in the Regency:

> [A] man in the mameluke costume came up to me and to my surprise addressed me in Sicilian ... He said if I understood Italian he wished to tell me something that I did at last convinced him of by answering him – He said his name was Mohammet ... and till only very lately was 'Kaid' of this place [Qatrun] and 'Tegerry', that now a Black slave had been sent by the Sultan [of Dirke] to supersede him, an Indignation he could not just put up with & was going to quit Fezzan ... I feel awkwardly situated ... if he goes with me it may be said I enticed him. I have told him I cannot take him, he says ... "when you are gone two or three days I will follow". I am certain he will so should anything be said about it this is the case. Betray his intentions to the People I of course cannot and prevent his going if he pleases I cannot.⁴⁷

Meanwhile, the actions of France vis-à-vis Mohammed Ali of Egypt had led to unexpected complications in the relationship between the Pasha of Tripoli and Britain. Yusuf Qaramanli especially feared British collusion and military action against him, as Mohamed Ali formulated plans to conquer Algiers, Tunis and Tripoli. On 1 March 1830, Warrington wrote home about the affair:

> Sir, I have the honor to Inform you that yesterday morning a vessel arrived from Leghorn [Livorno] bringing the news that France had entered into an alliance with Mohamed Ali to subjugate the three Regencies of Barbary, Tripoli, Tunis and Algiers and that England and Russia would co.operate in the measure.
> Shortly after hearing this Report, I saw the Sardinian Consul who read me a Letter, confirming the same, and He added that the French Ambassador had officially communicated the Event to the court of Florence ... The Bashaw impressed on my mind the extreme Importance of the case and the great Interest it had excited and He requested me [to] communicate the circumstances to the British Government, the Admiral and to the Lieutenant-Governor of Malta and that he would freight a vessel purposely.
> I replied that as this was a Question of that Political magnitude, I could not take any step without His Highness would commit to Paper His Sentiments and the accompanying Letter will afford further Information. The Bashaw appears

to believe it perfectly true France intends to assist Mohamed Ali, and grounds His only hope that England is not a Party. His Highness took a Retrospect of about 170 years, during which Peace and good will had always manifested itself between the Respective Governments and that He trusted England found no just cause to discontinue that Friendship and Harmony.[48]

This report from the British consul indicates a series of changing dynamics in the region, including the growing power of Mohamed Ali and an ambitious France. While Tripoli sought reassurance that its long-established friendship with Britain would strengthen the Regency's position against external threats, Consul Warrington was eager to communicate to the British government intelligence on the latest French manoeuvres in Egypt.

Britain in the Mediterranean

Following the capture of Malta, Britain's occupations of the Ionian Islands and Aden signified a growing imperial power that was attempting to formulate a coherent policy in order to maintain the integrity of the Ottoman Empire. Britain's naval bases fortified British defences east of Gibraltar and west of Mahon in Minorca, strengthening British influence in the region. Meanwhile, British strategic priorities, both political and economic, continued apace. Alliances and military cooperation with the Ottoman Empire – such as the training of the Ottoman cavalry – primarily against French imperial ambitions, were bolstered with the appointment of the Earl of Elgin (1766–1841) as the first British ambassador to Istanbul in November 1798.[49]

The question over the future of the Greek isles was a politically explosive one by the time of the second abdication of Napoleon and the Treaty of Paris in 1815. With the threat once more of a Russian invasion of Ottoman lands, the Greeks began to revolt in 1821.[50] The British government viewed the future of the Greek isles as a matter of utmost concern that would shape its strategic priorities and the future of the eastern Mediterranean as well as the Middle East. In 1818, Maitland was sent to undertake secret negotiations with the representative of the Ottoman Porte, Ali Pasha of Tepeceleni/Ioannina, only three years after the Paris Treaty was concluded. Maitland wrote to Robert Liston, British ambassador at Istanbul on 14 November 1818 to explain the precarious negotiations over the status of the island of Parga in the region of Preveza. He also wrote of the assistance he had already provided to Parga's neighbours on the island of Paxò (Paxos), as he felt the two were inextricably linked on the threat of emigration. Maitland continued:

> Many of the Pargauists who now talk of emigrating will alter their tones – and that I have always considered the issuing [of] Proclamations as a farce till the amount of such indemnity was declared … the Pargauists would be fairly treated by receiving an indemnification of £150,000 … You must be aware how

apt whenever any opening of this kind is made, the Bashaw's [sic] Ministers are to avail themselves of it, and I am now pressed extremely by Colovò [Spiros Kolovos, advisor to Ali Pasha of Ioannina/ Tepedeleni] to make this Declaration.

In the mean time however to give the vizier a most unequivocal proof of our intention, I have directed as great a part of the Militia of Parga to be disbanded as possible, and as the People of the Island of Paxò were always in the habits of grinding their corn at Parga, I have ordered Wind Mills to be erected at Paxò, as a necessary step previous to the evacuation: In measures which seem to give Colovò and His Master equal satisfaction.

I cannot give up Parga until the indemnity is made good ... Parga is not to be ceded till the Porte gives in its accession to the Treaty of Paris of 1815 relative to the Ionian Islands, and about this the Bashaw [sic] pretends to be extremely staggered.[51]

In this charged political standoff, this case brings into focus the role of the 'man on the spot' because Maitland was 'somewhat embarrassed' and later apologetic that he had already issued a figure to settle the dispute without first receiving official instruction. Accordingly, British agents, including Warrington, had followed a well-established path in the discharge of their responsibilities and in pursuing a course of action they felt was in the best interests of Britain.

In returning to Tripoli, one of the recurring points of contention was the capture of Greek prizes and slaves. While vessels and their crew continued to be seized in the waters of the Mediterranean by the Pasha's naval officers, Tripoline cruisers also periodically captured and enslaved Greek subjects by conducting raids on coastal settlements in the eastern Mediterranean. These included the port of Milo (Milos) and Candia (Heraklion) over the first three decades of the 1800s.[52] The British consul made the strongest representations he could for the release of prizes and captives, and his leverage in these negotiations subsequently increased with the support of the Exmouth Treaty of 1816, explicitly prohibiting White (Christian) slavery.

In conjunction with the negotiations of Pellew in 1816 – Warrington gave his enthusiastic and whole-hearted support to a proposal for an 'institution for the relief' of slavery in the Regency.[53] This institution was introduced to the consul by Sidney Smith 'for the relief and amelioration of the sufferings of Christian slaves' brought into Tripoli.[54] In this case, Warrington, like his superior, acted without any official guidance or instruction from the government.[55] As a result, the consul was rebuked after he had officially engaged the other consuls in Tripoli – including the Swedish and American – in the endeavour. Warrington went so far as to submit an account of the initial expenditure that was required to establish the institution – a not insignificant sum of $28,884 that the Lords Commissioners were categorically not inclined to pay.[56] Warrington was further censured for insulting Sir Sidney Smith, whom he blamed for misleading him about the long-term financial backing and governmental support for such a 'benevolent institution'.[57] Despite these 'miscommunications', Warrington, on 29 June 1823, continued to write of the British government's favourable position with, and influence over, the reigning Qaramanli dynasty:

At the audience yesterday His Highness desired me to communicate Privately to you that the Dey of Algiers has written Him very strongly for being so much inclined to favour the English in the Greek Question, as well as allowing Travellers to pass into the Interior and in consequence when the war is at an end He may expected to be well paid for it.

The Bashaw [sic] said 'I not only like the English, but it is my Policy & best Interest to keep in with them, because I well know they can make me, and I hope they will shortly convince Algiers a second time on that point'.

It is my opinion the Bashaw [sic] courts the Protection of England. In communicating the Bashaw's sentiments, you will consider me His Echoe as I should not presume to comment on such a delicate affair.[58]

Understandably, the Pasha sought to fortify the city as a result of real or perceived threats from Hussein Dey, Mohamed Ali, the French, and the Ottoman Porte. The consul, however, revealed in his dispatches that he feared the defences were in fact part of Ottoman designs against the Greeks.[59] Other information periodically included an account of the city of Tripoli's strengths by land and sea as well as its naval force.

Meanwhile, the British vice-consuls at Benghazi and Derna monitored the activities of Egypt and supported the work of the exploratory missions. They also monitored the caravan trade with the south. The vice-consular reports included some information on the trade and traffic in slaves from the interior.[60] The vice-consuls were placed on strategic points of the major trade routes to and from the interior of the 'Great Sudan' (see Figure 12).

British 'Offices' beyond Tripoli

Under the direction of Consul Warrington, and greatly accelerated by the series of joint government and African Association exploratory missions, the consul developed an extensive system of representation and intelligence-gathering in the Regency of Tripoli during the reign of Yusuf Qaramanli. By 1824, this network of agents extended as far south as Kuka and as far east as Derna, and was unprecedented in the Regency, if not the whole of Ottoman North Africa. While the Colonial Department continuously ensured that more than adequate British representation was maintained in Tripoli, it was down to the person and vision of Consul Warrington to substantially expand the British presence and 'offices' beyond the borders of the Regency. Following Murray's disapproval of Warrington's conduct and the consul's suspension of diplomatic relations with Yusuf Qaramanli, Major J. Fraser was promptly dispatched as vice-consul to Tripoli and duly arrived at the end of November 1830.[61] Joseph Dupuis was also subsequently posted as vice-consul at Tripoli to monitor and report on Warrington's work. The consul unsuccessfully attempted to have Dupuis moved to the position of vice-consul at Benghazi. Warrington utilized his own informal – and personal – network of contacts in England as well as in Tripoli to develop an expansive network of vice-consular agents. Prior to the nomination of a British-born vice-consul, Giacomo Rofsoni was appointed by Consul Warrington to the office at Benghazi in 1822. Warrington later selected Benedetto Regiginiani and Pietro Caravana as vice-consuls successively to Derna (1822 and 1831, respectively). These vice-consuls chosen by Warrington were already acquaintances, if not close friends, with the consul, and he held them in high esteem, in stark contrast to his disdain for the majority of his Maltese subjects in the Regency.[62] When Giacomo Rofsoni's vice-consulship ended, Thomas Wood replaced him as vice-consul at Benghazi in May 1827.

Although there is little explicitly mentioned in Warrington's dispatches, his friend and British naval surgeon Dr John Dickson must have gathered intelligence from the court of Yusuf Qaramanli, and relayed it to the consul. Dickson, as personal physician to Yusuf Qaramanli, had gained access to the most private aspects of the Pasha's day-to-day life, as well as other Qaramanli family members. The Admiralty, as early as 1817, had hoped that Dickson could be employed 'to great advantage' while in Tripoli, but for reasons that remain unclear, ordered him to withdraw from the service of the Pasha in December 1826.[63]

Following the nomination of John Tyrwhitt on 12 December 1821 to the vice-consular post at Kuka, Ernest Toole was recruited as a temporary agent in August 1823 because of Tyrwhitt having become ill.[64] Unfortunately, on 1 November 1824, Tyrwhitt died at his post.[65] Toole had also acted as assistant to Major Denham in Bornu until his own (Toole's) death following ten days of fever in May 1824.[66] Beyond the Regency of Tripoli, the British consul took advantage of the launch of exploratory missions in the 1820s to appoint, from within the ranks, at least two individuals, Toole to Kuka, and Oudney to Murzuq. There is no evidence to suggest, however, that Warrington received any official direction either in support of, or opposition to, his recruitment of vice-consuls in this way. On the contrary, his recommendations did not interfere with the original work of the missions and complemented the intelligence-gathering priorities of the government.

In short, the growth of the vice-consular network symbolized the growth in interest and activity in the region. If Warrington's ambitions had been realized to the full, British agents would have become firmly established in the kingdoms of Central Africa, including Kanem-Bornu.

The exploratory missions throughout the 1820s generated an enormous amount of correspondence and the transmission of information about the discoveries and encounters of the explorers, specifically Laing, Denham, Oudney and Clapperton. At the start of their travels, Consul Warrington wrote of the fantastical story (but which at the time he believed was a reliable account) of the ability to reach, as part of the course of the Nile, 'Grand Cairo' in forty days from Timbuktu. Nevertheless, such accounts provide important evidence that such information was requested by the British government, and that information was obtained with a view to assisting in the British exploration of the African interior.[67] Other information provided by the locals included details of the towns and tribes, such as the Kingdom of Kanem-Bornu and the Tebu people.[68] The ultimate goal of the South and Southeastern Missions was to find the source of the Niger river and to establish the best method of introducing 'into the interior of Africa specimens of British manufactures'.[69]

While the missions were delayed and diverted by the Pasha, other events also thwarted the explorers' ambitions. This was never the more so than when Dixon Denham parted ways with fellow explorers in November 1822, following allegations of misconduct against Hugh Clapperton.[70] As a result, the party and its correspondence became fragmented and the government in turn became frustrated at not having received maps and papers relative to the work of the missions.[71]

Some members of the exploratory missions, such as Oudney and Clapperton, developed closer relationships with each other and with the consul. Others, such as Denham, fostered relations with political figures within the government and tribal leaders in and beyond the Regency. These relationships directly and indirectly served British imperial interests in the region.[72] In November 1817, Warrington wrote to Earl Bathurst:

> It appearing to me that it is the Intention of the British Government to attempt Exploring Africa from this Quarter I have therefore availed myself of every opportunity to gain that Information which may facilitate an object so Interesting to the world at large.[73]

The official correspondence from the consul at Tripoli continued to suggest that Warrington communicated intelligence regarding access to and information on, the interior in response to official instructions.[74] His despatches detail accounts of the geography of the Sudan to Timbuktu, the course of the Niger river, and individuals of note who could further facilitate the work of the missions south of the Regency. Five years later, in December 1823, Warrington reiterated to Wilmot Horton the favourable circumstances for the missions and continued his reassurances that the explorers would receive a favourable reception:

> Permit me to observe should a Southern Party (as well as an Eastern & Western, be formed Mr Toole will execute His part to the satisfaction of His Majesty's Government. With proper attention to the great Bello of the Soudan country & to the Shaik of Bornou with a vigilant Eye to this Government, all Africa can be explored.[75]

With the assistance of the government and of the African Association, the British consul established an influential British presence at Tripoli and developed a series of effective formal and informal networks that enabled the bridgehead at Tripoli to successfully keep abreast of local and regional developments, as well as to serve wider British naval and political interests in the Mediterranean. Meanwhile, Warrington continued his attempts to direct the course of the missions, after their departure from Tripoli. In November 1822 he wrote to Undersecretary Wilmot Horton on the subject:

Should Major Denham go Eastward from Bornow to Dongola which I believe His Instructions order Him to do, He will have performed an Important Service.

But it appears to me desirable that Dr. Oudney and Lieutenant Clapperton (separate them and nothing will be done) should proceed Southward to Bergherme, Darfour, & Senaar, provided the Niger continues to run in that direction.[76]

In September 1824, with a view to promoting good relations with the Sudan, the British government made a gift of a Turkish scimitar to the Sultan, Mohamed Bello. This present highlights the government's efforts to secure the cooperation of Bello in allowing the explorers through his territories.[77] British agents – commercial, consular and diplomatic – played a vital and necessary part in advancing European access to, and knowledge of, the region. Laing's successful mission to Timbuktu of 1826 was quickly followed, in 1827, by a French counterpart, René Caillé (1799–1838).[78] There were, of course, other explorers before Laing, but the heightened British activity of the first half of the nineteenth century emphasizes the deep imperial rivalry at this time between Britain and France. London understood that active British political and diplomatic engagement was crucial in the protection and promotion of British economic and strategic interests in the region.

Intervention

British foreign policy during this period was more reactive and only partially coherent as a consequence of its opposition to French manoeuvres in the Mediterranean. In May 1798, to block any French attempt to cross the Persian Gulf, Dundas ordered that troops be sent to reinforce the British garrison at Perim. Accordingly, a fleet was dispatched under Admiral Blankett to the Rea Sea via the Cape of Good Hope. This order was placed 'as early as June 1798' when the British government lacked any confirmation on the 'ultimate destination of the French fleet'.[79]

Rather like the British government's later ambivalence towards the 1807 Treaties of Tilsit, the cooperation extended to the Convention of al-'Arish (1800) was ultimately rescinded by Lord Keith.[80] Smith was admonished for signing the convention without prior discussion with, or the sanction of, the government.[81] The uncertainty about how to progress in the eastern Mediterranean was as much to do with the rapid reformulation of alliances, as with the failure of the Second Coalition, as well as the autonomy held by imperial agents across the Mediterranean.

The consul also corresponded with, and cultivated intelligence from, British subjects and agents in Tripoli, Tunis, Egypt, Malta, Livorno, as well as from his own vice-consular personnel.[82] Despite frequently displaying independence from London, the consul still had to rely upon a range of people to facilitate his day-to-day transactions with the Qaramanli Diwan and with the public at large. This was especially the case for Warrington who, in stark contrast to his two predecessors Lucas and Langford, did not display skills in any European or 'Oriental' language.

At the same time, due to his remoteness from the centre (London) and the relatively slow communication system, he also maintained an independence which distinctly shaped Britain's imperial interests in the region. Distance was a significant factor in shaping the careers of diplomatic agents and the work they did in the Regency and throughout the Mediterranean, particularly with the British governor at Malta, and later, the British ambassador to Istanbul.[83]

During the period from 1795 to 1832, British agents had been accused of interference in the politics of Tripoli on several occasions, and they appeared to grow in frequency with the consulship of Warrington. In November 1801, following Tripoli's declaration of war on the United States of America, Acting Consul Bryan McDonogh defended himself against charges that he had 'stimulated' the Regency into declaring war on the United States.[84] These allegations were refuted, and McDonogh provided some documents as evidence of his innocence in the event, including a statement of support by the Danish consul in Tripoli, as well as an earlier communication with Timothy Pickering, the American secretary of state.[85] In his own defence, in a letter to the Duke of Portland, McDonogh wrote:

> There are European agents in this place whom I know to be the professed enemies of his Majesty's late Consul Lucas and mine, for no other reason but envy, knowing the growing power and the British interest with this government.[86]

By 1810, however, Yusuf Qaramanli reacted decisively to an attempt by Consul Langford to impress his view upon the Pasha, on a matter of 'controversy' between a Maltese and a Tripoline Jew. Running at Langford with a pistol in hand, and in front of his Diwan, Yusuf Qaramanli declared that he was 'the master in his own house'.[87] Following this 'gross insult', the British consul felt compelled to decline raising the British flag over the consulate. This action signified the temporary cessation of friendly relations between Britain and Tripoli, and, once again, was an act disapproved of by the British government. Unlike Warrington's similar actions in years to come, this incident resulted in the end of Langford's consular career in Tripoli when he was promptly ordered to return to London in May 1811.[88] Much to the anger of the secretary of state, Langford did not depart Tripoli until January 1812.[89] Despite this serious diplomatic incident which had caused the Pasha to place Consul Langford under house arrest, the issue of the influence wielded by the British consul at Tripoli continued to remain an issue.

Despite the orders of the Colonial Department, Warrington continued involving himself in the local politics of the Regency, including between Yusuf Qaramanli and challengers to his authority in both Tripoli and Fezzan.[90] In 1824, an affair of high political importance had arisen between Yusuf Qaramanli and Sheikh Abd' al-Jalil Saif al-Nasser of Fezzan. On the pretext of securing the well-being of the explorers while they travelled through Murzuq and beyond the borders of Fezzan, Yusuf Qaramanli ordered that Sheikh Saif al-Nasser's wife and children be conveyed to Tripoli as hostages. Warrington viewed this event as an opportunity for him to extend the influence of Britain further south by offering himself as a 'mediator' in the affair.[91] He communicated secretly with Saif al-Nasser about the welfare of his family and took every opportunity to impress on the Sheikh that the hostage situation was nothing to do with Britain – that he, as consul, was doing everything in his power to secure their release. Warrington wrote to the secretary of state on the affair in April 1824:

> It is certainly most unpleasant not having had any communication from the Mission for such a time, however, I feel fully persuaded they are doing well, and that the arrival of the children will remove every obstacle. I have always entertained but one opinion respecting the Shaiks children, and on the principle of Honor and sound Policy I have exerted myself to get them restored to their Parent.[92]

In another case, in 1827, Consul Warrington had been accused by the Swedish consul of interfering in the sale of a merchant schooner.[93] The charges were considered sufficiently serious to cause the Swedish government to make an official representation of their consul's complaints to the Colonial Department. On 7 November 1827, Warrington wrote to the undersecretary of state to refute the accusations of interference levelled against him by the Swedish consul:

> Each charge is answered separately ... as for my having the Power to prevent a British merchant selling His Vessel to the Bashaw [sic], my Honorable and worthy Friend might well suppose that He could walk into Mr. Mantons Shop & forbid the disposal of the Implements of His Industry for fear of their being directed against Himself, as suppose a Merchant can be prevented selling His Property to the Bashaw.[94]

In October 1831, the consul confirmed that the Pasha would not keep his promise of safety to the wife and children of Sheikh Saif al-Nasser.[95] The consul wrote home frustrated that the Pasha had refused all proposals to mediate on his behalf with al-Nasser, although he hastened to add, following his promises as to what he could achieve as a result of the crisis, that he still maintained popularity and 'good will with the Interior'.[96] Despite being instructed not to interfere any further, Warrington continued to communicate with al-Nasser and offered the continuing 'friendship' of Britain to the Sheikh, in secret and without Yusuf Qaramanli's knowledge.[97] On 5 October 1831, Warrington wrote to Hay to justify his latest actions; 'when He has behaved in that handsome manner in allowing senna to an Enormous amount to freely pass, because it is British Property, such conduct would elicit an answer from me'.[98] The serious conflict between the Sheikh and the Pasha continued until 20 December 1831, when Consul Warrington wrote to Abd' al-Jalil Saif al-Nasser to inform him that, through his diligent mediation, he had finally obtained the release of his wife and children and that they were now safely at his property in the Menshia.[99]

In 1827, a politically significant event arrived at the doorstep of Consul Warrington in the person of Prince Jaffer of the Kingdom of Wadai. The heir apparent had arrived destitute in Tripoli, because of the death of his father and the consequent challenge to his right to accede the throne.[100] According to Consul Henry Salt (1780–1827) in Egypt, the prince was 'about' twenty-two years of age, conversant in Arabic and with some knowledge of Persian. Salt added that the prince was 'without pretensions, with a very interesting countenance, polite in his manners, and from his superiority of mind likely, should he ever return, to be of great use to his countrymen'.[101] There are a number of possible explanations for the instability in Wadai. First, that the prince had to escape due to a disputed succession and protracted civil war following the death of Muhammad Abd' al-Karim Sabun (d.1815) that continued until 1838 when the Sultan of Darfur Mohamed al-Hussein (1838–74) intervened. The second cause could have been that war was waged against Wadai by one of its neighbours, Bornu, Bagirmi, or Darfur. And the third scenario was continuing instability following Mohamed Ali's conquest of the neighbouring territories of Sennar and Kordofan in 1821. According to Warrington, the young prince had sought the protection and assistance of the British flag. It was decided that it was best to get the heir apparent to Egypt and thence to Mecca without delay. The prince was subsequently sent from Tripoli to Alexandria, where he was received by Consul Salt. Like Warrington, Salt firmly believed that through the continued assistance to Prince Jaffer, the British government would be able to 'obtain an influence in the heart of Africa'.[102] Unfortunately, money had become an issue, as Warrington had not sent the prince with any financial support. In frustration, Salt subsequently complained that the prince had been 'thrown upon his hands' without adequate provision and raised the question of how his expenses might be defrayed. He went on to request that the African Association might interest itself in the case, given the benefit it would bring by enhancing British influence in the interior.[103] By the summer of 1827, however, the season had passed for the prince to be conveyed on to Mecca. And, seven years after his first arrival to the British consulate in Egypt, the prince had still not been conveyed on, either to England or Mecca. In consequence, Prince Jaffer asked that he be assisted to return home to Wadai. On 13 July 1827, the consul wrote to Lord Dudley to ask for some direction:

> This [the Prince's return to Wadai] will not be possible for some months at least and by this time as he is left absolutely 'penniless'. I beg leave to receive your Lordship's instructions whether I may be permitted to advance the money requisite for his maintenance & his journey as also to what amount.
>
> I should myself think that in a private way as I have recommended, his object may be attained if it should prove practicable, with a few hundred dollars.
>
> I should also beg leave to be informed in case he should not be able to return by this route whether I may be permitted to send him to England, as this may be done by sea at a very trifling expense.[104]

Salt's hope was that, if he could at least remove the prince elsewhere, he could free himself from the responsibility, and the cost, of looking after him. He suggested that, once in England, the prince would 'connect himself with the African Society or with some other Association' that would help him make his journey home.[105]

The predicament in which Salt found himself was due to Warrington's actions and government instructions.

Another example of the consul's 'mediation' in local affairs came in 1831, following serious clashes between the tribe of Haleefa and Yusuf Qaramanli. The head of the tribe, Sheikh Mohamed Haleefa, like his father before him, had been murdered on the orders of Yusuf Qaramanli.[106] Mohamed Haleefa's brother, Wooma, had recently succeeded his brother and had taken refuge in the consul's garden because the Pasha had ordered him to be strangled. The consul believed that the attempt to murder Wooma was a result of information provided by Wooma on the complicity of the Pasha in the murder of his son-in-law Laing five years previous. In September 1831, Warrington detailed Haleefa's desperate situation and the assistance he had provided:

> He arrived in some state of agitation, and His manly features as pallid as Death, telling me His murderers were still in pursuit. That he had left his Pistols & had nothing to defend himself. He wished me to lend him fire arms. I replied no – but pointing to the corner of the Room said there is a Rifle with Powder and Ball – he took the hint, loaded it with at least ten Balls, threw himself across his horse, and was off as quick as thought.[107]

As a result, Warrington concluded that his actions had 'secured the Gratitude of the formidable Tribe & given me unbounded Influence ... The Tribe of Haleefa allowed my People to Pass with money 400 Spanish dollars & supplies to Godames [Ghadames] when the Bashaw's [sic] Troops dare not show their face in that District'.[108]

The consul maintained a not altogether private opinion on who should prevail in the succession dispute that was being waged in Tripoli between the heir apparent, Ali Qaramanli, and one of Yusuf Qaramanli's grandsons, Mohamed. Warrington was, once again, explicitly prohibited from intervening in an affair that the British government considered not to be in the British interest. Despite this, the consul maintained his ambition that Tripoli should become a British colony.[109] In fact, Warrington frequently wrote on the subject and believed his actions would help ensure that Mohamed Qaramanli would become the next ruler of the Regency. Ultimately, Ali Qaramanli, the heir apparent, became the new Pasha of Tripoli. The correspondence also emphasizes the growing confidence of the consul after seventeen years as His Majesty's most senior representative in Tripoli. Despite Warrington's justifications of his expansive activities while consul at Tripoli, his decision-making in the Regency increasingly went beyond the exercise of influence in the interests of the British government, to active intervention in the affairs of the Regency.

A number of strategic concerns collided in the immediate post-Napoleonic era that directly helped to shape the British presence in the Regency of Tripoli, during the last substantive reign of a Qaramanli dynast, Yusuf Pasha. The location of the port of Tripoli – a gateway to both the Sudan and to the Mediterranean – meant that the consul was uniquely placed to report on a range of imperial interests that extended from Cádiz to Istanbul. The consul had developed an effective formal and informal network around him that communicated intelligence on political and military developments in Egypt, the Sudan and the eastern Mediterranean, as well as in the Regency of Tripoli itself. By acting as the 'man on the spot' the British consul helped to shape British imperial interests in Tripoli and the interior. In part, Warrington's expanding network of vice-consuls represented his ambitions for Britain in North and Central Africa and contributed to a powerful British presence and successful intelligence-gathering network in and beyond the borders of the Regency. The consul was able to exercise an unprecedented level of influence and a great deal of personal intervention in the affairs of Yusuf Qaramanli through the bridgehead, and the enlistment of local cooperation by the consul. This was based on an established, though unofficial, practice of autonomous decision-making and activity of some overseas government agents.

In the Pasha's kidnap of al-Nasser's family, and as the succession battle between Ali and Mohamed Qaramanli has shown, the consul's interference appeared to achieve little for any party. Rather, Warrington's determined 'mediation' served only to exacerbate relations between local powers, and to weaken the authority of the Qaramanli dynasty. The consul's isolation and length of service certainly contributed to his acting 'on the spot' and, in so doing, Warrington inadvertently affected British policy in the region. The consul at Tripoli and the British government together helped to shape both British interests and intelligence-gathering priorities in North Africa. British agents' activities reflected the strategic concerns of the British government in the Mediterranean, before and after the Greek revolt of 1821. The reports of the consul from Tripoli provide an insight into the consul's imperial ambitions in the interior of Africa, on behalf of the British Empire. That some of the consul's interventions may have come to little is a separate issue, but it nevertheless speaks to the person and power that an individual imperial agent could wield outside of the parameters of formal empire.

Chapter 8

CONCLUDING REMARKS: CONSULS AND EMPIRE-BUILDING IN NINETEENTH-CENTURY NORTH AFRICA

As a protected imperial presence in Tripoli, British involvement and activity in the Regency of Tripoli during the reign of Yusuf Qaramanli has revealed the extent of British ambitions in the region. The British consul's interests and activities culminated in the development of a British bridgehead in Tripoli. This was achieved through the influential role of the consul as the 'man on the spot' and his autonomy in developing and defining British ambitions in the Regency and in Africa. Through the successful enlistment of a variety of local agents, and through the development of an expansive vice-consular network, Consul Warrington extended British representation, and the protection and promotion of British interests as expressed by the government, other British agents and himself. He was able to do so because of the changing political scene in the Mediterranean, and growing British imperial strength, as well as his personal charisma and professional skill in the performance of his duties. From the perspective of London at the time, the bridgehead at Tripoli promised much for extending the reach of British influence in Africa. While political developments after 1830 had a negative effect upon the work of the British consul, such events were viewed as having occasioned only a temporary setback to the bridgehead, rather than as an indication of the end of Britain's protected presence in Tripoli. The conclusions here provide a fuller account of Tripoli's place in British strategic priorities, the person and role of the British consul and the extent of British – official or unofficial – ambitions in both the Mediterranean and Africa.

The consular archives provide clear evidence not only of British interests but also of the potential of Tripoli and the kingdoms of the interior as markets to be exploited for the economic and political benefit of British Empire. In this way, the British consular archives, through qualitative and quantitative means, highlight the extent of British imperial ambitions at the beginning of the nineteenth century.

The dynamics behind the British presence in the Regency have been traced to several sources – firstly, the historical autonomy and diplomatic privilege of the consuls to Algiers, Tunis and Tripoli; secondly, European power-rivalry; and thirdly, the re-encounter with the resources of the African interior. In turn, and within this context, the imperial bridgehead at Tripoli contributed to the development of British policy formulation. The activities of the British consul and the various networks he fostered around him provide a clear indication of the importance of Tripoli in intelligence-gathering and in the supply of British garrisons in the Mediterranean. The alliances and connections maintained by the consul as the 'man on the spot' provide evidence not of a British 'informal empire' but rather that imperial ambitions and subsequent policy could, and did, come from a number of unexpected quarters. These included the relationships fostered by the consul with other British agents and the local political elite, as well as his other activities in the Regency.

In Tripoli, the ultimate aim of exercising influence over the Pasha was achieved through the person and skill of the British consul. The political and economic realities faced by the Qaramanli government, coinciding with the end of the Napoleonic Wars, facilitated the consul's political position. With the continual decline in revenues from prize-taking, slave trading and annual tribute payment from European states, Tripoli needed to establish new trading partnerships. Yusuf Qaramanli was prepared to modify his previous stance towards treaty negotiations in order to foster increased trade with Europe. Consul Warrington exploited the opportunity to enhance his standing by acting as mediator in the treaty negotiations of 1818, but failed to grasp the opportunity offered by the Pasha to remind those European states of their commercial agreements. Continued British support to develop trading partnerships with Europe would have established a closer relationship between Britain and Tripoli, and would have served the consul's later ambitions well. Instead, in 1826, Yusuf Qaramanli declared war on the parties that failed to honour their treaty agreements. These included Sardinia, the Papal States and Naples.[1] Warrington's failure to mediate again proved a catastrophic error in judgement by the consul. A lasting British imperial presence in the Regency necessitated a viable local trading economy. Without the much-needed revenue from new trading agreements, Yusuf Qaramanli could not rebuild the economy and maintain the political stability that was necessary as the basis for a closer partnership with Britain. Furthermore, the Pasha was faced with a loss of political and moral authority over his subject territories that could no longer be salvaged. One of the final blows to the legitimacy of the Qaramanli dynasty came as a result of a protracted insurrection in Fezzan. The year 1831 marked country-wide rebellions and resulted in the loss of Murzuq to Abd' al-Jalil Saif al-Nasser. Meanwhile, the powerful presence of the consul had established an imperial bridgehead in Tripoli that fostered relationships with tribal leaders in the hinterlands of the Regency and tied together a disparate array of imperial activities.

This bridgehead could not have operated without a significant level of cooperation between the consul, other British agents in the Regency and members of the local population, including the landed elite. Relationships between the British consul and the notables of the Qaramanli Diwan – such as with Hajj Mohamed Bait-al-Mal – highlight the paramountcy of the promotion of British interests. On close consideration of the correspondence, this cooperation also extended to notables of the elite, including Hassuna D'Ghies, whose family had assisted the explorers on their travels through the southern territories of the Regency. Both Hassuna D'Ghies and his father Mohamed appeared to act as cultural intermediaries by facilitating a hospitable reception at several points for the missions. The dispatches of the consul provide evidence of the use of financial reward and gifts to ministers such as Mohamed Bait-al-Mal to smooth the way for future cooperation.

After 1826, the consul's undesirable influence in Tripoli appears to have soured Warrington's relations with local notables. His growing interference in local affairs, combined with his belief that Hassuna D'Ghies, and others, had colluded with the French consul in the murder of his son-in-law Alexander Gordon Laing, resulted in D'Ghies's loss of position, wealth and status. This event underscored how volatile relationships could be in Tripoli and how the consul was able to exercise an unusual level of influence over the reigning Pasha, Yusuf Qaramanli.

The House of Commons did not answer D'Ghies's 1834 petition for the restitution of his property and reputation by an investigation and removal of Warrington. A friend of D'Ghies, James Scarlett MP, publicly spoke of how His Majesty's consul at Tripoli had destroyed the standing and property of an honourable and respectable family. No matter the reasons behind the behaviour of the consul, it was the effect of his intervention which was of significance.

Each of the three successive British consuls to Tripoli were men of skill and ability, despite various shortcomings that have been indicated by the consular records. While financial problems afflicted two of the consuls, the consular post at Tripoli was certainly not a professional 'last resort' nor was it an undesirable position that few in the consular service wanted to fill. Appointments to Tripoli, Tunis or any of their neighbours were competitive and required a level of patronage to obtain. Competition for consular vacancies was fierce and the appointment to the level of consul general required ability, as well as connections. By 1826, in an effort to improve the pay for the 'Barbary consuls', Undersecretary Hay reflected:

> His Lordship [the Secretary of State Earl Bathurst] is decidedly of opinion that the salaries of these Officers [Consuls General] are much too low for their adequate maintenance and remuneration; and considering the very peculiar nature of their situations and of the duties which they have to perform, as well as the importance of holding out a fair inducement to persons of character and ability to undertake the Charge of His Majesty's interests in those inhospitable Countries.[2]

The 'peculiar' aspect of the consul's position was a reference to the historical exceptionalism in the management of the consuls to Algiers, Tunis and Tripoli and the inherited tradition of the exercise of diplomatic privilege. As Consuls Langford and Warrington detailed, they did not hesitate to threaten the Pasha of Tripoli if they deemed it an expedient step in the protection of British interests. The experience and diplomatic skills which the consuls brought to the role is clearly evident. Lucas and Langford demonstrated their long service in the consular establishments in Morocco and Tripoli. With this, they were both employed at alternate stages of their career as 'Oriental Interpreters' for his Majesty's government and displayed proficiency, if not fluency, in Arabic, Turkish and Italian. Consul Warrington, as the exception, relied instead on a network of local go-betweens including his own children and servants to translate and interpret. Nevertheless, his skill at persuading through financial incentive or political manipulation had hitherto been unheard of in Tripoli. Warrington commented on his powerful presence and the extent of his political powers in the Regency, as well on his 'close' connections to the sovereigns of the interior. His influence over Yusuf Qaramanli in the last decade of the Pasha's reign was publicly noted by former ministers and those close to the Qaramanli family. At the height of his power, the consul exercised a role in the displacement, dismissal and fortunes of notables, as well as contributing to the growing instability in the Regency.

Consul Warrington also introduced a number of initiatives in the Regency, with the cooperation of his European colleagues. These endeavours served to emphasize his ambition and expansive vision for Britain in the Regency of Tripoli. With the permission of Yusuf Qaramanli, he proposed a programme for a wide-scale vaccination programme of the subjects of the Regency, as well as a Board of Health to be established at Tripoli. These initiatives were in direct response to the devastating impact of various epidemics on the local population and are important in highlighting the practice of initiative and autonomy by the consul. On the religious front, Warrington attempted to improve the standing of the church beyond the tiny Franciscan convent by obtaining a place of worship and resident Father for the consul's British – mainly Maltese – subjects and by establishing a cemetery within which to inter fellow Protestants. The consul also assisted the Swedish consul's attempt to circulate copies of the Bible in the city – an act strictly forbidden by the Regency's laws – by providing a safe haven for the books. The Swedish and British consular correspondence explicitly suggest at least acquiescence by the Pasha in the presence and distribution of Christian religious material and indicate that he was motivated less by a concern about the observance of local laws and more by a desire to obtain pecuniary compensation from the Swedish government for the 'prohibited' activities. This event raises further questions about the lack of official support of the British consul for at least some of his actions. Here, the Colonial Department did not state an opinion or position on the subject, but rather left it to the consul and the British Bible Society, and Warrington's subsequent appeals to the Bishop of Malta. In the city, a Protestant cemetery was established where at least one of Consul Warrington's children was interred. Warrington's efforts to promote British interests in the Regency were unrelenting. Unfortunately, the consul's development of local health programmes, as well as his promotion of other causes, often met with a lack of willingness from the government to provide the necessary financial support for these initiatives. This drive to curtail overseas spending was not unique to Tripoli, however, but the prevailing attitude of the British government in all its activities abroad, with one or two exceptions, during the early nineteenth century. The success of the British presence in Tripoli, in likeness to its presence in the Bight of Benin and elsewhere, was dependent on a number of favourable circumstances coinciding to create a lasting imperial presence. The British government's reluctance to dispense financial resources overseas was only one part of a complex picture that also required favourable local circumstances and a determined 'man on the spot'.

The British bridgehead at Tripoli encapsulated the activities of a series of networks from Tripoli in the service of British imperial interests. An operational imperial bridgehead effectively came into being with the joint exploration missions of the African Association and the government. Moreover, it suggested that the imperial ambitions of the consul helped to define the work of these networks – whether through proposing the course that the exploratory missions should adopt, or by shaping the recruitment to, and development of, a vice-consular network in and beyond the Regency. While the explorers were concerned with ascertaining the source of the Niger river (among other activities), various members contributed to the consul's vice-consular personnel, and the missions acted as a catalyst in Consul Warrington's refinement of his ambitions to utilize Tripoli to establish a profitable trade with Central and West Africa, most notably with Sultan Bello of the Sokoto Caliphate. The correspondence of the consul also reveals his personal desire for a permanent British settlement in Tripoli, like the British colonies in the West Indies, as well as to promote British exploitation of the regional economies of Central and West Africa. Inadvertently, the consul highlighted what other officials may have forgotten, that is, that British merchants had in the past established trade in British manufactures in territories as far inland as Timbuktu. Moreover, Warrington also emphasized the prominence of Tripoli in gaining access to the interior of Africa, through the caravan routes that directly connected Tripoli to Kano in Hausaland and Kuka in Kanem-Bornu via the strategically important towns of Ghadames and Murzuq in the Regency of Tripoli. The data extracted from the returns of British trade with the Regency for 1823–31 provide further evidence of the consul's ambitions and helped to shape his dispatches to the secretary and undersecretary of state. The role played by the consul in establishing and directing a number of activities emphasize his freedom to pursue imperial ambitions as he saw fit. The British government, specifically in the form of the Secretary of State Bathurst, however, was mainly concerned with the consul's primary function of exercising influence over Yusuf Qaramanli in the service of *existing* British concerns. These included the regular supply of provisions to British naval garrisons stationed in the Mediterranean, the suppression of the trade in slaves (particularly White ones) and the protection of British subjects and British vessels in the Mediterranean. Under these circumstances, and so long as these needs were being met, the secretary of state saw no reason and felt no pressure to prevent the downfall of the Qaramanli dynasty and the subsequent re-occupation of Tripoli by Ottoman forces in 1835.

The intelligence-gathering process, both of the consul and his personal as well as vice-consular network, underscored the continuity of Britain's concern over the imperial ambitions of France and Russia after the termination of the Napoleonic Wars. Keen to do whatever necessary to protect Britain's commercial empire in India, the British government, by extension, also had a vested interest in maintaining the integrity of the Ottoman Empire. The desire to maintain the status quo in the eastern Mediterranean embroiled Britain in the region for decades to come, long after the anti-Ottoman Greek revolts of 1821. The ambitions of Mohamed Ali and

Ibrahim Pasha, along with French-supported military activity in Egypt remained a key concern. The consul's reports also increasingly faced inward, to the local politics of the Regency, including developments in the Sudan, to territories as far southeast as the Kingdom of Wadai. The assistance provided to an heir-apparent of Wadai indicated a subtle but nevertheless official level of growing interest in the governments of Central and Eastern Africa in the medium- to long-term.

As the 'man on the spot' the consul also attempted to promote friendly relations with the tribal leaders and sovereigns south of Tripoli. This meant that Warrington intervened in local affairs, including through the persistent mediation for the safe return of Abd' al-Jalil Saif al-Nasser's family. The consul's utilization of go-betweens has re-emphasized the influential role of the consul as the 'man on the spot', despite the requests of both the Colonial Department and of Yusuf Qaramanli to not interfere in the internal affairs of the Regency.

Tripoli's strategic location was emphasized when British naval agents utilized the favourable base of Tripoli to undertake a detailed survey of the Regency's coastline as far as Egypt. In the final months of Yusuf Qaramanli's reign, Warrington pursued his own interests and actively supported one side in the succession dispute – which he had been explicitly requested to refrain from. His repeated acts of intervention in affairs, with which the British government was decidedly not interested, serve to underscore just how freely the consul at Tripoli acted during the first decades of the nineteenth century.

New avenues for research in the history of modern Tripoli and British imperial engagement in the region are numerous. From the perspective of British engagement, and in the light of the person and agency of the consuls to Tripoli, a revision is needed of British interests and activities in North Africa in the early nineteenth century. Following the call of Anthony Kirk-Greene in 1974, this book has investigated the person, careers and activities of three British consuls, including Consul Warrington, that were stationed in Tripoli during the last substantive reign of a Qaramanli dynast. The project of examining the political consulates of G. B. Gagliuffi, George Crowe and Dixon Denham from the mid-nineteenth century, however, must remain a future project for another scholar of African history.[3]

ANNOTATED INDEX OF NAMES

Abd' al'-Rahman, Abraham, Gibraltan Jewish merchant resident in Tripoli and former broker to British Consul Richard Tully in the late eighteenth century.

à Court, Sir William (1779–1860), 1st Baron Heytesbury, after appointments to Naples 1801–7 and then Vienna in 1807, à Court became First Commissioner in Malta in 1812, then Envoy Extraordinary to the Barbary States, 1813–14.

al-Ahmar, Mohamed, in 1820 succeeded Mohamed al-Mukni as governor of Fezzan.

Ali Pasha of Ionnina/Tependeleni (1740–1822), ruler of Ottoman Albania, and territories in the eastern Ottoman empire. Subsequently challenged the authority of the Ottoman Porte and was killed in 1822.

Amor, Sidi, no biographical information available.

Antonio, Father and Apostolic Prefect of Tripoli between 1814 and 1824.

Bainbridge, Captain William (1774–1833), US naval officer, commanded the US frigate *Philadelphia*, lost in 1803 in Tripoli harbour.

Bait-al-Mal, Hajj Mohamed (born c.1793), Khaznadar or chief to the Pasha's treasury and advisor to Yusuf Qaramanli, initially trained as a secretary in the Pasha's Diwan, and had also been dispatched on to embassies to Istanbul.

Bathurst, Earl Henry (1762–1834), known as Lord Apsley, 3rd Earl Bathurst in 1794; secretary of state for war and the colonies in June 1812–April 1827.

Beaussier, Bonaventure (b.1748), French consul to Tripoli from 1802 to at least 1813.

Beechey, Henry William (1788/1789–1862), explorer and painter of northern Africa, vice consul to Benghazi in 1822.

Bello, Sultan Mohamed (1781–1837), third sultan of the Sokoto Caliphate.

Bentham, Jeremy (1748–1832), Utilitarian philosopher and jurist. Close friend of Hassuna D'Ghies. With a view to political reform, Bentham undertook a Civil and Constitutional Code for Tripoli and Greece in the early 1820s.

Bentinck, Lord William Henry Cavendish (1774–1839), duke of Portland, governor of Madras in 1803–7, returned to England to serve in the Peninsular campaigns (1807–14), then commander-in-chief of British forces in Sicily.

Borghul, Ali, Ottoman officer, temporarily ruled the Regency of Tripoli in 1793–5 in the name of Sultan Selim III.

Brahim Rais, in 1794 a captain of the Port to the Pasha of Tunis.

Bruce, James (1730–1794), after his appointment as consul to Algiers in 1763–5, he travelled through North Africa, Egypt and Syria. In 1768, Bruce undertook work on the sources of the Nile.

Bu Khalloum, Hameda, also referred to as 'Bobaker' or Abubakr Bu Khalloum, accompanied travellers on their mission to Bornu in 1822–3.

Bunbury, Lieutenant Colonel Thomas (1791–1862), British naval officer, served in the Peninsular campaigns and returned to London to serve in government after the Battle of Toulouse (1814).

Buttabel, Head Marabout, a religious leader and man of influence in Tripoli. Buttabel also maintained close connections to al-Kanemi of Kanem-Bornu.

Caillé, René (1799–1838), French explorer of Africa who reached Timbuktu in 1828 and published an account of his travels thereon.

Camden, Earl John Jeffreys Pratt (1759–1840), secretary of state for war and the colonies in 1804–5.

Caravana, Pietro (d.1832), British vice-consul to Derna in 1832.

Carstensen, J. A. Danish, chargé d'affaires and later consul to Tripoli, 1814–c.1824.

Casalaina (d.1832), brother-in-law to Pietro Caravana.

Cassiano, Father Pacifico da Monte, Apostolic Prefect of Tripoli in c.1800.

Castlereagh, Viscount Robert Stewart (1769–1822), 2nd Marquess of Londonderry, secretary of state for war and the colonies in 1805–6 and 1807–9.

Clapperton, Lieutenant Hugh (1788–1827), explorer of northern and central Africa. In 1822, Clapperton was dispatched on a mission to Bornu with Walter Oudney and Dixon Denham.

Clot, Antoine Berthelemy (1793–1868), French surgeon appointed surgeon-in-chief by Mohamed Ali and founded the Qasr al-Aini (initially called the Abu Za'bal hospital). Clot was later awarded the title 'Bey' for his services.

Codrington, Vice Admiral Sir Edward (1770–1851), served in the Napoleonic wars, the Greek wars of Independence and, in 1827, defeated the Egyptian-Ottoman fleet at the Battle of Navarino Bay.

Coen, Joseph, Jewish broker to consul Richard Tully in 1794.

Collingwood, Lord Cuthbert (1748–1810), 1st Baron Collingwood, appointed vice admiral in 1804, commander-in-chief of the Mediterranean fleet in 1805, fought with Nelson in the Battle of Trafalgar (1805).

Colovò, see 'Kolovos, Spiros'.

Coxe, Charles D., American consul to Tripoli in 1832.

Crocillo, Dr Pietro Francesco, personal physician to Yusuf Qaramanli in 1810, and later Neapolitan consul to Tripoli in 1828.

Denham, Major Dixon (1786–1828), explorer of northern and central Africa, member of the Bornu mission from Tripoli in 1822.

D'Ghies, Fatima, sister to Hassuna D'Ghies, married to Yusuf Pasha's son, Mustafa Qaramanli.

D'Ghies, Hassuna (1792–1836 or 1837), Tripoline notable, and brother-in-law to Ali Qaramanli – later Pasha of Tripoli – and his brother Mustafa

Qaramanli. Ambassador to London, France and Holland in 1821–5; succeeded his father, Mohamed D'Ghies, as minister for foreign affairs in 1826–9.

D'Ghies, Khadija, sister to Hassuna D'Ghies, married to Yusuf Pasha's son and successor, Ali Qaramanli.

D'Ghies, Mohamed (d.1816), father of Hassuna D'Ghies. The first minister or the minister for foreign affairs to Yusuf Qaramanli until his death.

D'Ghies, Mohamed, younger brother of Hassuna D'Ghies.

D'Ghies, Seid, younger brother of Hassuna and Mohamed D'Ghies.

Dickson, Dr John, surgeon in the Royal Navy, personal physician to the Pasha after the termination of the service of Pietro Crocillo and later Portuguese chargé d'affaires in 1828.

Dundas, Henry, 1st Viscount Melville (1742–1811), secretary of state for war and the colonies, First Lord of the Admiralty.

Dupré, M., French consul to Tripoli, succeeded Baron Rousseau in 1830.

Dupuis, Joseph (1789–1874), British vice-consul to Tripoli, 1826–36.

Elliot-Murray-Kynynmound, Sir Gilbert (1751–1814), 1st Earl of Minto, viceroy of Anglo-Corsican Kingdom in 1794, later became Governor-General of India 1807–13.

Farfara, Leon (d.1805), agent and banker in Tripoli, including to Consul Simon Lucas. Broker to Yusuf Qaramanli until his death.

Georgia, Mustafa, see 'Gurji, Mustafa'.

Goderich, Lord Viscount Frederick John Robinson (1782–1859), Undersecretary for war in 1809, and secretary of state in 1827.

Gordon, Lieutenant Colonel Sir James Willoughby (1772–1851), 1st Baronet, military secretary in 1804–9, commissary-in-chief to the Forces in 1809, quartermaster general to the Forces in 1811–51.

Goulburn, Henry (1784–1856), undersecretary for home affairs in 1810–12, and undersecretary for war and the colonies in 1812–21.

Gråberg of Hemsö, Count Jacob Florence (1776–1847), Swedish consul to Tripoli in 1823–8.

Grosvenor, Lord Richard (1795–1869), visited the Regencies of Algiers, Tunis and Tripoli in 1830.

Gurji, Mustafa (born c.1789), also referred to as Mustafa 'Georgia' by the British consul. Gurji was son-in-law to Yusuf Qaramanli, by 1824 and had been Captain of the Port for a number of years. In 1832, fled and sought British protection in Tripoli.

Haleefa, Sheikh Mohamed, head of tribe from Gharian, repeatedly challenged the authority of Yusuf Qaramanli.

Haleefa, Sheikh Wooma, brother of Sheikh Mohamed Haleefa who was murdered on Yusuf Qaramanli's orders in Gharian. Their father was also previously murdered by the Pasha in Tripoli. Wooma, on fleeing Tripoli, became the new head of the tribe of Haleefa.

Hamet, Sidi (born c.1747), prime minister and brother-in-law to Yusuf Qaramanli.

Hammuda Pasha (1759–1814), full name Muhammad ibn Ali, Bey of Tunis, 1777–1814.

Hassan, Hassan al-Faqih (b.1781) Merchant in Tripoli in the early 1800s, who chronicled the political and economic life of Tripoli.

Hawkesbury, Lord Charles Jenkinson, also known as 1st Earl of Liverpool (1729–1808), president of the Board of Trade in 1786–1804.

Hay, Robert William (1786–1861), private secretary to Sir Henry Dundas in 1821–3 and permanent undersecretary of state in 1825–36.

Hillman, William, carpenter and seaman; relation of Walter Oudney and accompanied the Bornu mission in 1822.

Horton, Robert John Wilmot (1784–1841), undersecretary of state for war and the colonies in 1821–8; later governor of Ceylon (Sri Lanka) in 1831–7.

Huskisson, William (1770–1830), undersecretary of state in 1795–1801, president of the Board of Trade in 1823–7, secretary of state for war and the colonies in 1827–8.

al-Hussein, Mohamed (1838–1874) succeeded his father, Mohamed Fadl, as Sultan of Darfur. During his reign, al-Hussein maintained friendly trading relations with the Sultanate of Wadai and Egypt in the first half of the nineteenth century.

Ibrahim Pasha (1789–1848), eldest son of Mohamed Ali of Egypt. Fought the al-Wahhab's on behalf of the Porte in the Yemen and later led campaigns across the Morea and Syria.

d'Itabayana, Baron Manuel Rodrigues Gameiro Pessoa, (d.1846), Brazilian minister plenipotentiary to Lisbon and Brazilian diplomatic representative at the Congress of Vienna in 1814–15.

d'Italinski, Andrey Yakovlevich (1743–1827), Russian ambassador to Istanbul in 1802–6 and 1812–16.

Jaffer, Prince (b.c.1805), heir apparent to Kingdom of Wadai.

al-Kanemi, Muhammad al-Amin (1776–1837), shehu of Kanem-Bornu.

Knudsen, Andreas Peter, Danish consul to Tripoli from c.1824 to at least 1828, referred to simply as 'Peter Knudsen' in the consular correspondence.

Kogia, Mustafa, bey of Tunis' (Hammuda Pasha's) prime minister in 1794.

Kolovos, Spiros, advisor and interpreter to Ali Pasha of Ioannina/ Tepedeleni.

Laing, Major Alexander Gordon (1794–1826), African explorer and son-in-law to British consul in Tripoli. Laing was assassinated on his departure from Timbuktu in September 1826.

Langford, William Wass (born c.1768) British consul to Tripoli from 1804 to 1812.

Lucas, Simon (d.1801), British consul to Tripoli from 1793 to 1801.

Lyle, Peter, see entry on Murad Rais.

Lyon, Lieutenant George Francis (1795–1832), British naval officer, who accompanied Ritchie as far as Sockna. In 1820 Lyon was appointed as Ritchie's successor by Earl Bathurst.

Maitland, Sir Thomas (1760–1824), governor of Malta in 1813–24.

McDonogh, Bryan, British acting consul from 1801 to 1803. Later Portuguese consul to Tripoli.

Mohamed Ali (1769–1849), pasha and viceroy of Egypt from 1805 to 1848. Mohamed Ali crushed the ruling mamluk class and established his own dynasty. He asserted his independence from the Ottoman Porte and undertook administrative, health and economic reforms in Egypt.

Mohamed, Dorby, emissary of Mohamed Ali, arrived in Tripoli in 1822 to obtain settlement of debts between the Regency of Tripoli and Egypt.

Morier, J. Philip, British consul to Egypt in 1805–6.

al-Mukni, Hajj Mohamed (born c.1764), bey and one of Yusuf Qaramanli's close advisors, governor of Fezzan in 1820; appointed bey of Benghazi in 1824.

Murad Rais (born c.1764), formerly known as Peter Lyle, arrived in the Regency of Tripoli in 1794; Lyle fled and 'turned Turk' following the alleged embezzlement of British cargo on board the *Hampden of London*. Appointed as 'High Admiral' by Yusuf Qaramanli in the 1820s.

Murray, Sir George (1772–1846), secretary of state for war and the colonies from 1828 to 1830.

Napean, Sir Evan (1752–1822), 1st Baronet; permanent undersecretary of state for the Home Office in 1782–91, undersecretary of state for war in 1794 and secretary to the Board of Admiralty in 1795–1804.

al-Nasser, Sheikh Abd' al-Jalil Saif, head of the tribal confederacy of the Awlad Suliman, continually challenged the authority of Yusuf Qaramanli, son-in-law to the emperor of Morocco.

Naudi, Saverio/Xavier (born c.1768), exiled Maltese, French and American chargé d'affaires in 1802. In the 1820s was a broker to Yusuf Qaramanli.

O'Brien, Richard Henry (1759–1824), American consul to Algiers in 1798.

Oudney, Dr Walter (1790–1824), naval surgeon and explorer of central Africa, contributed to the publication of *Narrative of Travels and Discoveries in Northern and Central Africa in the Years 1822, 1823, and 1824* by Dixon Denham, Hugh Clapperton and Walter Oudney.

Park, Mungo (1771–1806), explorer of western Africa and the Niger. Park published an account of his travels, *Travels in the Interior Districts of Africa*.

Peacocke, Sandford, brother-in-law to consul William Wass Langford.

Pearce, Captain Robert (c.1797–1825), Royal Navy officer, died accompanying Hugh Clapperton on an exploratory mission into the interior of Africa in 1825.

Pelham, Lord Thomas (1756–1826), 2nd Earl of Chichester, home secretary in 1801–3.

Pellew, Edward (1757–1833), 1st Viscount Exmouth, commander-in-chief of the Mediterranean fleet in 1811–14. Successfully bombarded Algiers in 1816 and subsequently established the Exmouth Treaty with the Regencies of Algiers, Tunis and Tripoli banning enslavement of Christian subjects.

Penrose, Rear Admiral Sir Charles Vinicombe (1759–1830), commander-in-chief of the Mediterranean fleet in 1814–15.

Qaramanli, Ali, son and rightful heir of Yusuf Pasha and claimed the throne in 1832 after a protracted civil war with Mohamed ibn Mohamed ibn Yusuf ibn Ali Qaramanli, the challenger to the throne.

Qaramanli, Brahen, son of Yusuf Pasha, no further biographical information available.

Qaramanli, Hamed ibn Ali ibn Ahmad, elder brother of Yusuf Pasha, was briefly new Pasha of Tripoli from January 1795 to June 1795, following expulsion of Ali Borghul. Later appointed bey of Benghazi and Derna.

Qaramanli, Hamet ibn Yusuf (d.1828), a son of Yusuf Pasha.

Qaramanli, Mahmoud (1800–1820), fourth son of Yusuf Pasha, died of typhus following an epidemic that swept Tripoli in 1820.

Qaramanli, Mohamed ibn Yusuf (d.1828), eldest son of Yusuf Pasha, returned from an exile in Egypt in 1820, subsequently appointed bey of Derna.

Qaramanli, Yusuf ibn Ali ibn Ahmad (1766–1838), Pasha of Tripoli in 1795–1832.

Reade, Sir Thomas (1782–1849), British consul to Tunis in 1824–49.

Ritchie, Dr Joseph (1788–1819), surgeon and explorer of northern Africa, died having reached Sockna.

Rofsoni, Giacomo, British vice consul to Benghazi from 1822 to 1826; appointed Tuscan consul to Tripoli in 1827.

Rousseau, Jean-Baptiste-Louis-Jacques-Joseph (1780–1831), French consul to Tripoli in 1823–9. Recalled to Paris following allegations that he was involved in the theft of the papers of Alexander Gordon Laing.

Sabun, Muhammad Abd' al-Karim (d.1815) Sultan of Wadai until his death in 1815.

al-Saghir ibn Mohamed, al-Mukhtar, (d.1847), a Sheikh and Marabout ('holy man') of the Qadiriyya order, from Azawad/Azwad and in 1825, chief of Timbuktu. Close relationship with Sultan Muhammad Bello.

Schembri, Gaetano, principal agent for Qaramanli in Malta. Schembri was also occasionally employed by others, including Pat Wilkie as Navy victualler in Malta in 1810.

Somerville, James, secretary to Pat Wilkie in 1812, and proconsul to Tripoli in 1813–14.

Smith, Sir William Sidney (1764–1840), Royal Navy officer, supporter of the anti-slavery campaign, attended the Congress of Vienna in 1814–15; appointed admiral in 1821.

Smyth, Captain William Henry (1788–1865), Royal Navy officer, undertook extensive surveys of the North African coastline, and the wider Mediterranean in 1817 and 1823.

Souza, Don Gerardo José de, Spanish consul to Tripoli in 1796–1814.

el Targhi, Hateeta, a Tuareg chief who, in February 1825, accompanied the travellers south from Tripoli.

Toole, Ernest Stuart, acting British vice consul to Kuka in 1823.

Tully, Richard (d.1739), British consul to Tripoli from 1783 to 1793.

Tyrwhitt, John (d.1824), British vice-consul to Kuka in 1822–4.

Tyrwhitt, Sir Thomas (1762–1833), cousin of John Tyrwhitt, Member of Parliament in 1796–1812, and Gentleman Usher of the Black Rod in 1812–32.
Vincenzo, Father and Apostolic Prefect of Tripoli in 1824.
al-Wahhab, Abd', this is a reference to the grandson of the Muhammad ibn Abd' al-Wahhab (1703–1792) of Najd, founder of the Wahhabi religious movement in central Arabia.
Warrington, Hanmer George (1776–1847), British consul to Tripoli in 1814–46. Warrington had seven sons and three daughters with his wife Jane.
Wellesley, Sir Henry (1773–1847), 1st Baron Cowley, British envoy to Spain in 1809–21.
Werry, Francis (1745–1832), British consul to Smyrna (Izmir) in 1805–29.
Wilkie, Patrick (Pat) (d.1813), British proconsul to Tripoli from 1812 to 1813, formerly Navy victualler in Malta at least from 1801 to 1810.
Windham, William (1750–1810), secretary of state for war and the colonies in 1806–7.
Wood, Thomas, succeeded Giacomo Rofsoni as British vice consul to Benghazi in May 1827. Married Consul Warrington's widowed daughter Emma Laing, and following her death, her sister Jane.

NOTES

Chapter 1

1 S. ElGaddari, *The Letters and Reports of British Consular and Diplomatic Agents in Tripoli, 1793-1832*. Camden Series (London: The Royal Historical Society and Cambridge University Press, 2020); S. J. Shaw, *History of the Ottoman Empire* (Cambridge: Cambridge University Press, 1977); H. Inalcik, S. Faroqhi, B. McGowan et al. (eds), *An Economic and Social History of the Ottoman Empire, 1300-1914* (Cambridge: Cambridge University Press, 1994); S. Faroqhi, *The Ottoman Empire and the World around It* (London: I.B. Tauris, 1997); D. Quataert, *The Ottoman Empire, 1700-1922* (Cambridge: Cambridge University Press, 2005); S. Deringil, *The Well-Protected Domains: Ideology and the Legitimation of Power in the Ottoman Empire 1876-1909* (London: I.B. Tauris, 2011).
2 D. C. M. Platt, *The Cinderella Service: British Consuls since 1825* (London: Longman, 1971); M. S. Anderson, 'Great Britain and the Barbary States in the Eighteenth Century', *Historical Research*, 29, 79 (1956): 87-107; H. I. Lee, 'The Supervising of the Barbary Consuls during the Years 1756-1836', *Bulletin of the Institute of Historical Research*, 23 (1950): 191-9.
3 J. Darwin, 'Imperialism and the Victorians: The Dynamics of Territorial Expansion', *English Historical Review*, 112, 447 (1997): 642; M. J. Reimer, *Colonial Bridgehead: Government and Society in Alexandria, 1807-1882* (New York: Routledge, 1998); A. Kirk-Greene, 'Towards a History of the Colonial Service', *African Affairs*, 73, 290 (1974): 108. Cf. M. Lynn, 'Consul and Kings: The Role of the "Man on the Spot", and the Seizure of Lagos, 1851', *Journal of Imperial and Commonwealth History*, 10, 2 (1982): 150-67; D. McLean, *War, Diplomacy and Informal Empire and the Republics of La Plata, 1836-1853* (London: I.B. Tauris, 1994).
4 Darwin, 'Imperialism and the Victorians', 642.
5 Ibid., 628.
6 A. K. Bennison, 'Liminal States: Morocco and the Iberian Frontier between the Twelfth and Nineteenth Centuries', *Journal of North African Studies*, 6, 1 (2001): 11-28.
7 E. Rossi, 'Tripoli', in E. J. Brill, *Encyclopedia of Islam*, Volume 4 (Leiden: Brill, 1934), 814-18.
8 Ibid. See also C. Féraud and A. Bernard, *Annales Tripolitaines* (Tunis: Librairie Tournier, 1927).
9 H. A. S. Johnston, *The Fulani Empire of Sokoto* (London: Oxford University Press, 1970).
10 K. Folayan, *Tripoli during the Reign of Yusuf Qaramanli* (Ile-Ife: University of Ife Press, 1979).
11 These territories covered a vast expanse of central Africa, from northeast Nigeria, Chad and the Sudan.
12 This position was re-stated in a speech given by Queen Victoria to both Houses of Parliament on 16 January 1840. A printed copy is contained in The National

Archives, London (TNA), Foreign Office and predecessors: Political and Other Departments: General Correspondence before 1906, Tripoli, Series I and II (hereafter FO) 160/3.

13 The dates stated are the periods of service of Lucas, Langford and Warrington as Consuls to Tripoli. E. Baigent, 'Lucas, Simon (*fl. c.*1766–1799)', in *Oxford Dictionary of National Biography* (Oxford University Press, 2004). Available online: https://doi.org/10.1093/ref:odnb/17144. Some details in Lucas's entry are incorrect, as Acting Consul Bryan McDonogh reported that Lucas had died on 4 May 1801 as an 'old man', TNA, FO 76/5, McDonogh to Portland, 15 May 1801. McDonogh's account is further supported by Lucas's memorial wherein Lucas wrote that he had begun his consular career in 1768, TNA, Home Office (hereafter HO) 46/16/112, Folios 301A–306: Memorial of Simon Lucas to William Grenville, 20 Aug. 1790. Langford (Bef. 9 Dec. 1772–25 April 1817), www.eliotsofporteliot.com/familytree/getperson.php?personID=I01831&tree=eliot1; *The Naval Chronicle*, volume 37, April 1817, 440; *Bath Chronicle and Weekly Gazette*, 8 May 1817; PROB 11/1609/251. With thanks to Richard Pennell for directing me to these sources. Warrington was born in 1776 in Acton, Denbighshire, and died in 1847 at Patras. For further details, see J. Wright, 'Warrington, Hanmer George (1776–1847)', in *Oxford Dictionary of National Biography* (Oxford University Press, Jan. 2008). Available online: https://doi.org/10.1093/ref:odnb/71826.

14 C. Bayly, *The Birth of the Modern World, 1780–1914* (Oxford: Oxford University Press, 2004). See also J. Darwin, *The Empire Project: The Rise and Fall of the British World System, 1830–1970* (Cambridge: Cambridge University Press, 2011); and P. E. Lovejoy, 'Commercial Sectors in the Economy of Nineteenth-Century Sudan: The Trans-Saharan Trade and the Desert-Side Salt Trade', *African Economic History*, 13 (1984): 85–116.

15 Folayan, *Tripoli during the Reign of Yusuf Qaramanli*; N. Lafi, *Une Ville du Maghreb entre Ancien Régime et Réformes Ottomanes: Genèse des Institutions Municipales à Tripoli de Barbarie (1795–1911)* (Paris: L'Harmattan, 2002); J. M. Abun-Nasr, *A History of the Maghrib* (Cambridge: Cambridge University Press, 1975); A. Moalla, *The Regency of Tunis and the Ottoman Porte, 1777–1814: Army and Government of a North-African Eyalet at the End of the Eighteenth Century* (London: RoutledgeCurzon, 2004); and K. Ben Srhir, *Morocco during the Embassy of John Drummond Hay, 1845–1886* (London: RoutledgeCurzon, 2004); J. A. O. C. Brown, *Crossing the Strait: Morocco, Gibraltar and Great Britain in the 18th and 19th Centuries* (Leiden: Brill, 2012); N. Erzini, *Moroccan-British Diplomatic and Commercial Relations in the Early 18th Century: The Abortive Embassy to Meknes in 1718* (Durham: Institute of Middle Eastern and Islamic Studies, University of Durham, 2002); L. J. Hume, 'Preparations for Civil War in Tripoli in the 1820s: Ali Karamanli, Hassuna D'Ghies and Jeremy Bentham', *Journal of African History*, 21, 3 (1980): 311–22.

Chapter 2

1 R. J. Gavin, *Aden under British Rule 1839–1867* (London: C. Hurst, 1975); Z. H. Kour, *The History of Aden 1839–1872* (London: Frank Cass, 1981); D. Kilingray, M. Lincoln and N. Rigby (eds), *Maritime Empires: British Imperial Maritime Trade in the*

Nineteenth Century (Woodbridge: Boydell Press, 2004); P. Morgan, *The Decline and Fall of the British Empire, 1781–1997* (London: Vintage, 2008).
2. A. T. Mahan, 'The Mediterranean and Italy', in *The Influence of Sea Power on the French Revolution and Empire*, Volume 1 (Boston: Little & Brown, 1894), 206.
3. A. B. Rodger, *The War of Second Coalition, 1798–1801: A Strategic Commentary* (New York: Oxford University Press, 1964).
4. TNA, FO 76/5, Simon Lucas to Duke of Portland, Tripoli, 9 Apr. 1797.
5. P. Kennedy, *The Rise and Fall of British Naval Mastery* (London: Allen Lane, 1976); A. T. Mahan, *The Influence of Sea Power on the French Revolution and Empire*, 2 Volumes. (London: Sampson Low & Marston, 1892).
6. R. W. Bullard, *Britain and the Middle East: From the Earliest Times to 1950* (London: Hutchinson's University Library, 1951), 30–1.
7. J. Darwin, *After Tamerlane: The Rise and Fall of Global Empires, 1400–2000* (London: Penguin, 2008), 214.
8. R. Holland, *Blue-Water Empire: The British in the Mediterranean since 1800* (London: Penguin, 2013), 10.
9. B. Arthur, *How Britain Won the War of 1812: The Royal Navy's Blockades of the United States, 1812–1815* (Woodbridge: Boydell Press, 2011); Kennedy, *The Rise and Fall of British Naval Mastery*; J. D. Grainger, *The British Navy in the Mediterranean* (Woodbridge: Boydell Press, 2017); B. Lavery, *Nelson's Navy: The Ships, Men and Organisation 1793–1815* (Oxford: Osprey Publishing, 2020).
10. Brown, *Crossing the Strait*, 186.
11. Ibid., 186–7.
12. A. R. H. al-Jabarti, S. Moreh, R. L. Tignor, E. W. Said and L. A. Fauvelet de Bourriene, *Napoleon in Egypt: Al-Jabarti's Chronicle of the French Occupation, 1798* (Princeton, NJ: Markus Wiener, 2004); J. R. Cole, *Napoleon's Egypt: Invading the Middle East* (New York: Palgrave Macmillan, 2007); D. Dykstra, 'The French Occupation of Egypt', in M. W. Daly (ed.), *The Cambridge History of Egypt: Volume 2: Modern Egypt from 1517 to the End of the Twentieth Century* (Cambridge: Cambridge University Press, 2008), 113–38; C. J. Esdaile, *The Wars of Napoleon* (London: Routledge, 2019); M. Broers, *Napoleon: Soldier of Destiny* (London: Faber & Faber, 2014).
13. Darwin, *After Tamerlane*, 182; M. W. Daly (ed.), *The Cambridge History of Egypt: Volume 2: Modern Egypt from 1517 to the End of the Twentieth Century* (Cambridge: Cambridge University Press, 1998).
14. Mahan, 'The Mediterranean and Italy', 253.
15. Ibid., 282; R. C. Anderson, *Naval Wars in the Levant, 1559–1853* (Liverpool: Liverpool University Press, 1952); Rodger, *The War of the Second Coalition*; Ingram, *In Defence of British India: Great Britain in the Middle East, 1775–1842* (London: Frank Cass, 1984); T. W. C. Blanning, *The French Revolutionary Wars, 1787–1802* (London: Arnold, 1996); Marshall (ed.), *The Oxford History of the British Empire: Volume 2: The Eighteenth Century*; R. Muir, *Britain and the Defeat of Napoleon, 1807–1815* (New Haven, CT: Yale University Press, 1996); and J. Black, *Britain as a Military Power, 1688–1815* (Abingdon: Routledge, 2014).
16. Bullard, *Britain and the Middle East*, 31.
17. R. Morriss, 'Smith, Sir (William) Sidney (1764–1840)', *Oxford Dictionary of National Biography* (Oxford University Press, 2009). Available online: https://doi.org/10.1093/ref:odnb/25940. On Smith's responsibilities in Istanbul and his secondment to the Turkish Navy in 1795, see Ingram, *In Defence of British India*, 37.

18. TNA, FO, 76/6, Horatio Nelson to Yusuf Qaramanli, Vanguard, Palermo, 28 Apr. 1799, in ElGaddari, *Letters and Reports*, 59.
19. Holland, *Blue-Water Empire*, 11.
20. A. T. Mahan, 'The Mediterranean from 1799 to 1801', in *The Influence of Sea Power on the French Revolution and Empire*, Volume 1 (Boston: Little & Brown, 1894), 299 and 324. On Phélippeaux, see Ghislain de Diesbach and Robert Grouvel, *Échec à Bonaparte: Louis-Edmond de Phélippeaux, 1767–1799* (Paris: Perrin, 1979).
21. E. Ingram, 'A Preview of the Great Game in Asia – I: The British Occupation of Perim and Aden in 1799', *Middle Eastern Studies*, 9, 1 (1973): 1–18.
22. Holland, *Blue-Water Empire*, 12.
23. Mahan, 'The Mediterranean from 1799 to 1801', 329; TNA, FO 76/8, James Somerville to Lieutenant Colonel Bunbury, Tripoli, 8 Mar. 1813, in ElGaddari, *Letters and Reports*, 128.
24. C. J. Bartlett, *Great Britain and Sea Power, 1815–1853* (Oxford: Clarendon Press, 1963), 59.
25. Bullard, *Britain and the Middle East*, 33.
26. D. Beales, 'Canning, George (1770–1827)', *Oxford Dictionary of National Biography* (Oxford University Press, Sept. 2014). Available online: https://doi.org/10.1093/ref:odnb/4556; Bartlett, *Great Britain and Sea Power*, 77. Cf. H. W. V. Temperley, *The Foreign Policy of Canning, 1822–1827: England, the Neo-holy Alliance, and the New World* (London: Frank Cass, 1925); R. Muir, *Britain and the Defeat of Napoleon*; W. Hinde, *George Canning* (London: Collins, 1973).
27. A. Porter and W. R. Louis (eds), *The Oxford History of the British Empire: Volume 3: The Nineteenth Century* (Oxford: Oxford University Press, 1999); C. I. Hamilton, 'Naval Power and Diplomacy in the Nineteenth Century', *Journal of Strategic Studies*, 3, 1 (1980): 74–88; Kennedy, *The Rise and Fall of British Naval Mastery*; J. Samson (ed.), *The British Empire* (Oxford: Oxford University Press, 2001); J. R. Seeley, *The Expansion of England* (London: Macmillan, 1914).
28. Holland, *Blue-Water Empire*, 40.
29. Pw Jd 52/1, Sir William à Court to Lord William Bentinck, Tripoli, 2 Oct. 1813. This letter is made available by kind permission of the University of Nottingham Manuscripts and Special Collections.
30. TNA, FO 76/16, Sir William à Court to Robert Wilmot, London, 5 May 1822, in ElGaddari, *Letters and Reports*, 190.
31. The Royal African Company was founded in 1660 as 'The Company of Royal Adventurers Trading to Africa' and was later renamed the 'African Company of Merchants' in the second half of the eighteenth century.
32. The ten English forts were (from West to East): Appolonia (Beyin), Dick's Cove (Fort Metal Cross, Dixcove); Succondee (Fort George, Sekondi); Commenda (Komenda); Cape Coast Castle; Annanaboe (Fort William, Anomabo); Tantumquerry; Winnebah; Fort James, Accra; and Whydah. E. C. Martin, 'The English Establishments on the Gold Coast in the Second Half of the Eighteenth Century', *Transactions of the Royal Historical Society*, Fourth Series, 5 (1922): 169.
33. Malachi Postlethwayt in Martin, 'The English Establishments on the Gold Coast', 170–1.
34. Bullard, *Britain and the Middle East*, 30; G. D. Clayton, *Britain and the Eastern Question: Missolonghi to Gallipoli* (London: University of London Press, 1971), 35.
35. TNA, FO 76/5, Simon Lucas to Henry Dundas, Tripoli, 6 Feb. 1795, in ElGaddari, *Letters and Reports*, 44.

36 TNA, FO 76/27, Hanmer Warrington to R. W. Hay, Tripoli, 10 Mar. 1820, in ElGaddari, *Letters and Reports*, 281.
37 Inalcik, Faroqhi, McGowan et al., *An Economic and Social History of the Ottoman Empire*; Faroqhi, *The Ottoman Empire*; K. Fahmy, 'The Era of Muhammad 'Ali Pasha', in M. W. Daly (ed.), *The Cambridge History of Egypt: Volume 2: Modern Egypt from 1517 to the End of the Twentieth Century* (Cambridge: Cambridge University Press, 2008), 139–79; Folayan, *Tripoli during the Reign of Yusuf Pasha Qaramanli*; Moalla, *The Regency of Tunis*.
38 Holland, *Blue-Water Empire*, 31.
39 Ibid., 35.
40 On Liverpool, see Sir T. Lawrence, 'Jenkinson, Robert Banks, Second Earl of Liverpool (1770–1828)', in *Oxford Dictionary of National Biography* (Oxford University Press, 2004). Available online: https://doi.org/10.1093/ref:odnb/14740.
41 Bartlett, *Great Britain and Sea Power*, 56.
42 Darwin, *After Tamerlane*, 165.
43 Holland, *Blue-Water Empire*, 43; Darwin, *After Tamerlane*, 210.
44 C. D. Hall, 'Pellew, Edward, First Viscount Exmouth (1757–1833)', in *Oxford Dictionary of National Biography* (Oxford University Press, May 2009). Available online: https://doi.org/10.1093/ref:odnb/21808.
45 Bartlett, *Great Britain and Sea Power*, 61.
46 Holland, *Blue-Water Empire*, 32–3.
47 Bartlett, *Great Britain and Sea Power*, 64; N. Thompson, 'Bathurst, Henry, Third Earl Bathurst (1762–1834)', in *Oxford Dictionary of National Biography* (Oxford University Press, Jan. 2008). Available online: https://doi.org/10.1093/ref:odnb/1696.
48 Holland, *Blue-Water Empire*, 48.
49 R. Bickers (ed.), *Settlers and Expatriates: Britons over the Seas* (Oxford: Oxford University Press, 2010).
50 W. St Clair, *That Greece Might Still Be Free: The Philhellenes in the War of Independence* (Cambridge: Open Book, 2008); M. Miliori, 'Europe, the Classical Polis, and the Greek Nation: Philhellenism and Hellenism in Nineteenth Century Britain', in R. Beaton and D. Ricks (eds), *The Making of Modern Greece: Nationalism, Romanticism & The Uses of the Past (1797–1896)* (London: Routledge, 2009), 65–77; T. J. B. Spencer, *Fair Greece! Sade Relic: Literary Philhellenism from Shakespeare to Byron* (London: Weidenfeld & Nicolson, 1954).
51 Cf. Holland, *Blue-Water Empire*, 43; Kennedy, *The Rise and Fall of British Naval Mastery*.
52 Cf. P. von Hess, 'Commander Panagiotis Kefalas Plants the Flag of Liberty upon the Walls of Tripolizza, after the Siege of Tripolitsa'. Available online: https://commons.wikimedia.org/wiki/File:Panagiotis_Kefalas_by_Hess.jpg; and H. Serrur, 'Death of a Greek Soldier during the Siege of Tripolizza'. Available online: https://en.wikipedia.org/wiki/Tripoli,_Greece#/media/File:Douai_chartreuse_serrur_soldat_grec.jpg.
53 Holland, *Blue-Water Empire*, 48.
54 Ibid.
55 Ibid., 9; Bartlett, *Great Britain and Sea Power*, 55.
56 Bartlett, *Great Britain and Sea Power*, 63; R. Thorne, 'Stewart, Robert, Viscount Castlereagh and Second Marquess of Londonderry (1769–1822)', in *Oxford Dictionary of National Biography* (Oxford University Press, May 2009). Available online: https://doi.org/10.1093/ref:odnb/26507.

57 TNA, FO 76/15, Hanmer Warrington to Earl Bathurst, Tripoli, 26 Mar. 1821, in ElGaddari, *Letters and Reports*, 176. Cf. TNA. FO 76/11, Hanmer Warrington to Earl Bathurst, Tripoli, 9 Nov. 1817, in ElGaddari, *Letters and Reports*, 156.
58 *A Treatise upon the Trade from Great-Britain to Africa ... By an African Merchant* (London, 1772); Robert Norris, *Memoirs of the Reiyn of Bossa Ahadee, King of Dahomy An Inland Country of Guiney, to which Are Added the Author's Journey to Abomey, the Capital, and A Short Account of the African Slave Trade* (London, 1789); and Archibald Dalzel, *The History of Dahomy, an Inland Kingdom of Africa, Compiled from Authentic Memoirs* (London, 1793).
59 TNA, FO 76/23: Hanmer Warrington to Vice Admiral Sir Edward Codrington, Tripoli, 15 Nov. 1827, in ElGaddari, *Letters and Reports*, 260.
60 A. Sattin, *Lifting the Veil: British Society in Egypt 1768–1956* (London: J. M. Dent, 1988), 16.
61 Ibid., 22–3.
62 A. Eden, *Full Circle: The Memoirs of Sir Anthony Eden* (London: Cassell, 1960), 424.
63 Darwin, 'Imperialism and the Victorians', 630.
64 TNA, FO 76/9, various reports from Warrington, including, Warrington to Bathurst, 27 July 1815; Warrington, 'Extracts from *A Short Account of Tripoli in the West*' (1844), on the topics of: 'Desert', 'Mountains', 'Rain', 'Temperature', 'Population', 'Districts' and 'Sovereigns of the Interior'. Less than a year later, in June 1816, Charles Robert Prinsep wrote to Viscount Castlereagh with a document entitled 'Grounds of an Opinion in Favour of Colonizing the Africa Coast of the Mediterranean from Great Britain', TNA, FO 8/2, Prinsep to Castlereagh, 26 June 1816.
65 Holland, *Blue-Water Empire*, 22.
66 Darwin, *After Tamerlane*, 162 and 211; Holland, *Blue-Water Empire*, 51.
67 K. Fahmy, *All the Pasha's Men: Mehmed Ali, His Army and the Making of Modern Egypt* (Cairo: American University in Cairo Press, 2002); Fahmy, 'The Era of Muhammad 'Ali Pasha'; A. L. al-Sayyid Marsot, *Egypt in the Reign of Muhammad Ali* (Cambridge: Cambridge University Press, 1994); H. Dodwell, *The Founder of Modern Egypt – A Study of Muhammad 'Ali* (Cambridge: Cambridge University Press, 1931, reprinted 1977).
68 Bartlett, *Great Britain and Sea Power*, 84.
69 Holland, *Blue-Water Empire*, 89.
70 Darwin, *After Tamerlane*, 162.
71 Bartlett, *Great Britain and Sea Power*, 58.
72 Bullard, *Britain and the Middle East*, 35.

Chapter 3

1 C. A. Swanson and D. W. Knox (eds), *Naval Documents Related to the United States' Wars with the Barbary Powers*, Volumes 1–6 (Washington, DC: US Government Printing Office, 1939–44).
2 A. W. Ould Cheikh, 'A Man of Letters in Timbuktu', in S. Jeppie and S. Bachir Diagne (eds), *The Meanings of Timbuktu* (Cape Town: Human Sciences Research Council of South Africa Press, 2008), 231–48; E. N. Saad, *Social History of Timbuktu: The Role of Muslim Scholars and Notables 1400–1900* (Cambridge: Cambridge University

Press, 1983); and Ş. Pamuk, *A Monetary History of the Ottoman Empire* (Cambridge: Cambridge University Press, 2004).
3   C. A. Bayly, *Imperial Meridian: The British Empire and the World, 1780–1830* (Harlow: Longman, 1989), 14.
4   TNA, FO 76/5, Lucas to Duke of Portland, 30 June 1795, in ElGaddari, *Letters and Reports*, 48–51. On Sultan Selim III's final attempt to permanently remove the Qaramanli family from the throne at Tripoli, see TNA, FO 76/5, Lucas to John King, 12 and 15 Feb. 1794, and Lucas to Portland, 9 Apr. 1797, in ElGaddari, *Letters and Reports*, 39–41 and 56–8. On Portland, D. Wilkinson, 'Bentinck, William Henry Cavendish Cavendish-, Third Duke of Portland (1738–1809)', in *Oxford Dictionary of National Biography* (Oxford University Press, Jan. 2008). Available online: https://doi.org/10.1093/ref:odnb/2162. On King, see S. M. Lee, 'King, John (1759–1830)', in *Oxford Dictionary of National Biography* (Oxford University Press, Jan. 2008). Available online: https://doi.org/10.1093/ref:odnb/64119.
5   TNA, FO 76/5, Lucas to Portland, 5 Apr. 1797.
6   On Pelham, see D. R. Fisher, 'Pelham, Thomas, Second Earl of Chichester (1756–1826)', in *Oxford Dictionary of National Biography* (Oxford University Press, Jan. 2008). Available online: https://doi.org/10.1093/ref:odnb/21799.
7   TNA, FO 76/5, McDonogh to Pelham, 2 Dec. 1802, in ElGaddari, *Letters and Reports*, 67–9.
8   Ibid.
9   TNA, FO 76/7, Langford to Liverpool, 10 July 1811, in ElGaddari, *Letters and Reports*, 72–5.
10 Ibid. 'Shake Seffannafsar' is likely to be Sheikh Saif al-Nasser of Fezzan.
11 Ibid.
12 *Report of Secretary of State relative to the Mediterranean Trade. Communicated to the House of Representatives and to the Senate*, 30 Dec. 1790 and 3 Jan. 1791, in Swanson and Knox (eds), *Naval Documents Related to the United States' Wars with the Barbary Powers: Volume 1: Naval Operations Including Diplomatic Background from 1785 through 1801* (Washington, DC: US Government Printing Office, 1939).
13 Ibid.
14 Valensi, *Le Maghreb Avant la Prise d'Alger, 1790–1830* (Paris: Flammarion, 1969); Moalla, *The Regency of Tunis*.
15 UCL, Bentham MSS, Box 24/474, D'Ghies to John Quincy Adams, 3 Feb. 1823. Quincy Adams was the US secretary of state, addressed by D'Ghies (and in translation by Bentham) as the 'Anglo-American United States' and reflected D'Ghies's desire to build on his relationship with Britain, and to extend cooperation to a new power with ambitions in the Regency.
16 UCL, Bentham MSS, Box 24, D'Ghies, various letters and interviews.
17 TNA, FO 76/5, Lucas to Dundas, 6 Feb. 1795, in ElGaddari, *Letters and Reports*, 44–7.
18 Ibid.
19 UCL, Bentham MSS, Box 24/438, D'Ghies interview with Jeremy Bentham, 25 Jan. 1823. While it is unclear when Mohamed D'Ghies took on his official role, we do know that he had held the position for more than a decade, according to the consular correspondence, until his death in late 1825, or early 1826. Warrington added that 'the Death of that most excellent man old Mr. D'Ghies the event took place some months since … A short time since all the Consuls received a Circular from the Bashaw announcing the appointment of Mr. Hassuna D'Ghies as Minister for Foreign Affairs', see TNA, FO 76/20, Warrington to Bathurst, 20 Feb. 1826. Hassuna D'Ghies held the

position of 'Minister for Foreign Affairs' for three years from 1826 to 1829, until he was replaced by his younger brother, Mohamed.
20 TNA, FO 76/5, Lucas to Dundas, 30 June 1795, in ElGaddari, *Letters and Reports*, 48–51.
21 Ibid.
22 Ibid.
23 These figures are for the greater Tripoli area, which includes the lands outside the city walls and expands to the Menshia. The figure for Fezzan, while inclusive of the inhabitants of Murzuq, includes 'all inland and south of Tripoli', Hassuna D'Ghies's interview with Jeremy Bentham, 18 Sept. 1822., UCL, Bentham MSS, Box 24. There are more conservative recent figures, estimating the population of Tripoli at 15,000–20,000, but that the population of the entire Regency had numbered 400,000. Cf. Rossi, 'Tripoli'; Lafi, *Une Ville du Maghreb*, 25.
24 TNA, FO 76/18, Warrington to Bathurst, 5 July 1824; and TNA, FO 76/23, Warrington to Hay, 20 Mar. 1828, in ElGaddari, *Letters and Reports*, 225–6. By comparison, in early 1828, Warrington wrote, though he may have underestimated the numbers, that the French Consul had 'no more than five or six resident subjects' in Tripoli, TNA, FO 76/23, Warrington to Hay, 20 Mar. 1828. See also Rossi, 'Tripoli'. On the role of the Maltese and Greek diaspora (amongst others) in the Mediterranean and the Maltese as the largest entrepreneurial network in Tripoli, see I. Baghdiantz McCabe et al. (eds), *Diaspora Entrepreneurial Networks, Four Centuries of History* (Oxford: Berg, 2005).
25 G. H. Warrington, 'Extract from *A Short Account of Tripoli in the West*', *Journal of the Royal Geographical Society of London*, 14 (1844): 106. The decrease in the number of the Maltese population in Tripoli between 1828 and 1844 was because of a number of factors that included the political instability in the city (as a result of the succession dispute) and the wider Regency (because of the Pasha's loss of authority).
26 UCL, Bentham MSS, Box 24/81–2, various, including Bentham, 'Account of Tripoli', based on notes and interviews with D'Ghies, 4 Oct. 1822, and Bentham MSS, Box 24/387, 'Jeremy Bentham to John Quincy Adams for Tripoli', 13 Jan. 1823.
27 UCL, Bentham MSS, Box 24/16, D'Ghies, various interviews with Bentham.
28 TNA, FO 76/27, Warrington to R. W. Hay, 9 Sept. 1830.
29 On Grosvenor, see H. R. Tedder, 'Grosvenor, Richard, Second Marquess of Westminster (1795–1869)', rev. K. D. Reynolds, in *Oxford Dictionary of National Biography* (Oxford University Press, 2004). Available online: https://doi.org/10.1093/ref:odnb/11670.
30 Grosvenor, *Extracts from the Journal of Lord R. Grosvenor: Being an Account of His Visit to the Barbary Regencies in the Spring of 1830* (London: Darf, 1986), 7.
31 BL, 8156 DF4: *Tracts on Slavery*, D'Ghies, *A Letter Addressed to James Scarlett*, 12 May 1822.
32 On Peter Lyle's alleged embezzlement of British cargo at Petras and elsewhere, as well as Lyle's 'abandonment' of his wife and five children in Wapping, London, see TNA, FO 76/5, Lucas to Dundas, 5 June 1794.
33 TNA, FO 76/18, Warrington to Wilmot Horton, 20 Feb. 1824.
34 On Saverio Naudi (also misspelt 'Nandi' in some of the correspondence), his close relationship to both the British consul and the Pasha, as well as the request from Count Shimmelman to the British government to remove him, see TNA, FO 76/8, Langford to Bathurst, 23 Feb. 1813; TNA, FO 76/19, extract of dispatch from the Minister at Copenhagen, H. W. W. Wynn to Canning, 13 Nov. 1825.

35 TNA, FO 76/7, Langford to Oakes, 18 Sept. 1811; TNA, FO 76/7, Langford to Liverpool, 6 Sept. 1810.
36 On Abraham Abd' al-Rahman (also called 'Abraham de Hardy Abudarham' and a British subject), see TNA, FO 76/5, Lucas to Dundas, 30 Jan. 1794, in ElGaddari, *Letters and Reports*, 32–9; TNA, FO 76/8, Langford to Liverpool, 20 Feb. 1811; and TNA, FO 76/7, Oakes to Langford, 12 Sept. 1811.
37 The Qadi (alternately spelt as Kadi, Kadey) was the minister of justice. The Qadi 'hears appeals from every Judicatory and places and displaces the members. He judges with open doors'. There were, according to the Tripoline Ambassador to London in 1822; 13, 14 and 15 judicatories for Tripoli, and 3–4 in Fezzan, with 3, 5 or 7 judges in each judicatory. UCL, Bentham MSS, Box 24, various papers, including D'Ghies's question-and-answer session with Bentham, 18 Sept. 1822. See also TNA, FO 76/29, Yusuf Qaramanli to Warrington, Dec. 1831. This letter was written sometime between 9 and 14 Dec. 1831, because it was provided in reply to a letter from the British consul dated 6 Dec. 1831, and Warrington then sent a response to the Pasha's original letter that was dated 14 Dec. 1831.
38 For details of daily entries in the consular or 'Office Diary' – the period 1 Jan. to 30 June 1829 is enclosed in a letter in TNA, FO 76/25, from Warrington to Hay, 26 Aug. 1829; and for 1 July to 31 Dec. 1829 is enclosed in a letter in TNA, FO 76/27, from Warrington to Hay, 17 Feb. 1830. Individuals designated as British subjects and therefore under the protection of the British flag expanded with British activity in the Mediterranean and included Corsicans, Sicilians, Greeks and Neapolitans; TNA, FO 76/5, Lucas to Dundas, 20 Oct. 1794, in ElGaddari, *Letters and Reports*, 42–4; TNA, FO 76/12, Maitland to Robert Liston, 14 Nov. 1818; and TNA, FO 76/20, Warrington to Bathurst, 13 July 1826, in ElGaddari, *Letters and Reports*, 246–9.
39 A Diwan was effectively a Cabinet or Council.
40 P. E. Lovejoy, 'Commercial Sectors in the Economy of the Nineteenth-Century Central Sudan: The Trans-Saharan Trade and the Desert-Side Salt Trade', *African Economic History*, 13 (1984): 98.
41 Senna is a species of the African Cassia tree and was used for medicinal purposes. On the prominence and re-export of senna from Tripoli to Europe, see Lydon, *On Trans-Saharan Trails: Islamic Law, Trade Networks and Cross-Cultural Exchange in Western Africa* (Cambridge: Cambridge University Press, 2009), 93; Bovill, *Caravans of the Old Sahara* (London: Oxford University Press, 1933); Boahen, 'The Caravan Trade in the Nineteenth Century', *Journal of African History*, 3, 2 (1962): 349–59; J. K. Thornton, *Africa and the Africans in the Making of the Atlantic World, 1400–1880* (Cambridge, Cambridge University Press, 1998); D. Eltis and S. L. Engerman (eds), *The Cambridge World History of Slavery: Volume 3: AD 1420–AD 1804* (Cambridge: Cambridge University Press, 2011); D. Richardson, 'The British Empire and the Atlantic Slave Trade, 1660–1807', in P. J. Marshall (ed.), *The Oxford History of the British Empire: Volume 2: The Eighteenth Century*, 440–64; Lovejoy, *Transformations in Slavery*; H. J. Fisher, *Slavery in the History of Muslim Black Africa* (London: Hurst, 2001).
42 Lovejoy, 'Commercial Sectors', 99.
43 Lovejoy, 'Commercial Sectors'; E. W. Bovill, *The Golden Trade of the Moors* (London: Oxford University Press, 1958).
44 Lovejoy, 'Commercial Sectors', 89; cf. George Francis Lyon, *A Narrative of Travels in Northern Africa in the Years 1818, 19, and 1820; Accompanied by Geographical Notices of the Sudan, and of the Course of the Niger* (London: John Murray, 1821); Jacopo

Gräberg di Hemsö, 'Prospetto del Commercio di Tripoli d'Africa, e delle sue relazioni con quello dell'Italia', *Antologia*, volume 30 (1827): 3–29; A. M. Altaleb, 'The Social and Economic History of Slavery in Libya (1800–1950).' PhD thesis (University of Manchester, 2015).

45 Salamé, *Narrative of the Expedition to Algiers in the Year 1816, Under the Command of the Right Honorable Admiral Viscount Exmouth* (London: John Murray, 1819).

46 Bayly, *Imperial Meridian*; Laidlaw, *Colonial Connections, 1815–45: Patronage, the Information Revolution and Colonial Government* (Manchester: Manchester University Press, 2005).

47 TNA, FO 76/7, Langford to Gordon, 25 Sept. 1810, in ElGaddari, *Letters and Reports*, 110–12; H. M. Chichester, 'Gordon, Sir James Willoughby, first baronet (1772–1851)', rev. R. T. Stearn, *Oxford Dictionary of National Biography* (Oxford University Press, May 2014). Available online: https://doi.org/10.1093/ref:odnb/1105.

48 TNA, FO 76/9, various reports from Warrington, including, Warrington to Bathurst, 27 July 1815; Warrington, 'Extracts from *A Short Account of Tripoli in the West*' (1844), on the topics of: 'Desert', 'Mountains', 'Rain', 'Temperature', 'Population', 'Districts' and 'Sovereigns of the Interior'. Consul Warrington was not the only person to propose a permanent British colony in the Regency. Less than a year later, in June 1816, Charles Robert Prinsep wrote to Viscount Castlereagh with a document titled 'Grounds of an Opinion in favour of Colonizing the Africa Coast of the Mediterranean from Great Britain', TNA, FO 8/2, Prinsep to Castlereagh, 26 June 1816.

49 D. W. Knox, 'Preface' in Swanson and Knox (eds), *Naval Documents Related to the United States' Wars with the Barbary Powers: Volume 1: Naval Operations including Diplomatic Background from 1785 through 1801*, v.

50 TNA, FO 76/5, McDonogh to Portland, 15 May 1801; and TNA, FO 76/5, Langford to York, 10 July 1804, in ElGaddari, *Letters and Reports*, 61–3 and 72–5.

51 Ibid.

52 Acting Consul McDonogh listed the following as composing the maritime force of the Pasha by December 1802, '3 ships mounting 28, 22 & 12 Guns, 1 Brig mounting 14 Guns, 3 Shambucks mounting 16, 12 and 9 Guns, 2 Kerlanguiskes mounting 12 and 9 Guns, 2 Galliots, 3 Tartans, 1 Brig of 16 Guns taken from the Americans, besides 10 Gun Boats which the Spaniards built for the Bashaw, mounting 12, 18 & 24 Pounders', TNA, FO 76/5, McDonogh to Pelham, 2 Dec. 1802, in ElGaddari, *Letters and Reports*, 67–9. Since his accession Yusuf Qaramanli had put concerted effort and resources into vastly improving the maritime and land forces of his Regency. This is particularly evident when McDonogh's account of the naval presence of the Pasha is contrasted with the insignificant resources at his disposal when he ascended the throne in 1795. Nevertheless, Tripoli maintained a cooperative relationship with Spain as, the consul wrote, that the Court of Spain had sent him '18 artificers, Black Smiths, Ships – Carpenters, and masons, with all their working Impliments, together with Masts and Stoves to fit out a Kebeck Cruizer of 16 Guns'. Alongside the aforementioned cruiser, the Pasha only possessed, according to the Consul, three 'lesser ones' which were constantly manned by Greeks. TNA, FO 76/5, Lucas to Dundas, 30 Jan. 1794, in ElGaddari, *Letters and Reports*, 32–9.

53 TNA, FO 76/23, Warrington to Murray, 1 Oct. 1828.

54 TNA, FO 76/5, McDonogh to Pelham, 2 Dec. 1802, in ElGaddari, *Letters and Reports*, 66–7.

55 TNA, FO 76/5, Langford to Camden, 20 Aug. 1804, in ElGaddari, *Letters and Reports*, 76–7.
56 TNA, FO 76/11, Penrose to John Wilson Croker, 5 June 1817; although the first American encounter with Derna was in fact in 1805. The reports of the British consul also contained details of apparent collusion between the United States and France, TNA, FO 76/11, Croker to Hamilton, 30 July 1817. For further details on Croker, see Lloyd, *Mr. Barrow of the Admiralty*, 86–8. On the close relationship between France and the United States, see various correspondences in Swanson and Knox (eds), *Naval Documents, Volumes 1–6*. See also UCL, Bentham MSS, Box 24/404, D'Ghies's interview with Bentham, constituting notes for a proposal to John Quincy Adams, 29 Jan. 1823. According to D'Ghies, if American troops took military possession of 'Barbary ... the natives would have nothing to fear', UCL, Bentham MSS, Box 24/16, D'Ghies interview with Bentham, 23 Jan. 1823.
57 Richard O'Brien to Thomas Jefferson, 8 June 1786, in Swanson and Knox (eds), *Naval Documents: Volume 1: Naval Operations including Diplomatic Background*. Apart from the latter examples, there is a notable absence of reportage on American activity in the Regency, in the consular correspondence of Lucas and both of his successors. It was not until 29 January 1823, when D'Ghies proposed that, in exchange for American military intervention and assistance to change the government of Tripoli it was to be made known that the 'US will not take permanent possession of the country (saving exception, if any, a port) nor exercise dominion nor infringe freedom of election'; UCL, Bentham MSS, Box 24, D'Ghies/Bentham to John Quincy Adams, 29 Jan. 1823.
58 Mohamed Qaramanli was Bey of Benghazi and was twenty-eight years old when his father had held a lavish wedding ceremony for him in Tripoli, and thirty-one years old when he fled and was subsequently exiled by Yusuf Pasha from the Regency. Britain had presented a gift of £125 to the Pasha on the wedding of Mohamed Bey. For further details on the career of Mohamed Qaramanli, see TNA, FO 76/5, McDonogh to Pelham, 29 Jan. 1803; TNA, FO 76/6, McDonogh to Camden, 2 Apr. 1805; TNA, FO 76/6, Langford to Castlereagh, 22 May 1809; TNA, FO 76/8, Langford to Liverpool, 17 Jan. 1812; TNA, FO 76/14, Warrington to Bathurst, 17 Nov. 1820, in ElGaddari, *Letters and Reports*, 175–6; TNA, FO 76/20, Warrington to Bathurst, 27 May 1826; Folayan, *Tripoli during the Reign of Yusuf Pasha Qaramanli*, 47–77.
59 It did not help that, as one of the Pasha's future ministers would explain to Jeremy Bentham, no firm lines were drawn between the finances of the government of Tripoli and those of the Qaramanli family. UCL, Bentham MSS, Box 24/4, Bentham, 'Account of Tripoli', 3 Oct. 1822.
60 TNA, FO 76/12, Warrington to Bathurst, 16 Apr. 1818; FO 76/29, Warrington to Hay, 19 June 1831, in ElGaddari, *Letters and Reports*, 295–6; Warrington to Yusuf Qaramanli; approximately 9 Dec. 1831; Warrington to Goderich, 19 Dec. 1831, in ElGaddari, *Letters and Reports*, 311; Warrington to Hay, 23 Dec. 1831, in ElGaddari, *Letters and Reports*, 311–13; and Warrington to Hay, 9 Feb. 1832, in ElGaddari, *Letters and Reports*, 316–17; Folayan, *Tripoli during the Reign of Yusuf Qaramanli*, especially chapter 4, 'The Abortive Imperial Scheme: 1817–1824', 78–105 and chapter 5, 'The Road to Revolution: 1825–1832', 106–42.
61 TNA, FO 76/23, Warrington to Hay, 20 Mar. 1828.
62 TNA, FO 76/5, Lucas to King, 12 Feb. 1794, in ElGaddari, *Letters and Reports*, 39–41.
63 TNA, FO 76/5, Lucas to King, 12 Feb. 1794 and TNA, FO 76/6, McDonogh to Pelham, 19 Feb. 1802, in ElGaddari, *Letters and Reports*, 39–41 and 64–6.

64 TNA, FO 76/6, Langford to unknown recipients, 15 Oct. 1806; TNA, FO 76/9, Warrington to Bunbury, 14 July 1814, in ElGaddari, *Letters and Reports*, 130–13; and FO 76/16, Warrington to Bathurst, 29 July 1822.
65 Folayan, *Tripoli during the Reign of Yusuf Pasha Qaramanli*, 118 and 121 in particular for details of tribute and securities to be paid to the Pasha by Sheikh Abd' al-Jalil Saif al-Nasser.
66 TNA, FO 76/31, Warrington to Hay, 9 Feb. 1832, in ElGaddari, *Letters and Reports*, 316–17.
67 Al-Mukni was sent to retake Fezzan in 1832, see TNA, FO 76/31, Warrington to Hay, 28 Jan. 1832, and TNA, FO 76/31, 24 Feb. 1832, in ElGaddari, *Letters and Reports*, 313–15 and 319–21; Folayan, *Tripoli during the Reign of Yusuf Pasha Qaramanli*, 51.
68 Folayan, *Tripoli during the Reign of Yusuf Pasha Qaramanli*, 118; TNA, FO 76/29, Warrington to Hay, 5 Oct. 1831, Warrington to [Abd' al-Jalil Saif al-] Nasser, 20 Dec. 1831, and Warrington to Hay, 23 Dec. 1831, in ElGaddari, *Letters and Reports*, 305–6 and 311–13.
69 TNA, FO 76/26, James Douglas, British Consul General to Morocco to unknown, 28 Oct. 1828; and TNA, FO 76/27, Warrington to Hay, 24 Feb. 1830.
70 TNA, FO 76/9, various dispatches, including Warrington to Bathurst, 20 Nov. 1815, in ElGaddari, *Letters and Reports*, 149–51; C. K. Webster, *The Congress of Vienna, 1814–1815* (London: Oxford University Press, 1918); H. W. V. Temperley and L. M. Penson (eds), *Foundations of British Foreign Policy: From Pitt (1792) to Salisbury (1902), or Documents, Old and New* (Cambridge: Cambridge University Press, 1938); H. A. Kissinger, *World Restored; Metternich, Castlereagh, and the Problems of Peace, 1812–22* (USA: Echo Point Books & Media, 2013); P. W. Schroeder, *The Transformation of European Politics, 1763–1848* (Oxford: Clarendon Press, 1994); A. Zamoyski, *Rites of Peace: The Fall of Napoleon and the Congress of Vienna* (London: Harper Perennial, 2007); M. Jarrett, *The Congress of Vienna and Its Legacy: War and Great Power Diplomacy after Napoleon* (London: I.B. Tauris, 2013); and B. E. Vick, *The Congress of Vienna: Power and Politics After Napoleon* (Cambridge, MA: Harvard University Press, 2014).
71 TNA, FO 76/9, Warrington to Bathurst, 20 Nov. 1815, in ElGaddari, *Letters and Reports*, 149–51.
72 TNA, FO 76/13, Maitland to Burghersh, 31 Jan. 1819; Warrington to Bathurst, 15 Apr. 1819; TNA, FO 76/14, Warrington to Bathurst, 17 July 1820, in ElGaddari, *Letters and Reports*, 170–1; TNA, FO 76/18, Warrington to Wilmot Horton, 14 Dec. 1820; TNA, FO 76/15, Warrington to Burghersh, 20 Apr. 1821; and TNA, FO 76/20, Warrington to Bathurst, 19 Feb. 1826, in ElGaddari, *Letters and Reports*, 241. See numerous correspondence on these agreements in TNA, FO 76/13, TNA, FO 76/20 and TNA, FO 76/22.
73 TNA, FO 76/20, Warrington to Bathurst, 19 Feb. 1826, in ElGaddari, *Letters and Reports*, 214; TNA, FO 76/17, Warrington to Wilmot Horton, 15 July 1823; TNA, FO 76/20, Warrington to Bathurst, 15 Apr. 1826, in ElGaddari, *Letters and Reports*, 244–5; and TNA, FO 76/21, Warrington to Hay, 28 Mar. 1827.
74 Folayan, *Tripoli during the Reign of Yusuf Pasha Qaramanli*, chapter 3, 'The Problems of Consolidation: 1806–1817', 47–77.
75 All monetary sums cited, apart from Sterling (and such figures are clearly denoted by '£' symbol), are in Spanish dollars. UCL, Bentham MSS, Box 24, D'Ghies proposal; TNA, FO 76/16, John Tyrwhitt to Warrington, 25 July 1822; TNA, FO 76/17, Warrington to Wilmot Horton, 22 Nov. 1823, in ElGaddari, *Letters and Reports*,

217–18; and TNA, FO 76/18, Warrington to Wilmot Horton, 7 Jan. 1824, in ElGaddari, *Letters and Reports*, 222–3. It should be noted however, that the conquest of Wadai as reported by Vice-Consul Tyrwhitt is disputed in later correspondence. The alternative proposal was that Mohamed Ali had sent troops there to capture Mamluks that had escaped the massacre in Cairo in 1811; TNA, FO 76/16, Warrington to Wilmot Horton, 19 Oct. 1822, in ElGaddari, *Letters and Reports*, 197–8.
76 TNA FO 76/16, Warrington to Wilmot Horton, 22 Nov. 1823; and FO 76/18, Warrington to Wilmot Horton, 7 Jan. 1824, in ElGaddari, *Letters and Reports*, 217–18 and 221–2. Awjila was a key point along the north-south caravan route in the east of the Regency. See Figures 1 and 5, depicting the Regency of Tripoli and relevant towns. Dorby's proposal to the Pasha of Tripoli to cede key towns in the Regency to Mohamed Ali questions the view that the Pasha of Egypt was not motivated to gain territorial acquisitions in the 'Barbary' states. In fact, though the French Proconsul Bernardino Drovetti did suggest the annexation of Algiers, Tunis and Tripoli in 1829, following Ali's 'newly constructed military machine', the consular correspondence from Tripoli clearly indicates that Egypt's westward ambitions began to take shape as early as 1823. Fahmy, 'The Era of Muhammad 'Ali Pasha', in Daly (ed.), *The Cambridge History of Egypt: Volume 2: Modern Egypt*, 165.
77 TNA, FO 76/17, Warrington to Wilmot Horton, 16 Nov. 1823, in ElGaddari, *Letters and Reports*, 216–17.
78 Ibid.
79 TNA, FO 76/17, Warrington to Wilmot Horton, 2 Dec. 1823, in ElGaddari, *Letters and Reports*, 218–19.
80 Ibid.
81 Ibid.
82 TNA, FO 76/12, Baron d'Itabayana to Warrington, 16 Dec. 1826 and Warrington to Baron d'Itabayana, 2 Feb. 1827, in ElGaddari, *Letters and Reports*, 253; and Warrington to Hay, 2 Feb. 1827. Manuel Rodrigues Gameiro Pessoa was the first Baron d'Itabayana and active at least from 1814 to 1815 when he was the Brazilian diplomatic representative at the Congress of Vienna. Thanks to Maria do Carmo Strozzi Coutinho at the Centro de História e Documentação Diplomática (Rio de Janeiro) for her assistance.
83 TNA, FO 76/12, Warrington to d'Itabayana, 2 Feb. 1827.
84 Roosevelt, 'Foreword' in Swanson (ed.), *Naval Documents*, iii. The United States continued, however, to sell sugar and coffee to the 'Ottomans', even after the dissolution of the Levant Company in 1825. Ingram, *Empire-building and Empire-builders* (London: Frank Cass, 1995), 34.
85 UCL, Bentham MSS, Box 24/404, D'Ghies interview with Bentham, 29 Jan. 1823.
86 TNA, FO 76/16, Warrington to Wilmot Horton, 1 June 1822, in ElGaddari, *Letters and Reports*, 191–2.
87 TNA, FO 76/9, Warrington to Stürmer, 15 Feb. 1815, in ElGaddari, *Letters and Reports*, 134–6.

Chapter 4

1 Civil unrest was usually a result of food shortages because of famine or drought, though it was also a consequence of a repeated refusal by the Arab tribes to pay

the required tribute to Yusuf Qaramanli. In a culmination of defiance, see united disobedience of several tribal leaders in TNA, FO 76/31, Warrington to Hay, 9 Feb. 1832, in ElGaddari, *Letters and Reports*, 316–17.

2   J-P. Daloz, *The Sociology of Élite Distinction: From Theoretical to Comparative Perspectives* (Basingstoke: Palgrave Macmillan, 2012); L. G. Vergara, 'Elites, Political Elites and Social Change in Modern Societies', *Revisita de Sociología*, 28 (2013): 32; A. Hourani, 'Ottoman Reform and the Politics of Notables', in A. Hourani, P. S. Khoury and M. C. Wilson (eds), *The Modern Middle East* (Berkeley: University of California Press, 1993), 83–110; S. Faroqhi, *The Ottoman Empire and the World Around It* (London: I.B. Tauris, 2011); and E. R. Toledano, 'The Emergence of Ottoman-Local Elites (1700–1900): A Framework for Research', in I. Pappé and M. Ma'oz (eds), *Middle Eastern Politics and Ideas: A History from Within* (London: Tauris Academic Studies, 1997); G. Mosca, *The Ruling Class* (London: McGraw Hill, 1939); V. Pareto, *The Rise and Fall of the Elites: An Application of Theoretical Sociology* (New Brunswick, NJ: Transaction, 1991); Abou-el-Haj, 'An Agenda for Research in History', 313; and M. J. Reimer, *Colonial Bridgehead: Government and Society in Alexandria, 1807–1882* (Cairo: American University in Cairo Press, 1997).

3   Hassan, H. al-Faqih, *Al-Yawmiyat al-Libiyya: 958–1248h./1551–1832* (Tripoli: Manchurat Jami'at al-Fatah, Markaz Jihad, 1984). Cf. Folayan, *Tripoli during the Reign of Yusuf Pasha* Qaramanli, 58–9; N. Lafi, 'Tripoli de Barbarie, 1795–1911: Genese et perennite de l'institution municipal.' PhD thesis (Université de Provence-Aix-Marseille 1, 1999).

4   Lafi, 'Tripoli de Barbarie', 9.

5   FO 76/18, Warrington to Horton, 28 Feb. 1824 and UCL, Bentham MSS, Box 24/15, D'Ghies's interview with Bentham, 23 Jan. 1823.

6   Altaleb, 'The Social and Economic History of Slavery in Libya', 58.

7   Hassan in Lafi, *Une ville du Maghreb*, 162.

8   A. Hourani, 'Ottoman Reform and the Politics of Notables', in A. Hourani, P. S. Khoury and M. C. Wilson (eds), *The Modern Middle East* (Berkeley: University of California Press, 1993), 87; TNA, FO 76/16, Hateeta el-Targhi to Warrington, no date (but late 1825); and FO 76/20, Hassuna D'Ghies to Mohamed al-Amin al-Kanemi, 24 March 1826.

9   TNA, 76/5, Lucas to Dundas, 6 Feb. 1795; FO 76/20, Warrington to Bathurst, 13 July 1826; FO 76/31, Warrington to Hay, 9 Feb. 1832; and FO 76/31, Warrington to Hay, 12 Feb. 1831, in ElGaddari, *Letters and Reports*, 44–7, 246–9 and 316–17.

10 Ibid. UCL, Bentham MSS, Box 24/16.

11 D'Ghies to John Quincy Adams, 3 Feb. 1823, Bentham MSS, Box 24, fo. 529; and fo. 477.

12 The Gharian is also proposed as a possible base for the receipt of arms and artillery during a period of political crisis for the reigning Pasha in the mid-1820s, and the place where Hassuna D'Ghies initially retreated on being accused of culpability in the murder of Major Laing in 1826; TNA, FO 76/33, various letters and statement from Hassuna D'Ghies to Viscount Goderich in the year 1832; UCL, Bentham MSS, Box 24/6, in particular an address from Hassuna D'Ghies to John Quincy Adams on the subject. Cf. Folayan, *Tripoli during the Reign of Yusuf Qaramanli*. UCL, Bentham MSS, Box 24, G.F. Lyon to Colonel Lyon, 19 Mar. 1819.

13 D'Ghies to Goderich, 'A Statement to the Right Honourable Lord Goderich, Secretary of His Britannic Majesty for the Colonies, concerning the Expedition of the late Major

Laing to Timbuctoo, and the Affairs of Tripoli, by the Shereeff Mohammed Hassuna D'Ghies, late Minister of the Pacha of Tripoli', CO 537/152.
14 UCL, Bentham MSS, Box 24/16, D'Ghies interview with Bentham, 30 Jan. 1823.
15 Hassan, *Al-Yawmiyat al-Libiyya*; Folayan, *Tripoli during the Reign of Yusuf Pasha Qaramanli*; and Lafi, *Une ville du Maghreb*.
16 Bentham, 'Codification Offer' of 8 May 1821, in UCL, Bentham MSS, Box 24, various drafts; and Schofield (ed.), *Securities against Misrule*.
17 UCL, Bentham MSS, Box 24/15, D'Ghies interview with Bentham, 23 Jan. 1823; and TNA, FO 76/18, Warrington to Wilmot Horton, 28 Feb. 1824; Folayan, *Tripoli during the Reign of Yusuf Pasha Qaramanli*, 158.
18 D'Ghies, 'The Petition of the Sheriff Mohamed Hassuna D'Ghies to the Honourable House of Commons', TNA, Colonial Office and Predecessors: Confidential General and Confidential Original Correspondence (hereafter CO) 537/152. Jeremy Bentham made a written record of at least some of his meetings with D'Ghies. There is also a body of correspondence in the consular records and elsewhere from D'Ghies to the Colonial Office and to various Members of Parliament, including James Scarlett. On Sir James Scarlett, MP, see G. F. R. Barker, 'Scarlett, James, First Baron Abinger (1769–1844)', rev. E. A. Cawthon, *Oxford Dictionary of National Biography* (Oxford University Press, Jan. 2009). Available online: https://doi.org/10.1093/ref:odnb/24783.
19 Folayan, *Tripoli during the Reign of Yusuf Pasha Qaramanli*, 58.
20 Ibid.; and FO 76/18, Warrington to Horton, 28 Feb. 1824.
21 Toledano, 'The Emergence of Ottoman-Local Elites', 161.
22 Cf. Folayan, *Tripoli during the Reign of Yusuf Pasha Qaramanli*; Lafi, *Une ville du Maghreb* and Moalla, *The Regency of Tunis*.
23 'Sheikh' is a title of respect accorded a head of a tribe, an elder or a chief. Lafi, *Une ville du Maghreb*, 95; and Folayan, *Tripoli during the Reign of Yusuf Pasha Qaramanli*, 59.
24 TNA, CO 537/152, D'Ghies to Goderich, (approximately 1823); TNA, FO 8/12, Wilmot Horton to Harrison, 30 Sept. 1824; O. A. R. El-Nagar, 'West Africa and the Muslim Pilgrimage: An Historical Study with Special Reference to the Nineteenth Century'. PhD thesis (School of Oriental and African Studies, University of London, 1969). See also entry for al-Mukhtar's father and brother, Sidi al-Mukhtar al-Kunti (1729–1811), and Ahmad al-Bakka'i al-Kunti (1803–1865) in E. K. Akyeampong and H. L. Gates Jr. (eds), *Dictionary of African Biography: Volume 1: ABACH-BRAND* (Oxford: Oxford University Press, 2012), 371–2 and 123. Cf. Saad, *Social History of Timbuktu*; and Ould Cheikh, 'A Man of Letters in Timbuktu'; Johnston, *The Fulani Empire of Sokoto*; and M. Last, *The Sokoto Caliphate* (New York: Humanities Press, 1967).
25 TNA, CO 537/152, D'Ghies to Goderich (approximately 1823).
26 Lafi, *Une ville du Maghreb*, 41.
27 TNA, FO 76/20 and TNA, FO 76/5, Lucas to Dundas, 30 Jan. 1794, in ElGaddari, *Letters and Reports*, 32–9.
28 Faroqhi, *The Ottoman Empire*, 46 in T. Insoll and B. Lecocq, *The Hajj from West Africa from a Global Historical Perspective (19th and 20th Centuries)* (London: Brill, 2012). Cf. J. S. Birks, 'The Mecca Pilgrimage by West African Pastoral Nomads, *Journal of Modern African Studies*, 15, 1 (1977): 47–58.
29 Lovejoy, 'Commercial Sectors', 109; Altaleb, 'The Social and Economic History of Slavery'; cf. J. Clancy-Smith, *Rebel and Saint: Muslim Notables. Populist Protest,*

Colonial Encounters (Algeria and Tunisia, 1800–1904) (Berkeley: University of California Press, 1994).
30 Faroqhi, *The Ottoman Empire*, 162.
31 K. Brown and J. Passon (eds), *Across the Sahara: Tracks, Trade and Cross-Cultural Exchange in Libya* (Cham, Switzerland: Springer International, 2020), 60; Lydon, *On Trans-Saharan Trails*, 103.
32 T. Insoll and B. Lecocq, *The Hajj from West Africa*; cf. Faroqhi, *The Ottoman Empire*, 192.
33 I. M. Shair and P. P. Karan, 'Geography of the Islamic Pilgrimage', *GeoJournal* 3/6 (1979): 599.
34 Hassan, *Al-Yawmiya al-Libiyya*; TNA FO 76/18/1/149, Warrington to Wilmot Horton, 28 Feb. 1824; Lafi, *Une ville du Maghreb*, 162; P. S. Khoury, 'The Urban Notables Paradigm Revisited', *Revue due monde musulman et de la Méditerranée*, 55–6 (1990): 215–30.
35 Ritchie and Lyon followed in the footsteps of the explorer Friedrich Conrad Hornemann who travelled to the territories of Fezzan and the Sudan in 1798–1801. E. Baigent, 'Ritchie, Joseph (*c*.1788–1819)', *Oxford Dictionary of National Biography* (Oxford University Press, 2004). Available online: https://doi.org/10.1093/ref:odnb/23677; and 'Lyon, George Francis [*alias* Said-ben-Abdallah]', *Oxford Dictionary of National Biography* (Oxford University Press, 2004). Available online: https://doi.org/10.1093/ref:odnb/17274.
36 TNA, FO 76/15, Warrington to Goulburn, 12 Dec. 1821, in ElGaddari, *Letters and Reports*, 186–7. C. Fyfe, 'Denham, Dixon (1786–1828)', *Oxford Dictionary of National Biography* (Oxford University Press, Jan. 2008). Available online: https://doi.org/10.1093/ref:odnb/7476; E. Baigent, 'Oudney, Walter (1790–1824)', *Oxford Dictionary of National Biography* (Oxford University Press, 2004). Available online: https://doi.org/10.1093/ref:odnb/20947; C. Fyfe, 'Clapperton, Hugh (1788–1827)', *Oxford Dictionary of National Biography* (Oxford University Press, Jan. 2008). Available online: https://doi.org/10.1093/ref:odnb/5433.
37 TNA, FO 76/15, Ritchie to Goulburn, Aug. 1818; and UCL, Bentham MSS, Box 24, G. F. Lyon to Colonel Lyon, 19 Mar. 1819. Four years later, D'Ghies extends the same hand of friendship and to the members of the new exploratory missions of Denham, Oudney and Clapperton, UCL, Bentham MSS, Box 24/523, Oudney to D'Ghies, 14 Apr. 1822. D'Ghies also provided his assistance (while in London) to Hugh Clapperton's uncle, one S. Clapperton, to convey letters on to the explorer beyond the territories of Tripoli, UCL, Bentham MSS, Box 24/535, Clapperton to D'Ghies, 31 Mar. 1823. See also TNA FO 76/16, Warrington to Wilmot Horton, 12 July 1822, in ElGaddari, *Letters and Reports*, 195–6. On the relative autonomy of Gharian from the authority of the Pasha of Tripoli, see TNA, FO 76/29, Warrington to Hay, 27 Sept. 1831, in ElGaddari, *Letters and Reports*, 302–4.
38 TNA, FO 76/19, Hateeta el-Targhi to Hanmer Warrington, no date.
39 TNA, FO 76/20, Warrington to Hay, 25 Mar. 1826.
40 Abubakr Bu Khalloum is also mis-identified in the correspondence as 'Ali Ben Moussa Bu Khalloom', TNA, FO 76/18, Warrington to Wilmot Horton, 24 Feb. 1824.
41 TNA, FO 76/16, Warrington to Wilmot Horton, 21 Aug. 1822.
42 TNA, FO 76/17, Warrington to Wilmot Horton, 2 Aug. 1823.
43 Ibid.
44 TNA, FO 76/17, Yusuf Qaramanli to Mohamed al-Amin al-Kanemi, 8 July 1823.
45 TNA, FO 76/17, Yusuf Qaramanli to al-Kanemi, 8 July 1823; Saad, *Social History of Timbuktu*; and Folayan, *Tripoli during the Reign of Yusuf Pasha Qaramanli*.

46 TNA, FO 76/19, Warrington to Bathurst, 24 May 1825, in ElGaddari, *Letters and Reports*, 232.
47 Ibid.
48 Tully, Miss. (ed.), *Letters Written during a Ten Year's Residence at the Court of Tripoli; Published from the Originals in the Possession of the Family of the Late Richard Tully, Esq.* 3rd edn (London: Cox and Baylis, 1819). Cf. P. Fleming, *The Siege at Peking* (Oxford: Oxford University Press, 1984).
49 TNA, FO 76/16, Warrington to Wilmot Horton, 1 June 1822, in ElGaddari, *Letters and Reports*, 191–2. Cf. TNA, FO 76/15, Hassuna D'Ghies to Wilmot Horton, 19 Dec. 1821.
50 TNA, FO 76/12 Yusuf Qaramanli to King George III, 11 May 1818.
51 TNA, FO 76/16, à Court to Wilmot Horton, 5 May 1822, in ElGaddari, *Letters and Reports*, 190–1.
52 De Souza's debts amounted in total to 57,776 Spanish dollars/piastres. There is some doubt on which currency because Consul Langford had written in 1811 that the above sum was in 'hard [Spanish] dollars', whereas Ambassador à Court had later described the amount as '57,776 piastres', TNA, FO 76/7, Langford to Wellesley, 21 July 1811, and à Court to Wilmot Horton, 5 May 1822; TNA, FO 76/8, Langford to Bathurst, 23 Feb. 1813; TNA, FO 76/16; BL, Heytesbury Papers Add. MSS 41512; Foreign Office, *British Foreign and State Papers, 1812–1814*. Volume 1, part 1 (London: James Ridgway, 1841), 190.
53 TNA, FO 76/16, à Court to Wilmot Horton, 5 May 1822, in ElGaddari, *Letters and Reports*, 190–1.
54 UCL, Bentham MSS, Box 24/15, D'Ghies interview with Bentham, 23 Jan. 1823; UCL, Bentham MSS, Box 24/6; TNA, FO 76/16, Warrington to Wilmot Horton, 12 July 1822.
55 TNA, FO 76/23, Warrington to Hay, 26 Mar. 1828, in ElGaddari, *Letters and Reports*, 262–3. By 25 July 1828, Bait-al-Mal refused to assist the consul in seeking redress over a dispute involving a Maltese subject, see TNA, FO 76/23, Warrington to Hay, 31 Dec. 1828; *Tripoli during the Reign of Yusuf Pasha Qaramanli*, 114.
56 TNA, FO 76/18, Warrington to Wilmot Horton, 28 Feb. 1824.
57 TNA, FO 76/17, Warrington to Wilmot Horton, 10 July 1823, in ElGaddari, *Letters and Reports*, 207.
58 TNA, FO 76/19, Warrington to Bathurst, 2 Oct. 1825, in ElGaddari, *Letters and Reports*, 236–8.
59 TNA, FO 76/23, Vice-Admiral Sir Edward Codrington to Warrington, 12 Nov. 1827, and Warrington to Codrington, 15 Nov. 1827, in ElGaddari, *Letters and Reports*, 260–1. On Sir Edward Codrington, see J. K. Laughton, 'Codrington, Sir Edward (1770–1851)', rev. R. Morriss, *Oxford Dictionary of National Biography* (Oxford University Press, Jan. 2008). Available online: https://doi.org/10.1093/ref:odnb/5796.
60 TNA, FO 76/27, Warrington to Murray, 18 Aug. 1830.
61 UCL, Bentham MSS, Box 24, various interviews conducted with Hassuna D'Ghies between 1822 and 1823.
62 UCL, Bentham MSS, Box 24/6 and 16; TNA, FO 76/16, Warrington to Wilmot Horton, 12 July 1822, in ElGaddari, *Letters and Reports*, 195–6.
63 D'Ghies, 'A Letter Addressed to James Scarlett, Esq. M.P. and Member of the African Institution on the Abolition of the Slave Trade'. Translated from French by Dr Kelly (Haymarket: J. Brethell, 1822). Copies of this address is held by the British Library, *Tracts on Slavery*, 8156 DF 4, and within the UCL Bentham Papers archive.

64 Original emphases. D'Ghies, 'A Letter Addressed to James Scarlett'.
65 Ibid.
66 Ibid.
67 Ibid.
68 Ibid. Original emphases.
69 UCL, Bentham MSS, Box, 24/558.
70 For Scarlett's defence of D'Ghies: 'The States of Barbary', HC Deb 19 Apr. 1836, Volume 32, cc1196–8. Available online: https://hansard.parliament.uk/Commons/1836-04-19/debates/96970bf3-ce87-48b6-b921-b95b744cf272/TheStatesOfBarbary; and TNA, FO 76/30, Scarlett to Hay, 24 Aug. 1831.
71 UCL, Bentham MSS, Box 24, G. F. Lyon to Colonel Lyon, 19 Mar. 1819.
72 Bentham, 'Securities against Misrule, adapted to a Mahommedan State and prepared with particular reference to Tripoli in Barbary', in UCL, Bentham MSS, Box 24, Bowring (ed.), *The Works of Jeremy Bentham: Volume 1*.
73 Hume, 'Preparations for Civil War in Tripoli in the 1820s: Ali Karamanli, Hassuna D'Ghies and Jeremy Bentham', 311–22.
74 In Scarlett's defence of D'Ghies: 'The States of Barbary'.
75 TNA, FO 76/16, Warrington to Bathurst, 29 July 1822.
76 TNA, FO 76/16, Warrington to Wilmot Horton, 12 July 1822, in ElGaddari, *Letters and Reports*, 195–6; TNA, FO 76/18, Warrington to Wilmot Horton, 28 Feb. 1824.
77 TNA, FO 76/16, Oudney to Warrington, 14 Apr. 1822.
78 TNA, FO 76/16, Warrington to Oudney and Denham, 29 May 1822.
79 Ibid.
80 TNA, FO 76/5, Lucas to Dundas, 5 June 1794.
81 TNA, FO 76/18, Warrington to Wilmot 10 Jan. 1824, Warrington to Wilmot Horton, 20 Feb. 1824; and TNA, FO 76/16, Warrington to Wilmot Horton, 10 June 1822, Warrington to Wilmot Horton, 12 July 1822, in ElGaddari, *Letters and Reports*, 195–6.
82 TNA, FO 76/20, Warrington to Bathurst, 27 Feb. 1826.
83 TNA, FO 76/20, Warrington to Knudsen, Feb. 1826; Andreas Peter Knudsen was a 'Candidate of Law', then Secretary (and temporary Acting Consul) to Consul Gierlew in Tunis around 1818–21. Knudsen was then promoted to the position of consul to Tripoli from 1822 to 1836. With thanks again to Gustaf Fryksén for his assistance.
84 TNA, FO 76/21, Warrington to Hay, 7 Nov. 1827.
85 May is given as Laing's approximate month of arrival in Timbuktu, as by 18 June 1826 Consul Warrington had received the news of Laing's entrance at that city from Hassuna D'Ghies, and several weeks must be set aside for the time that it would have taken a courier to deliver the news to D'Ghies from the interior to Tripoli. TNA, FO 76/20, Warrington to Bathurst, 18 June 1826. Laing's arrival could also have not taken place before 13 April 1826, because the consul's correspondence of the same date states that Laing had not yet reached Timbuktu, TNA, FO 76/20, Warrington to Hay, 13 Apr. 1826. The last correspondence received by Consul Warrington from Laing was dated 21 September 1826. TNA, FO 76/23, Warrington to Murray, 29 Aug. 1828, in ElGaddari, *Letters and* Reports, 268–9.
86 Rousseau had previously been the French consul to Basra, Aleppo and Baghdad; A. Mézin, *Les Consuls de France au siècle de lumières (1715–1792). Diplomatie et Histoire*: Volume 1 (Paris: Imprimerie Nationale, 1997), 528.
87 TNA, FO 76/23, Warrington to Murray, 29 Aug. 1828, in ElGaddari, *Letters and Reports*, 268–9. On Murray, S. G. P. Ward, 'Murray, Sir George (1772–1846)', *Oxford*

Dictionary of National Biography (Oxford University Press, Jan. 2008). Available online: https://doi.org/10.1093/ref:odnb/19608.
88 TNA, FO 76/26, Warrington to Murray, 25 and 27 May 1829.
89 TNA, FO 76/26, Rousseau to Warrington, 17 June 1829.
90 UCL, Bentham MSS, Box 24/16, D'Ghies interview with Bentham, 29 Jan. 1823.
91 TNA, FO 76/29, Warrington to Goderich, 24 June 1831; TNA, FO 76/29, Warrington to Hay, 27 Sept. 1831, in ElGaddari, *Letters and Reports*, 302–3.
92 TNA, CO 537/152, D'Ghies, 'Petition to the House of Commons', 1834.
93 Ibid.
94 TNA, FO 76/23, Warrington to Huskisson, 16 Apr. 1828.
95 Ibid.
96 TNA, FO 76/27, Warrington to Murray, 18 Aug. 1830, and TNA, FO 76/29, Warrington to Hay, 26 Jan. 1831.
97 Ibid.
98 TNA, FO 76/23, Warrington to Huskisson, 16 Apr. 1828; TNA, FO 160/3, Warrington to Ortez, 23 Apr. 1817.
99 Scarlett's defence of D'Ghies: 'The States of Barbary'.

Chapter 5

1 Bayly, *Imperial Meridian*.
2 Platt, *The Cinderella Service*; Anderson, 'Great Britain and the Barbary States', 106; and Lee, 'The Supervising of the Barbary Consuls'.
3 C. R. Middleton, *The Administration of British Foreign Policy, 1782–1846* (Durham, NC: Duke University Press, 1977); G. R. Berridge, *British Diplomacy in Turkey, 1583 to the Present: A Study in the Evolution of the Resident Embassy* (Leiden: Martinus Nijhoff, 2009); A. C. Wood, *A History of the Levant Company* (London: Routledge, 1964), 59–63; Platt, *The Cinderella Service*; R. A. Jones, *The Nineteenth-Century Foreign Office: Administrative History* (London: Weidenfeld and Nicolson, 1971), and Jones, *The British Diplomatic Service, 1815–1914* (Waterloo, ON: Wilfrid Laurier University Press, 1983); M. Mösslang and T. Riotte (eds), *The Diplomats' World: A Cultural History of Diplomacy, 1815–1914* (Oxford: Oxford University Press, 2008); Ben Srhir, *Britain and Morocco during the Embassy of John Drummond Hay*; L. Müller, *Consuls, Corsairs and Commerce: The Swedish Consular Service and Long-distance Shipping, 1720–1815* (Uppsala: Uppsala Universitet, 2004); R. T. Ridley, *Napoleon's Proconsul in Egypt: The Life and Times of Bernardino Drovetti* (London: Rubicon Press, 1998); L. Müller and J. Ojala, 'Consular Services of the Nordic Countries during the Eighteenth and Nineteenth Centuries: Did They Really Work?', in Boyce and Gorski (eds), *Resources and Infrastructures in the Maritime Economy1500–2000* (St. Johns, Newfoundland: International Maritime Economic History Association, 2002), 23–41; C. I. Chessell, 'Britain's Ionian Consul: Spiridion Foresti and Intelligence Collection (1793–1805)', *Journal of Mediterranean Studies*, 16, 1–2 (2006): 45–61; G. G. Gilbar, 'Resistance to Economic Penetration: The Kārguzār and Foreign Firms in Qajar Iran', *International Journal of Middle East Studies*, 43, 1 (2011): 5–23; F. de Goey, *Consuls and the Institutions of Global Capitalism, 1783–1914* (London: Pickering & Chatto, 2014); D. Lambert and A. Lester, *Colonial Lives across the British Empire: Imperial Careering in the Long Nineteenth Century* (Cambridge: Cambridge University Press,

2006); and Lester, 'Imperial Circuits and Networks: Geographies of the British Empire', *History Compass*, 4, 1 (2006): 121–41.
4   R. Hallett, *Records of the Africa Association* (London: Nelson, 1964), 26. A guide to Tripoli was previously written by one Vice-Consul Anthony Knecht in 1767, C. R. Pennell, 'Tripoli in the Mid Eighteenth Century: A Guidebook', *Revue d'histoire maghrébine*, 9, 25–6 (1982): 91–121.
5   Warrington, 'Extract from *A Short Account of Tripoli in the West*', 104–7.
6   TNA, FO 76/6, Circular to Consul Langford, April 1806.
7   TNA, FO 76/5, Langford to York, 10 July 1804; TNA, FO 76/7, Wilkie to Liverpool, 6 Feb. 1812, in ElGaddari, *Letters and Reports*, 72–5 and 123–4; *Cobbett's Annual Register*, 10 Sept. 1803.
8   TNA, FO 76/5, Lucas to Dundas, 22 Aug. 1793, in ElGaddari, *Letters and Reports*, 29–32.
9   TNA, FO 76/5, Lucas to Dundas, 22 Aug. 1793, in ElGaddari, *Letters and Reports*, 29–32. Langford returned to Tripoli in his new capacity as consul general on 26 June 1804; TNA, FO 76/5, Langford to York, 10 July 1803; and TNA, FO 76/5, Langford to York, 10 July 1804, in ElGaddari, *Letters and Reports*, 72–5. After unsuccessfully pursuing the post of British consul general to Tripoli, McDonogh later secured the Portuguese consulship to the Regency. TNA, FO 76/6, for a draft letter (from the Colonial Office) to Langford, December 1806; and TNA, FO 76/6, Langford to Windham, 28 Feb. 1807.
10 TNA, PROB 11/1414/268, Will of Simon Lucas, 25 Sept. 1804.
11 Langford duly arrived in London on 11 May 1812. TNA, FO 76/8, Langford to Liverpool, 11 May 1811; Langford to Liverpool, 29 Jan. 1812; and Langford to Bathurst, 17 June 1812. The latter two letters in ElGaddari, *Letters and Reports*, 122–3 and 126.
12 E. W. Bovill, 'Colonel Warrington', *Geographical Journal*, 131, 2 (1965): 161–6; TNA, HO 46/16/112, folios 301A–306: Lucas to Grenville, 20 Aug. 1790; TNA, FO 76/5, Lucas to Dundas, 20 Oct. 1794, in ElGaddari, *Letters and Reports*, 42–4.
13 P. Rée, 'Beechey, Henry William (1788/9–1862)', *Oxford Dictionary of National Biography* (Oxford University Press, Oct. 2006). Available online: https://doi.org/10.1093/ref:odnb/1948.
14 TNA, FO 76/5, Lucas to Turnbull, 14 Mar. 1798.
15 TNA, FO 76/5, McDonogh to Portland, 15 May 1801, in ElGaddari, *Letters and Reports*, 61–3.
16 TNA, PROB 11/1414/268, Will of Simon Lucas, 25 Sept. 1804; PROB 11/1999/237, 22 May 1844; and PROB 6/244, 1848, Wills of Hanmer Warrington; FO 76/5, Lucas to John King, 12 Feb. 1794; and FO 76/9, Warrington to Major General Bunbury, 14 July 1814, in ElGaddari, *Letters and Reports*, 130–1.
17 TNA, FO 76/6, Langford to Windham, 28 Feb. 1807.
18 TNA, FO 76/6, Windham to Langford, December 1806.
19 Ibid. TNA, FO 366/543, 'Rates and Regulations of Outfit to HM's Diplomatick Servt. Abroad'.
20 TNA, FO 76/6, Windham to Langford, Dec. 1806, and Maria Langford to Windham, 28 Dec. 1807.
21 TNA, FO 76/6, Maria Langford to Windham, 28 Dec. 1807.
22 TNA, FO 76/8, Langford to Liverpool, 29 Jan. 1812, in ElGaddari, *Letters and Reports*, 122–3.
23 TNA, FO 76/14, Somerville to Maitland, 26 Jan. 1815.

24 TNA, FO 76/13, Somerville to Maitland, 26 Jan 1815; TNA, FO 101/13, 'Certified Copy of Commission as Consul General in Tripoli and instructions to Consul General Crowe'.
25 TNA, FO 366/542, Orders in Council, 28 Feb. 1822; and House of Commons: Reports from the Committees: *Volume 2. Report from the Committee Appointed to Inquire into the Consular Offices* (London: 1835).
26 TNA, FO 76/8, Langford to Liverpool, 29 Jan. 1812, and Langford to Bathurst, 17 June 1812, in ElGaddari, *Letters and Reports*, 122–3 and 126.
27 TNA, FO 76/20, Warrington to Bathurst, 9 June 1826.
28 Ibid.
29 Grosvenor, *Extracts from the Journal*, 10.
30 Ibid.; TNA, MFQ 1/102, 'Watercolour of Consul Hanmer Warrington's country house near Tripoli' extracted from TNA, FO 76/14, and enclosed in a letter dated 20 Oct. 1820; Lyon, *A Narrative of Travels*.
31 For some details of Popham and his family, see H. Popham, 'Popham, Sir Home Riggs (1762–1820)', *Oxford Dictionary of National Biography* (Oxford University Press, Jan. 2008). Available online: https://doi.org/10.1093/ref:odnb/22541.
32 TNA, HO 46/16/112, Folios 301A–306: Lucas to Grenville, 20 Aug. 1790.
33 Ibid.
34 Ibid. According to Lucas, he had served as a vice-consul from 1768, and from 1784 to 1790 he had been employed as an interpreter by the British government. It is unclear what Lucas did in the intervening period from, approximately, 1777 to 1784.
35 Ibid.
36 This correspondence may be found as part of a proposal for the establishment of an 'Orientalist' department within British government. See 'Letter from Dr. John Gilchrist to the Right Honorable Lord Castlereagh, written in June, 1805, when that noble Lord was President of the Board of Controul, on the Utility of Appointing Oriental Interpreters to Government', in L. Dundas Campbell (ed.), *The Asiatic Annual Register* (1807). The author of the letter, Dr Gilchrist, also wrote that he was 'much astonished that an expert and respectable interpreter for Hindoostanee, Turkish, Arabic &c. is not more frequently required … there are British consuls in every quarter of the world, to act when requisite, as the protectors, defenders, and interpreters, of their countrymen abroad', ibid.
37 TNA, FO 76/5, Lucas to Dundas, 22 Aug. 1793, in ElGaddari, *Letters and Reports*, 29–32. In similar circumstances, Lucas's predecessor, Richard Tully, had also held a position as Oriental Interpreter in London. TNA, FO 76/5, Memorial of Richard Tully to Dundas, December 1780.
38 TNA, FO 76/8, Langford to Liverpool, 29 Jan. 1812, in ElGaddari, *Letters and Reports*, 122–3.
39 TNA, FO 76/20, Warrington to Bathurst, 17 Aug. 1826.
40 Grosvenor, *Extracts from the Journal*, 27; TNA, FO 76/9, Warrington to Bunbury, 8 July 1814; TNA, FO 76/14, Warrington to Bathurst, 30 May 1820.
41 TNA, FO 76/20, Warrington to Bathurst, 17 Aug. 1826.
42 A dragoman such as Mustafa essentially acted as a go-between for the consul with the Government of Yusuf Qaramanli, and he was also the primary translator and interpreter for Warrington. Placed alongside the consul's correspondence, the addition of 'Chief' to Mustafa's title suggests that he had more than one dragoman in his service.

43 TNA, FO 76/20, Warrington to Wilmot Horton, 10 July 1823, in ElGaddari, *Letters and Reports*, 207; TNA, FO 76/20, Warrington to Bathurst, 11 June 1826.
44 TNA, FO 76/29, Hay to Warrington, November 1831, and Warrington to Hay, 6 Dec. 1831.
45 TNA, FO 76/29, Warrington to Hay, 6 Dec. 1831.
46 TNA, FO 76/12, Yusuf Qaramanli to King George III, 11 May 1818.
47 Ibid.
48 Ibid.
49 TNA, FO 76/16, Warrington to Denham, 15 July 1822; Denham to Warrington, 11 Oct. 1822; and Warrington to Wilmot Horton, 19 Oct. 1822.
50 TNA, FO 366/542, Orders in Council, 28 Feb. 1822; and House of Commons: Reports from the Committees: Volume 2. *Report from the Committee Appointed to Inquire into the Consular Departments* (London: 1835).
51 TNA, HO 46/16/112, Folios 301A–306: Lucas to Grenville, 20 Aug. 1790.
52 Ibid.
53 Ibid. Lucas's patrons included Mr. Townshend (Lord Sydney at the time of the memorial being submitted), Lord North, General Elliot (Lord Heathfield), Evan Nepean and Sir Clement Cottrell.
54 TNA, FO 76/5, Lucas to King, 12 Feb. 1794; R. G. Thorne (ed.), 'King, John (1759–1830)', in *The History of Parliament: The House of Commons, 1790–1820* (London: Secker & Warburg, 1986). Available online: http://www.historyofparliamentonline.org/volume/1790-1820/member/king-john-1759-1830.
55 TNA, FO 76/5, Langford to Camden, 15 Dec. 1804.
56 Ibid.
57 TNA, FO 76/16, à Court to Wilmot Horton, 5 May 1822, in ElGaddari, *Letters and Reports*, 190–1.
58 See Pennell, 'The Social History of British Diplomats'; and Platt, *The Cinderella Service*, 10.
59 TNA, FO 76/5, Lucas to Portland, 30 June 1795, in ElGaddari, *Letters and Reports*, 48–51.
60 TNA, CO 160/3, A. Wood, 'Minute by His Excellency the Governor', in *Gazzetta del Governo di Malta*, 12 Oct. 1815; TNA, FO 76/9, Warrington to Bathurst, 20 Nov. 1815, in ElGaddari, *Letters and Reports*, 151–2.
61 TNA, FO 76/13, Warrington to Bathurst, 29 Dec. 1819, in ElGaddari, *Letters and Reports*, 163–4.
62 TNA, FO 76/14, Warrington to Bathurst, 1 Oct. 1820, in ElGaddari, *Letters and Reports*, 172–3.
63 So-called after Maitland, governor of Malta and first Lord High Commissioner of the United States of the Ionian Islands. G. F. Bowen, *The Ionian Islands under British Protection* (London, 1851); A. Porter, *The Oxford History of the British Empire: Volume III: The Nineteenth Century* (Oxford: Oxford University Press, 1999); M. Fusaro, 'Representation in Practice: The Myth of Venice and the British Protectorate in the Ionian Islands (1801–1864)', in M. Calaresu et al. (eds), *Exploring Cultural History: Essays in Honour of Peter Burke* (Farnham, Surrey: Ashgate, 2010), 309–26, especially 315; C. Paschalidi, *Constructing Ionian Identities: The Ionian Islands in British Official Discourses; 1815–1864*. PhD thesis (University College London, 2009).
64 TNA, FO 76/22, Watson to Huskisson, Dec. 1827.
65 TNA, FO 101/6 contains the large volume of documents generated by the *La Fortuna* case.

66 TNA, FO 76/17, Nepean to Bathurst, 2 May 1823. Though Nepean's date of death is wrong in the following entry, further details on his career may be obtained from R. G. Thorne (ed.), 'Nepean, Evan (1752–1822), of Loders Court, Dorset', in *The History of Parliament: The House of Commons, 1790–1820* (London: Secker & Warburg, 1986). Available online: http://www.historyofparliamentonline.org/volume/1790-1820/member/nepean-evan-1752-1822.
67 TNA, FO 76/29, Warrington to Hay, 12 Sept. 1831.
68 TNA, FO 76/31, Warrington to Hay, 28 Jan. 1832, in ElGaddari, *Letters and Reports*, 313–15; and TNA, FO 76/7, Langford to Liverpool, 12 Aug. 1811.
69 Marriage certificates for Emma Warrington and Alexander Gordon Laing, TNA, FO 76/19, 14 July 1825; and TNA, FO 76/26, Emma Laing and Thomas Wood, 13 April 1829.
70 TNA, FO 76/18, Warrington to Wilmot Horton, 7 Jan. 1824. There is no other currently known record of Walter Bornou Warrington, beyond Warrington's own announcement of his birth to Wilmot Horton on 7 Jan. 1824. In contradiction to Bovill's claims in 'Colonel Warrington' and to John Wright's assertion of the former in his *Oxford Dictionary of National Biography* entry on Warrington, *Burke's Landed Gentry* (1864) was correct in stating that Warrington had had seven sons and three daughters with his wife Jane. The last-born child, Walter Bornou, was simply not named. On Warrington's announcement of the death of Oudney, see TNA, FO 76/18, Warrington to Wilmot Horton, 7 Jan. 1824 and Warrington to Wilmot Horton, 12 Aug. 1824.
71 On the refusal of the secretary of state to appoint Dalzel, see TNA, FO 76/20, Warrington to Bathurst, 17 Aug. 1826, and on Charles Thornhill, see TNA, FO 76/23, Warrington to Huskisson, 19 Feb. 1828.
72 The surgeon's wife, Elizabeth Dickson (née Dalzel, 1790–1862) was interred in the Protestant cemetery in Tripoli. On Archibald Dalzel, see J. A. Rawley, 'Dalzel, Archibald (1740–1818)', *Oxford Dictionary of National Biography* (Oxford University Press, 2009). Available online: https://doi.org/10.1093/ref:odnb/47570; I. A. Akinjogbin, 'Archibald Dalzel: Slave Trader and Historian of Dahomey', *Journal of African History*, 7, 1 (1966): 67–78. Relations between the Warrington and Dickson families remained close throughout Warrington's time in Tripoli and at least to 1832. One of Warrington's daughters, Louisa, later married one Edward Dalzel Dickson, and became Louisa Buena Parry Dickson. According to her last will and testament, she named two of her sons after their grandfathers, Hanmer and John, TNA, FO, 161/6, 23 May 1849.
73 TNA, FO 76/18, Warrington to Wilmot Horton, 18 August 1824; and TNA, FO 76/20, Warrington to Bathurst, 19 Aug. 1826.
74 TNA, FO 76/7, Langford to Liverpool, 27 May 1811, and Langford to Liverpool, 15 July 1811, in ElGaddari, *Letters and Reports*, 116–18. On the connection of Sandford Peacocke to the Apreece family see, *The Gentleman's Magazine*, 71, 2, (1801): 1208, and 103, 2, (1833): 80–1. Cf. E. Burke, *The Annual Register* (1805).
75 TNA, FO 76/29, Warrington to Wood, 15 May 1831.
76 TNA, FO 75/5, McDonogh to Portland, 4 May 1801.
77 Folayan, *Tripoli during the Reign of Yusuf Qaramanli*.
78 TNA, C 13/83/21, and C 13/2101/9; TNA, FO 76/20, Warrington to Hay, 15 April 1826; TNA, FO 76/12, Warrington to Bathurst, 12 Dec. 1821, in ElGaddari, *Letters and Reports*, 244–5 and 186–7; TNA, FO 76/16, Denham to Warrington, 2 Mar. 1822.

79 TNA, FO 76/15, Warrington to Bathurst, 12 Dec. 1821, in ElGaddari, *Letters and Reports*, 186-7. Cf. TNA, C 13/83/21 and C 13/2101/9.
80 TNA, FO 76/20, Warrington to Bathurst, 25 June 1826.
81 Pennell, 'The Social History of British Diplomats'.
82 TNA, FO 76/27, Warrington to Murray, 18 Aug. 1830.
83 TNA, FO 76/8, Langford to Liverpool, 29 Jan. 1812, and Langford to Bathurst, 17 June 1812.
84 TNA, FO 76/5, Langford to Camden, 20 Aug. 1804, in ElGaddari, *Letters and Reports*, 76-7.
85 TNA, FO 76/5, Langford to Hawkesbury, 28 Aug. 1804, in ElGaddari, *Letters and Reports*, 77-79.
86 TNA, FO 76/6, Draft of letter to Langford, Dec. 1806.
87 TNA, FO 76/5, Langford to York, 22 Dec. 1803; TNA, FO 76/8, Langford to Bathurst, 17 June 1812, in ElGaddari, *Letters and Reports*, 126.
88 TNA, FO 76/8, Langford to Liverpool, 29 Jan. 1812, in ElGaddari, *Letters and Reports*, 122-3.
89 TNA, FO 76/18, Warrington to Wilmot Horton, 18 Aug. 1824.
90 Consul Coxe died in Tripoli on 23 September 1830, TNA, FO 76/27, Warrington to Hay, 26 Sept. 1830; TNA, FO 76/29, Warrington to Hay, 7 Nov. 1831; and TNA, FO 76/31, Warrington to Hay, 19 March 1832. The latter two correspondences in ElGaddari, *Letters and Reports*, 309 and 321.
91 This letter from Sir Thomas Tyrwhitt to the secretary of state has not been retained in the files of the consular correspondence.
92 TNA, FO 76/20, Warrington to Hay, 15 Apr. 1826.
93 Ibid. In the same letter Warrington writes of other debts he had accrued prior to taking up his consulship at Tripoli:

> Many more charge me 14 pr. cent. I have paid one creditor 580£ annuity secured on 31886£ odd for 16 years for the advance of £4400 which in part I received. I have paid 160£ annuity for a similar term secured the same sum on the advance of £1200. I have paid 130£ annuity for the same Term – I have for the advance of 1000£. I have paid 200£ annuity for 18 years on the advance of £1400 which Miss W. redeemed two years since that was secured on £6141. I But please God I may yet live to accomplish it as my Letters to my agent clearly demonstrate my anxiety to pay off these dreadful annuities – when the trifling debts will soon follow. I do not wish to excite Commiseration or Pity but I could a 'Tale unfold' that I have been most shamefully treated & which would exonerate me thoroughly in every act. TNA, FO 76/20, Warrington to Hay, 15 Apr. 1826.

94 TNA, FO 76/20, Warrington to Hay, 10 May 1826.
95 For further biographical information on Gråberg, see *Svenskt Biografiskt Lexicon* (Dictionary of Swedish National Biography), 'Gråberg', Available online: http://sok.riksarkivet.se/SBL/Presentation.aspx?id=13259. Consul Gråberg was a prolific writer, for a detailed account of his work, see L. J. E. G. (ed.), *Notice Biographique sur le Chevalier Jacques Gråberg de Hemsö* (1831). A copy of this publication is contained within TNA, FO 76/29. There are also extensive consular records in Swedish bound with the British consul's correspondence in TNA, FO 76/21; FO 160/49-50, and FO 160/52-4.
96 Ibid.

97 John Thornton, according to the Society, was a Christian philanthropist who provided support to the founders George Cussons and John Davies. The Bible Society was renamed the Naval and Military Bible Society in 1804 to distinguish it from the newly formed British and Foreign Bible Society. The Society still holds to its 1779 mission: 'For purchasing Bibles to be distributed among British Soldiers and Seamen of the Navy, to spread abroad (by the blessing of God) Christian knowledge and reformation of manners.' The Naval and Military Bible Society is now known as the Naval, Military and Air Force Bible Society (hereafter NMAFBS); http://www.nmafbs.org/about-us/. See also TNA, FO 76/20, John Thornton to Hay, 19 July 1826; G. Goodwin, 'Jowett, William (1787–1855)', rev. H. C. G. Matthew, *Oxford Dictionary of National Biography* (Oxford University Press, 2004). Available online: https://doi.org/10.1093/ref:odnb/15145. On Thornton, see the biographical entry for his father, Samuel Thornton by M. Reed, 'Thornton, Samuel (1754–1838)', *Oxford Dictionary of National Biography* (Oxford University Press, Oct. 2009). Available online: https://doi.org/10.1093/ref:odnb/27362.
98 TNA, FO 76/23, John Barker, HM Consul at Alexandria, to Dudley, 1 Dec. 1827; TNA, FO 76/23, Hay to Backhouse, 14 July 1828. Cf. J. Kidd, *The Churches of Eastern Christendom* (Abingdon: Routledge, 2010), 448.
99 TNA, FO 76/23, Barker to Dudley, 1 Dec. 1827.
100 TNA, FO 76/27, Warrington to Hay, 28 Sept. 1830.
101 TNA, FO 76/6, Langford to Windham, 11 Apr. 1807, in ElGaddari, *Letters and Reports*, 84–5.
102 BL, Heytesbury Papers Add. MS 41512, Wilkie, 'Observations on Tripoli in the West'; TNA, FO 76/16, Warrington to Wilmot Horton, 19 Oct 1822, in ElGaddari, *Letters and Reports*, 197–8. See also, A. Porter, 'Religion, Missionary Enthusiasm and Empire', in Porter and Louis, *The Oxford History of the British Empire: Volume 3*; Porter, 'Commerce and Christianity': The Rise and Fall of a Nineteenth-Century Missionary Slogan', *Historical Journal*, 28, 3 (1985): 597–621; and J. Osterhammel, 'Britain and China, 1842–1914', in Porter and Lewis (eds), *The Oxford History of the British Empire: Volume 3: The Nineteenth Century*.
103 TNA, FO 76/16, Warrington to Wilmot Horton, 19 Oct. 1822, in ElGaddari, *Letters and Reports*, 197–8.
104 TNA, FO 76/6, Langford to Windham, 4 Apr. 1807, in ElGaddari, *Letters and Reports*, 83–4.
105 TNA, FO 76/27, Warrington to Hay, 28 Sept. 1830.
106 A. H. Tawil, *Khafaya Jadid al Muthirah Takshifuha Maqbarat Tarabulus al-Burutistantiyah*. Tripoli: Markaz Jihad al-Libiyin lil-Dirasat al-Tarikhiyah, 2008.
107 TNA, FO 76/27, Warrington to Hay, 7 Feb. 1830.
108 TNA, FO 76/27, Warrington to Murray, 3 Oct. 1830.
109 TNA, FO 76/12, Warrington to Hay, 24 Sept. 1827.
110 TNA, FO 76/11, Warrington to Bathurst, 20 Nov. 1817.
111 TNA, FO 76/23, Warrington to Huskisson, 16 June 1828, in ElGaddari, *Letters and Reports*, 265.
112 TNA, FO 76/27, Warrington to Murray, 5 Nov. 1830, in ElGaddari, *Letters and Reports*, 289–90.
113 Ibid.
114 Ibid.
115 Ibid.
116 TNA, FO 366/542, Orders of Council, 28 Feb. 1822.

Chapter 6

1. Darwin, 'Imperialism and the Victorians', 629.
2. Lynn, 'Consul and Kings: British Policy, "the Man on the Spot", and the Seizure of Lagos, 1851', 150–67.
3. Particularly southwest into modern-day Mali and other territories west of the Niger river.
4. For some discussion of the British view on the French occupation, see proceedings of the 'Algerine Commission' in T. Foster (ed.), *The Westminster Review*, Volume 22, 1835.
5. Lynn, 'Consul and Kings'.
6. Darwin, *The Empire Project*, 150.
7. Wood, *A History of the Levant Company*; C. Laidlaw, *The British in the Levant Trade and Perceptions of the Ottoman Empire in the Eighteenth Century* (London: I.B. Tauris, 2010); Darwin, *The Empire Project*; P. J. Cain and A. G. Hopkins, *British Imperialism, 1688–2000*, 2nd edn (Harlow: Longman, 2001).
8. Darwin, *The Empire Project*, 151 and 161.
9. Laidlaw, *Colonial Connections*; J. Onley, *The Arabian Frontier of the British Raj Merchants, Rulers, and the British in the Nineteenth-century Gulf* (Oxford: Oxford University Press, 2007); McLean, *War, Diplomacy and Informal Empire*; A. Varnava, *British Imperialism in Cyprus, 1878–1915: The Inconsequential Possession* (Manchester: Manchester University Press, 2009); V. T. Harlow, *The Founding of the Second British Empire: Volume 2: 1763–93* (London: Longmans, 1964); J. Gallagher and R. Robinson, 'The Imperialism of Free Trade', *Economic History Review*, 6, 1 (1953): 1–15; Robinson et al., *Africa and the Victorians: The Official Mind of Imperialism* (Basingstoke: Macmillan, 1981); Marshall, *The Oxford History of the British Empire: Volume 2: The Eighteenth Century*; Bayly, *Imperial Meridian*; Bayly, *The Birth of the Modern World*; Darwin, *The Empire Project*; Platt, 'The Imperialism of Free Trade: Some Reservations', *Economic History Review*, 21, 2 (1968): 296–306; Platt, *The Cinderella Service*; Cain and Hopkins, *British Imperialism*.
10. The Río de la Plata, or River Plate, covers territory that is now divided between the states of Uruguay and Argentina. Bayly, *Imperial Meridian*, 10. This idea, is in turn, built on Vincent Harlow's 'potentialities of Asia and Africa' in Harlow, *The Founding of the Second British Empire, 1763–93*; McLean, *War, Diplomacy and Informal Empire*; Varnava, *British Imperialism in Cyprus*.
11. Gallagher and Robinson, 'The Imperialism of Free Trade', cf. McLean, *War, Diplomacy and Informal Empire*; Robinson et al., *Africa and the Victorians*; A. G. Hopkins, 'The Victorians and Africa'; Fieldhouse, *The Theory of Capitalist Imperialism*; C. C. Eldridge (ed.), *British Imperialism in the Nineteenth Century* (New York: St. Martin's Press, 1984); Darwin, 'Imperialism and the Victorians'; and Onley, *The Arabian Frontier of the British Raj*.
12. P. J. Marshall, *Bengal: The British Bridgehead: Eastern India 1740–1828: The New Cambridge History of India* (Cambridge: Cambridge University Press, 1987); M. E. Yapp, *The Making of the Modern Near East, 1792–1923* (Oxford: Oxford University Press, 1987); Reimer, *Colonial Bridgehead: Government and Society in Alexandria*; McLean, *War, Diplomacy and Informal Empire*; Lynn, 'Consul and Kings'; and J. P. Parry, 'Steam Power and British Influence in Baghdad, 1820–1860', *Historical Journal*, 56, 1 (2013): 145–73.

13 E. N. Rothman, *Brokering Empire: Trans-Imperial Subjects between Venice and Istanbul* (Ithaca, NY: Cornell University Press, 2012); Lambert and Lester, *Colonial Lives across the British Empire*; Killingray et al., *Maritime Empires: British Imperial Maritime Trade in the Nineteenth Century*; J. Samson, *British Imperial Strategies in the Pacific, 1750–1900* (London: Routledge, 2021); Lester, 'Imperial Circuits and Networks'; Stoler, 'Imperial Debris: Reflections on Ruins and Ruination', *Cultural Anthropology*, 23, 2 (2008): 191–219.

14 Abou-el-Haj, 'An Agenda for Research in History', 314. While several studies have extracted information where available on the slave and salt trades, these details have been isolated from the full reports of trade included within the consular archives pertaining to Tripoli. Lovejoy, 'Commercial Sectors in the Economy of the Nineteenth-Century Central Sudan'; G. Baer, 'Slavery in Nineteenth Century Egypt', *Journal of African History*, 8, 3 (1967): 417–41; and J. Wright, *The Trans-Saharan Slave Trade* (London: Routledge, 2007). The notable exceptions are studies on Nordic (particularly Swedish) commercial engagement with North African states. See Müller, *Consuls, Corsairs, and Commerce*; and Müller, 'Swedish Consular Reports as a Source of Business Information', 1700–1800', *International Economic History Congress* (Helsinki, 2006): 1–12; and on British trade with Morocco, Brown, *Crossing the Strait*.

15 S. Haggerty, *'Merely for Money?' Business Culture in the British Atlantic, 1750–1815* (Liverpool: Liverpool University Press, 2012), 162; Lester, 'Imperial Circuits and Networks'; Hoek, 'Parallel Arc Diagrams: Visualizing Temporal Interactions', *Journal of Social Structure*, 12, 7 (2011): 11–25; and J. Haggerty and S. Haggerty, 'Visual Analytics of an Eighteenth-Century Business Network', *Enterprise and Society*, 11, 1 (2009): 1–25.

16 C. A. Bayly, *Empire and Information: Intelligence-gathering and Social Communication in India 1780–1870* (Cambridge: Cambridge University Press, 1996); Darwin, *The Empire Project*.

17 Darwin, 'Imperialism and the Victorians', 629.

18 TNA, FO 76/16, Warrington to Wilmot Horton, 4 July 1822.

19 Cf. Daly (ed.), *The Cambridge History of Egypt: Volume 2: Modern Egypt*; J. C. Herold, *Bonaparte in Egypt* (New York: Harper & Row, 1962); and D. Chandler, *The Campaigns of Napoleon* (London: Weidenfeld & Nicolson, 1993).

20 TNA, FO 76/12, Warrington to Bathurst, 16 Apr. 1818; TNA, FO 76/2, Warrington to Hay, 22 Apr. 1820; TNA, FO 76/20, Warrington to Bathurst, 27 Feb. 1826, in ElGaddari, *Letters and Reports*, 242–4; TNA, FO 76/27, Warrington to Hay, 9 Sept. 1830.

21 M. Duffy, 'World-Wide War and British Expansion, 1793–1815', in P. J. Marshall (ed.), *The Oxford History of the British Empire: Volume 2: The Eighteenth Century* (Oxford: Oxford University Press, 1998), 196. On Dundas's term as secretary of state, see Sainty (ed.), *Office-Holders in Modern Britain: Volume 6: Colonial Office Officials, 1794–1870* (London: Institute of Historical Research, University of London, 1976), 8. On his life and career, including as secretary for war, president of the Board of Control (for India) and First Lord of the Admiralty, see M. Fry, 'Dundas, Henry, first Viscount Melville (1742–1811)', *Oxford Dictionary of National Biography* (Oxford University Press, May 2009). Available online: https://doi.org/10.1093/ref:odnb/8250.

22 Duffy, 'World-Wide War and British Expansion, 1793–1815', 196.

23 TNA, FO 76/7, Langford to Wellesley, 21 July 1811, in ElGaddari, *Letters and Reports*, 118–19; TNA, FO 76/8, Langford to Bathurst, 23 Feb. 1813; TNA, FO 76/16, à

Court to Wilmot Horton, 5 May 1822, in ElGaddari, *Letters and Reports*, 190–1; BL, Heytesbury Papers Add. MSS 41512; Foreign Office, *British Foreign and State Papers, 1812–1814*. Volume 1, Part 1 (London: James Ridgway, 1841), 190.
24 TNA, FO 76/11, Warrington to Bathurst, 9 Nov. 1817, in ElGaddari, *Letters and Reports*, 156–7; and BL, Heytesbury Papers Add. MSS 41512.
25 Langford departed Tripoli in January 1812, and until Warrington arrived in Tripoli in November 1814, Wilkie had been dispatched as British proconsul from 20 January 1812. Fifteen months later, on 20 July 1813, and for reasons that remain unclear, Wilkie was replaced by Somerville.
26 TNA, FO 76/20, Warrington to Bathurst, 9 June 1826.
27 TNA, FO 76/16, Carstensen to Warrington, 11 Sept. 1822, and Warrington to Bathurst, 14 Sept. 1822.
28 TNA, FO 76/16, Carstensen to Warrington, 11 Sept. 1822.
29 TNA, FO 160/35, various correspondence with fellow consuls in North Africa, as well as TNA, FO 160/37 and TNA, FO 160/38 for communication with the Russian Ambassador A. Italinsky in Büyükdere – the summer residence of the Ambassador on the Bosphorus, in the province of Istanbul – as well as others, including British naval officials in Malta.
30 TNA, FO 76/20, Warrington to Bathurst, 17 Aug. 1826; TNA, FO 76/17, Oudney to Warrington, 14 July 1820; Warrington to Wilmot Horton, 11 Mar. 1823; Warrington to Oudney, 25 Aug. 1823, and Warrington to Wilmot Horton, 6 Oct. 1823; TNA, FO 76/16, Denham to Warrington, 2 Mar. 1820, and TNA, FO 76/16, Denham to Warrington, 11 Oct. 1822.
31 TNA, FO 76/17, Warrington to Hay, 5 Oct. 1831, in ElGaddari, *Letters and Reports*, 305–6.
32 TNA, FO 76/17, Warrington to Wilmot Horton, 31 Mar. 1820.
33 Bayly, *Imperial Meridian*, 248.
34 TNA, FO 76/11, Croker to Hamilton, 30 July 1817, and Hamilton to Goulburn, 1 Aug. 1817.
35 TNA, FO 76/20, Warrington to Bathurst, 17 Aug. 1826; and TNA, FO 76/17, Oudney to Warrington, 14 July 1820; Warrington to Wilmot Horton, 11 Mar. 1823; Warrington to Oudney, 25 Aug. 1823, and Warrington to Wilmot Horton, 6 Oct. 1823; TNA, FO 76/16, Denham to Warrington, 2 Mar. 1820; and TNA, FO 76/16, Denham to Warrington, 11 Oct. 1822.
36 TNA, FO 76/20, Warrington to Hay, 25 June 1826, in ElGaddari, *Letters and Reports*, 245–6.
37 TNA, FO 76/19, Warrington to Bathurst, 9 Feb. 1825, in ElGaddari, *Letters and Reports*, 228–30.
38 Bayly, *Imperial Meridian*.
39 S. Zubaida, 'Cosmopolitanism in the Middle East', Research Center for International Political Economy and Foreign Policy Analysis (RECIPE), Issue 12, *Amsterdam Middle East Papers* (Amsterdam International Studies, 1997), and Zubaida, 'Middle Eastern Experiences of Cosmopolitanism', in S. Vertovec and R. Cohen (eds), *Conceiving Cosmopolitanism: Theory, Context and Practice* (Oxford: Oxford University Press 2002), 33–8.
40 Bayly, *Imperial Meridian*.
41 TNA, FO 76/5, McDonogh to Pelham, 2 Dec. 1802, in ElGaddari, *Letters and Reports*, 67–9.
42 TNA, FO 76/18, Warrington to Wilmot Horton, 29 Sept. 1824.

43 TNA, FO 76/12, Warrington to Bathurst, 17 Apr. 1818, in ElGaddari, *Letters and Reports*, 160.
44 Lovejoy, 'Commercial Sectors in the Economy of the Nineteenth-Century Central Sudan'.
45 TNA, FO 76/12, Warrington to Bathurst, 17 Apr. 1818, in ElGaddari, *Letters and Reports*, 160.
46 Ibid.
47 On the prominence and re-export of senna from Tripoli to Europe, see Lydon, *On Trans-Saharan Trails*, 93; Bovill, *Caravans of the Old Sahara*; Boahen, 'The Caravan Trade in the Nineteenth Century'; Thornton, *Africa and the Africans in the Making of the Atlantic World*; Eltis and Engerman, *The Cambridge World History of Slavery*; Richardson, 'The British Empire and the Atlantic Slave Trade, 1660–1807', 440–64; Lovejoy, *Transformations in Slavery*; Fisher, *Slavery in the History of Muslim Black Africa*.
48 Lovejoy, 'Commercial Sectors in the Economy of the Nineteenth-Century Central Sudan'.
49 TNA, FO 76/19, Warrington to Wilmot Horton, 24 July 1825; TNA, FO 76/18, Warrington to Wilmot Horton, 18 Aug. 1824; TNA, FO 76/19, Warrington to Bathurst, 22 June 1825; and Lynn, 'Consul and Kings', 151.
50 Laidlaw, *Colonial Connections*, in particular chapter 7, 'An Information Revolution', 169–99.
51 TNA, FO 76/7, Langford to Gordon, 25 Sept. 1810, in ElGaddari, *Letters and Reports*, 110–12; and TNA, FO 76/9, various reports from Warrington.
52 TNA, FO 76/12, Warrington to Bathurst, 17 Apr. 1818, in ElGaddari, *Letters and Reports*, 160.
53 See trade returns in TNA, FO 76/30.
54 Egypt was also in short supply of coal. See Fahmy, 'The Era of Muhammad 'Ali Pasha', 161.
55 TNA, FO 76/15, Warrington to Bathurst, 14 Feb. 1821, and Warrington to Bathurst, 26 Mar. 1821. The latter correspondence in, ElGaddari, *Letters and Reports*, 176–7.
56 TNA, FO 76/15, Warrington to Bathurst, 26 Mar. 1821, in ElGaddari, *Letters and Reports*, 176–7; and TNA, FO 76/15, Warrington to Bathurst, 14 Feb. 1821; W. Edwards, *Notes on British History: Part IV: 1793–1901* (London: Rivingtons, 1958).
57 Nelson to Wilkie, 10 Feb. 1804, in N. H. Harris (ed.), *The Dispatches and Letters of Vice Admiral Viscount Nelson*, Volume 5 (Cambridge: Cambridge University Press, 2011).
58 TNA, FO 160/3, Beaussier to Wilkie, 28 Mar. 1812. On Beaussier, see Mézin, *Les Consuls de France, Volume 1*, 132.
59 TNA, FO 366/542, Orders of Council, 28 Feb. 1822; House of Commons: Reports from the Committees: Volume 2. *Report from the Committee Appointed to Inquire into the Consular Departments*; and House of Lords Sessional Papers: *Report from the Select Committee (of the House of Commons) on Consular Establishment; together with the Minutes of Evidence, and Appendix*, 26 (22 August 1835), 1–204.
60 TNA, FO 76/19, Warrington to Laing, 11 Oct. 1825.
61 TNA, FO 76/23, Warrington to Evers, 20 Apr. 1828. On the treaty mediated for His Holiness Pope Pius VII with Tripoli and signed by Warrington on 24 Dec. 1818, see TNA, FO 76/13; TNA, FO 76/20; and TNA, FO 76/22.
62 TNA, FO 76/5, Lucas to Portland, 4 Sept. 1799.
63 TNA, FO 76/5, King George III to Yusuf Qaramanli, 9 Sept. 1797.

64 TNA, FO 76/7, Langford to Liverpool, 25 June 1810.
65 Ibid.
66 Hallett, *Records of the Africa Association*, and Hallett, *The Penetration of Africa*.
67 TNA, FO 76/16, Oudney to Warrington, 17 Sept. 1822. Hillman was also formerly a shipwright in the Royal Navy. TNA, FO, 8/12, Wilmot Horton to Croker, 27 Apr. 1822.
68 TNA, FO 76/13, Warrington to Bathurst, 29 Dec. 1819, in ElGaddari, *Letters and Reports*, 163–4; TNA, FO 76/18, Denham to Warrington, 20 Jan. 1824; Tyrwhitt to Warrington, 23 May 1824; and Warrington to Wilmot Horton, 18 Aug. 1824; TNA, FO 76/19, Warrington to Bathurst, 22 June 1825; and TNA, FO 76/29, Wood to Hay, 19 Aug. 1831.
69 TNA, FO 76/20, Warrington to Bathurst, 17 Aug. 1826; TNA, FO 76/17, Oudney to Warrington, 14 July 1820; Warrington to Wilmot Horton, 11 Mar. 1823; Warrington to Oudney, 25 Aug. 1823, and Warrington to Wilmot Horton, 6 Oct. 1823; TNA, FO 76/16, Denham to Warrington, 2 Mar. 1820.
70 Cf. TNA, FO 76/18, various correspondences, including Warrington to Oudney, 2 June 1824; FO 76/11, Warrington to Bathurst, 22 Aug. 1817; TNA, FO 76/17, Warrington to Wilmot Horton, 10 July 1823, in ElGaddari, *Letters and Reports*, 207.
71 *Caledonian Mercury*, 2 May 1822.
72 TNA, FO 76/18, Warrington to Wilmot Horton, 24 Feb. 1824; and TNA, FO 76/29, Warrington to Hay, 12 Sept. 1831; TNA, FO 76/17, Denham to Warrington, 4 Apr. 1823.
73 TNA, FO 76/16, Beechey to Warrington, 6 June 1822; Warrington to Wilmot Horton, 14 Mar. 1822; Tyrwhitt to Warrington, 25 July 1822, Warrington to Wilmot Horton, 4 Nov. 1822, and Oudney to Warrington, 14 Jan. 1823.
74 TNA, FO 76/17, Denham to Clapperton, 11 Apr. 1823, Clapperton to Warrington, 11 July 1823; and Warrington to Wilmot Horton, 4 Nov. 1823, the latter correspondence in ElGaddari, *Letters and Reports*, 210–12.
75 TNA, FO 76/17, Denham to Clapperton, 11 Apr. 1823; TNA, FO 76/17, Oudney to Warrington, 14 Jan. 1823.
76 TNA, FO 76/16, Warrington to Wilmot Horton, 4 Nov. 1822; and Oudney to Warrington, 14 Jan. 1823.
77 TNA, FO 76/11, Penrose to Croker, 25 Jan. 1817.
78 TNA, FO 76/20, Warrington to Bathurst, 27 Feb. 1826, in ElGaddari, *Letters and Reports*, 242–4.
79 Ibid.
80 TNA, FO 76/5, Lucas to King, 15 Apr. 1794; Langford to Camden, 15 Dec. 1804; and TNA, FO 76/9, Warrington to Bunbury, 14 July 1814, in ElGaddari, *Letters and Reports*, 130–1.
81 TNA, FO 76/5, Lucas to Dundas, 5 Sept. 1794.
82 TNA, FO 76/5, Lucas to Dundas, 5 June 1794.
83 TNA, FO 76/29, Warrington to Goderich, 30 Sept. 1831, in ElGaddari, *Letters and Reports*, 304. Cf. Pennell, 'The Social History of British Diplomats', 363.
84 TNA, FO 76/29, Warrington to Goderich, 30 Sept. 1831, in ElGaddari, *Letters and Reports*, 304. On Goderich, P. J. Jupp, 'Robinson, Frederick John, First Viscount Goderich and first earl of Ripon (1782–1859)', *Oxford Dictionary of National Biography* (Oxford University Press, May 2009). Available online: https://doi.org/10.1093/ref:odnb/23836.

85 TNA, FO 76/10, Warrington to Melville, 5 Aug. 1816, in ElGaddari, *Letters and Reports*, 152–3. On Melville, M. Fry, 'Dundas, Robert Saunders, second Viscount Melville (1771–1851)', *Oxford Dictionary of National Biography* (Oxford University Press, 2008). Available online: https://doi.org/10.1093/ref:odnb/8260; E. J. Edwards, *A Concise History of Small-Pox and Vaccination in Europe* (London: H.K. Lewis, 1902); L. V. Kuhnke, *Lives at Risk: Public Health in Nineteenth-Century Egypt* (Berkeley: University of California Press, 1990); D. Arnold, *Colonizing the Body: State Medicine and Epidemic Disease in Nineteenth-Century India* (Berkeley: University of California Press, 1993); and Curtin, *Death by Migration*. Cf. The pioneering work of Spanish physician Francisco Javier de Balmis (1753–1819) on taking the smallpox vaccine to Spanish colonies in 1803.
86 Grosvenor, *Extracts from the Journal*, 22.
87 BL, Heytesbury Papers Add. MS 41512, and TNA, FO, 76/20, Dickson to Warrington, 24 Mar. 1826, and Dickson to Yusuf Qaramanli, 20 Dec. 1826., TNA, FO 76/31, Warrington to Goderich, 24 Jan. 1832.
88 TNA, FO 76/31, Warrington to Goderich, 24 Jan. 1832.
89 TNA, FO 76/10, Warrington to Melville, 5 Aug. 1816; TNA, FO 76/20, in ElGaddari, *Letters and Reports*, 152–3; TNA, FO 76/20, Dickson to Yusuf Qaramanli, 20 Dec. 1826.
90 Fahmy, 'The Era of Muhamed 'Ali Pasha', 168–9. Clot was awarded the title 'Bey' for his services. Fahmy writes that Dr Clot was from Marseille and, in 1825, had arrived in Egypt and later founded the Qasr al-Aini (initially called the Abu Za'bal hospital); Fahmy, 'The Era of Muhamed 'Ali Pasha', 161 and 166.
91 TNA, FO 76/17, Warrington to Robert Wilmot, 17 Oct. 1823, in ElGaddari, *Letters and Reports*, 209–10.
92 TNA, FO 76/19, Warrington to Hay, 24 Dec. 1824; TNA, FO 76/20, Warrington to Bathurst, 20 June 1826; TNA, FO 76/29, Warrington to Goderich, 19 Dec. 1831, in ElGaddari, *Letters and Reports*, 311; and official trade returns submitted by the consul general for Benghazi and Tripoli in TNA, FO, Tripoli, Series I and II.
93 TNA, FO 76/15, Warrington to Bathurst, 4 Nov. 1821, in ElGaddari, *Letters and Reports*, 185–6. Folayan, 'Tripoli-Bornu Political Relations', and Folayan, *Tripoli during the Reign of Yusuf Pasha Qaramanli*; see also numerous correspondences in TNA, FO 76/29 on the conflict with Sheikh Abd' al-Jalil Saif al-Nasser; Lester, 'Imperial Circuits and Networks'.

Chapter 7

1 TNA, FO 76/5; TNA, FO 76/5, Langford to York, 10 July 1804, in ElGaddari, *Letters and Reports*, 72–5; TNA, FO 76/11, Penrose to Croker, 25 Jan. 1817; and TNA, FO 76/16, Warrington to Wilmot Horton, 26 Aug. 1822.
2 TNA, FO 76/17, Warrington to Wilmot Horton, 10 July 1823, in ElGaddari, *Letters and Reports*, 207.
3 Bayly, *Imperial Meridian*.
4 Anderson, *The Eastern Question*, 51.
5 Cf. M. Mazower, *The Greek Revolution: 1821 and the Making of Modern Europe* (London: Allen Lane, 2021); P. M. Kitromilides and C. Tsoukalas, *The Greek Revolution: A Critical Dictionary* (Cambridge, MA: Belknap Press, 2021);

C. W. Crawley, *The Question of Greek Independence: A Study of British Policy in the Near East 1821–1833* (Cambridge: Cambridge University Press, 1930). On Egypt, al-Jabarti et al., *Napoleon in Egypt: Al-Jabarti's Chronicle of the French Occupation*; Cole, *Napoleon's Egypt*; Dykstra, 'The French Occupation of Egypt'.
6 See Laidlaw's and Louise Guenther's work on New Zealand, the Cape and Brazil, respectively; Laidlaw, *Colonial Connections*; Guenther, 'The British Community of 19th Century Bahia: Public and Private Lives'. See also Darwin, *The Empire Project*; R. Hyam, *Britain's Imperial Century, 1815–1914: A Study of Empire and Expansion* (London: Palgrave Macmillan, 2002); and Cain and Hopkins, *British Imperialism, 1688–2000*.
7 The consular correspondence usually took three months from Tripoli to London, via Malta or Livorno. This is confirmed by the 'date received' stamp on the correspondence received by the Colonial Department from the consuls to Tripoli.
8 Bayly, *Empire and Information*, 1.
9 Ibid., 124.
10 Ibid., 55; S. Schaffer et al. (eds), *The Brokered World: Go-Betweens and Global Intelligence, 1770–1820* (Sagamore Beach, MA: Science History Publications, 2009); P. D. Curtin, *Cross-Cultural Trade in World History* (Cambridge: Cambridge University Press, 1984); and P. Horden and N. Purcell, *The Corrupting Sea: A Study of Mediterranean History* (London: Wiley-Blackwell, 2000).
11 Bayly, *Empire and Information*, 17 and 55; Stoler, *Along the Archival Grain*; Said, *Orientalism*; Said, *Culture & Imperialism*; Bhabha, *The Location of Culture*; and Foucault, *The Archaeology of Knowledge*.
12 Turnbull, 'Boundary-Crossing, Cultural Encounters and Knowledge Spaces', in Schaffer et al. (eds), *The Brokered World*, 387–428.
13 Cunningham (ed.), *The Early Correspondence of Richard Wood*.
14 Freitag and Wende (eds), *British Envoys to Germany, 1816–1866: Volume 1: 1816–1829*, xix; E. Prevelakis and K. Kalliataki Merticopoulou (eds), *Epirus, Ali Pasha and the Greek Revolution: Consular Reports of William Meyer from Preveza*, Volumes 1–2. Monuments of Greek History, Number 12, (Athens: Academy of Athens, 1996).
15 Bayly, *Empire and Information*, 48.
16 TNA, FO 76/6, Langford to Windham, 28 Feb. 1807, and Yusuf Qaramanli to King George III, 24 Feb. 1807.
17 Ibid.
18 Ingram, *In Defence of British India*, 205.
19 D. Dykstra, 'The French Occupation of Egypt', in Daly (ed.), *The Cambridge History of Egypt: Volume 2: Modern Egypt*.
20 Fahmy, 'The Era of Muhammad 'Ali Pasha', especially 165; Ridley, *Napoleon's Proconsul in Egypt*. Cf. R. W. Seton-Watson, who suggests that, in fact, it was suggested by Prince Jules Auguste de Polignac that France annexe Algiers, while Egypt would conquer Tunis and Tripoli. R. W. Seton-Watson, *Britain in Europe, 1789–1914* (London: Cambridge University Press, 1955).
21 Najd is an area to the east of the province of Hijaz, which flanks the Red Sea. In the early nineteenth century, the province extended as far north as the territories of Syria. J. Pinkerton (ed.), *A General Collection of the Best and Most Interesting Voyages and Travels in All Parts of the World*, Volume 10 (London: Longman, Hurst, Rees, Orme, and Brown; and Cadell and Davies, 1811), 81; TNA, FO 76/7, Langford to Liverpool, 1 Feb. 1810, in ElGaddari, *Letters and Reports*, 106–7.
22 D. Cummins, *The Wahhabi Mission and Saudi Arabia* (London: I.B. Tauris, 2009), 55.

23 TNA, FO 76/7, Langford to Liverpool, 1 Feb. 1810, in ElGaddari, *Letters and Reports*, 106–7.
24 TNA, FO 76/7, Langford to Gordon, 25 Sept. 1810, in ElGaddari, *Letters and Reports*, 110–12.
25 TNA, FO 76/7, Langford to Liverpool, 31 Mar. 1811.
26 TNA, FO 76/11, Warrington to Bathurst, 24 Aug. 1817, in ElGaddari, *Letters and Reports*, 155–6; TNA, FO 76/16, Warrington to Wilmot Horton, 4 Nov. 1822.
27 TNA, FO 76/20, Warrington to Hay, 26 June 1826, in ElGaddari, *Letters and Reports*, 246.
28 Ibid.
29 Ibid.
30 TNA, FO 76/12, Croker to Goulburn, 2 Feb. 1818. On Henry Goulburn, see G. F. R. Barker, 'Goulburn, Henry (1784–1856)', rev. David Eastwood, *Oxford Dictionary of National Biography* (Oxford University Press, Jan. 2008). Available online: https://doi.org/10.1093/ref:odnb/11148.
31 W. H. Smyth, *Memoir Descriptive of the Resources, Inhabitants, and Hydrography of Sicily and Its Islands* (London: John Murray, 1824).
32 Ibid. Cf. TNA, FO 76/13, Barrow to Goulburn, 23 Mar. 1819, and TNA, FO 76/15, Barrow to Goulburn, 22 Nov. 1821 on Penrose's and Bathurst's subsequent support of the repair of a ship belonging to Yusuf Qaramanli at the naval dockyard in Malta (despite the increased cost of repair totalling £1,700); TNA, FO 76/16, various correspondences including Hassuna D'Ghies to Wilmot Horton, 11 Feb. 1822; and TNA, FO 76/6, Langford to Castlereagh, 15 Oct. 1807.
33 Since 1799 at Acre, see Fahmy, 'The Era of Muhammad 'Ali Pasha', 141.
34 Fahmy, 'The Era of Muhammad 'Ali Pasha', 146–9; The Literary Panorama, *Volume 10. The Literary Panorama* (London: Coxe & Baylis, 1811), 120; Herold, *Bonaparte in Egypt*; and Chandler, *The Campaigns of Napoleon*.
35 TNA, FO 76/16, Warrington to Wilmot Horton, 19 Oct. 1822, in ElGaddari, *Letters and Reports*, 197–8.
36 TNA, FO 76/16, Oudney to Warrington, 17 Sept. 1822, and Warrington to Wilmot Horton, 19 Oct. 1822, the latter in ElGaddari, *Letters and Reports*, 197–8.
37 TNA, FO 76/16, Warrington to Wilmot Horton, 31 Dec. 1822.
38 TNA, FO 76/16, Warrington to Wilmot Horton, 10 Dec. 1822, in ElGaddari, *Letters and Reports*, 198–9.
39 Ibid.
40 TNA, FO 76/15, Warrington to Bathurst, 21 Sept. 1821; TNA, FO 76/16, Warrington to Oudney and Denham, 15 Apr. 1822; TNA, FO 76/18, Warrington to Wilmot Horton, 24 Feb. 1823.
41 TNA, FO 76/15, Warrington to Bathurst, 16 July 1821, in ElGaddari, *Letters and Reports*, 181–3.
42 A. Twells, *The Civilising Mission and the English Middle Class, 1792–1850: The 'Heathen' at Home and Overseas* (Basingstoke: Palgrave Macmillan, 2009).
43 TNA, FO 76/16, Clapperton to Warrington, 10 Sept. 1822.
44 TNA, FO 76/16, Warrington to Wilmot Horton, 31 Dec. 1822.
45 TNA, FO 76/18, Toole to Warrington, 27 Oct. 1823; TNA, FO 76/16, Warrington to Wilmot Horton, 4 Nov. 1822.
46 TNA, FO 76/16, Warrington to Wilmot Horton, 31 Dec. 1822.
47 TNA, FO 76/18, Toole to Warrington, 27 Oct. 1823.
48 TNA, FO 76/27, Warrington to Hay, 1 March 1830.

49 Spencer Smith had formerly been the most senior British agent at Istanbul. Dykstra, 'The French Occupation of Egypt', 121. On Elgin, see William St Clair, 'Bruce, Thomas, seventh earl of Elgin and eleventh earl of Kincardine (1766–1841)', *Oxford Dictionary of National Biography* (Oxford University Press, May 2013). Available online: https://doi.org/10.1093/ref:odnb/3759.

50 J. L. Comstock (ed.), *History of the Greek Revolution: Compiled from Official Documents of the Greek Government* (New York: William W. Reed, 1828).

51 TNA, FO 76/12, Maitland to Liston, 14 Nov. 1818. Kolovos was Ali Pasha's advisor, translator and secretary, and along with the merchant Constantino Monovarda, he was sent as 'commissioner' in the negotiations with Maitland at Corfu. Thank you to Mathieu Grenet who also suggested 'Spiros Kolovos' as the actual name of 'Colovò'. On Spiros Kolovos, see P. Aravantinos, Ιστορία Αλή πασά του Τεπελενλή, Εκ του Τυπογραφείου των Καταστημάτων Σπυρίδωνος Κουσουλίνος (Athens, 1895), 462; M. P. C. Pieri, *Compendio della storia del Risorgimento della Grecia dal 1740 al 1824: Volume 1* (Legros: Marazzani, 1858), 63; Efendi, *Mémoires sur la Grèce et l'Albanie pedant le gouvernement d'Ali-Pacha*.

52 In fact, there seemed to be a near-constant pursuit of Greek prizes. In November 1823, Warrington recorded that Qaramanli's officers had returned from a two-year cruise with captives from Candia (Heraklion). TNA, FO 76/17, Warrington to Wilmot Horton, 15 Nov. 1823, in ElGaddari, *Letters and Reports*, 215–16; and TNA, FO 76/6, Langford to Castlereagh, 4 Mar. 1809; G. Fisher, *Barbary Legend: Trade and Piracy in North Africa, 1415–1830* (Oxford: Clarendon Press, 1957); S. Dearden, *A Nest of Corsairs: The Fighting Karamanlis of the Barbary Coast* (London: John Murray, 1976); and Panzac, *The Barbary Corsairs*.

53 TNA, FO 76/9, Warrington to Smith, 15 July 1815, and Warrington to Bathurst, 21 July 1815, in ElGaddari, *Letters and Reports*, 141–4 and 144–5.

54 Ibid.

55 TNA, FO 76/9, Circular to the European Consuls 'in the Barbary States', written in French at Vienna, 2 Jan. 1815.

56 TNA, FO 76/9, Warrington to Bathurst, 21 July 1815, in ElGaddari, *Letters and Reports*, 144–5.

57 TNA, FO 76/9, Warrington to Smith, 15 July 1815, and Warrington to Bathurst, 21 July 1815, in ElGaddari, *Letters and Reports*, 141–4 and 144–5. On the eccentricity of Sir William Sidney Smith, since his appointment in 1798 to the Mediterranean on the *Tigre*, see G. Hill, *A History of Cyprus: Volume 4: The Ottoman Province. The British Colony, 1571–1948* (Cambridge: Cambridge University Press, 1952), 101; and Ingram, *In Defence of British India*, 37.

58 TNA, FO 76/17, Warrington to Wilmot Horton, 29 June 1823, in ElGaddari, *Letters and Reports*, 204–5.

59 TNA, FO 76/20, Warrington to Hay, 26 Dec. 1826.

60 TNA, FO 76/7, Langford to Liverpool, 25 June 1810; TNA, FO 76/18, Warrington to Wilmot Horton, 5 Mar. 1824; TNA, FO 76/18, Warrington to Wilmot Horton, 12 Aug. 1824.

61 TNA, FO 76/27, Fraser to Hay, 18 Nov. 1830, and Fraser to unknown, Dec. 1830; TNA, FO 76/31, Warrington to Hay, 25 Jan. 1832; TNA, FO 8/12, Wilmot Horton to Dupuis, 30 Sept. 1824.

62 TNA, FO 76/14, Warrington to Bathurst, 1 Oct. 1820, in ElGaddari, *Letters and Reports*, 172–3.

63 TNA, FO 76/11, Penrose to Croker, 25 Jan. 1817; TNA, FO 76/20, Dickson to Yusuf Qaramanli, 20 Dec. 1826.
64 TNA, FO 76/12, Warrington to Bathurst, 12 Dec. 1821, in ElGaddari, *Letters and Reports*, 186–7; TNA, FO 76/20, Warrington to Hay, 15 Apr. 1826.
65 TNA, FO 76/19, Mohamed Sadave to Warrington, 20 Mar. 1825. Sadave had been employed as a servant to Tyrwhitt at the British vice-consular office.
66 TNA, FO 76/18, Denham to Warrington, 10 May 1824, and Warrington to Wilmot Horton, 12 Aug. 1824.
67 TNA, FO 76/16, Warrington to Wilmot Horton, 12 July 1822.
68 TNA, FO 76/16, Oudney to Warrington, 14 Jan. 1823.
69 TNA, FO 76/27, Warrington to Murray, 12 Mar. 1830.
70 TNA, FO 76/16, Warrington to Wilmot Horton, 4 Nov. 1822.
71 TNA, FO 76/19, Warrington to Denham, 9 Feb. 1825.
72 TNA, FO 76/17, Warrington to Wilmot Horton, 20 Dec. 1823, in ElGaddari, *Letters and Reports*, 220–1; and TNA, FO 76/18, Warrington to Bathurst, 21 Apr. 1824.
73 TNA, FO 76/11, Warrington to Bathurst, 9 Nov. 1817, in ElGaddari, *Letters and Reports*, 156–7.
74 TNA, FO 76/16, Warrington to Wilmot Horton, 12 July 1822.
75 TNA, FO 76/17, Warrington to Wilmot Horton, 20 Dec. 1823, in ElGaddari, *Letters and Reports*, 220–1.
76 TNA, FO 76/16, Warrington to Wilmot Horton, 4 Nov. 1822.
77 TNA, FO 8/12, Wilmot Horton to G. Harrison, 30 Sept. 1824.
78 For the account of Caillié's journey, see R. Caillié, *Journal d'un voyage á Tembouctou et á Jenné dans l'Afrique Central: Volumes 1–3* (Paris, 1830).
79 Dykstra, 'The French Occupation of Egypt', 121.
80 On Keith, see C. H. H. Owen, 'Elphinstone, George Keith, Viscount Keith (1746–1823)', *Oxford Dictionary of National Biography* (Oxford University Press, May 2009). Available online: https://doi.org/10.1093/ref:odnb/8742.
81 Dykstra, 'The French Occupation of Egypt', 129.
82 TNA, FO 76/16, Carstensen to Warrington, 11 Sept. 1822.
83 Laidlaw, *Colonial Connections*; Guenther, 'The British Community of 19th Century Bahia'.
84 TNA, FO 76/6, McDonogh to Portland, 1 Nov. 1801, in ElGaddari, *Letters and Reports*, 63–4.
85 Ibid. The 'testimony' of Nielsen, the Danish consul, dated 27 Oct. 1801, and the above-mentioned letter from Pickering to McDonogh, 15 Jan. 1800, are enclosed with TNA, FO 76/6, McDonogh to Portland, 1 Nov. 1801, in ElGaddari, *Letters and Reports*, 63–4; TNA, FO 76/5, McDonogh to Pelham, 27 May 1802.
86 TNA, FO 76/6, McDonogh to Portland, 1 Nov. 1801, in ElGaddari, *Letters and Reports*, 63–4.
87 TNA, FO 76/7, Langford to Liverpool, 3 Dec. 1810, in ElGaddari, *Letters and Reports*, 114.
88 TNA, FO 76/7, Langford to Liverpool, 3 Dec. 1810; TNA FO 76/7, in ElGaddari, *Letters and Reports*, 114; Sir Hildebrand Oakes to Langford, 12 Sept. 1811. Oakes was lieutenant-general for Ordnance at Malta and from 4 June 1811, lieutenant-general in the Army. For further information on Oakes, see C. Doorne, 'Oakes, Sir Hildebrand, first baronet (1754–1822)', *Oxford Dictionary of National Biography* (Oxford University Press, 2004). Available online: https://doi.org/10.1093/ref:odnb/20426.

89 TNA, FO 76/8, Langford to Liverpool, 11 May 1811; Langford to Liverpool, 29 Jan. 1812, in ElGaddari, *Letters and Reports*, 122–3.
90 TNA, FO 76/19, Warrington to Bathurst, 22 June 1825.
91 TNA, FO 76/17, Toole to Warrington, 18 Oct. 1823; and TNA, FO 76/18, Warrington to Wilmot Horton, 2 Feb. 1824.
92 TNA, FO 76/18, Warrington to Bathurst, 21 Apr. 1824; TNA, FO 76/18, Tyrwhitt to Warrington, 23 Mar. 1824, in Warrington to Bathurst, 21 Apr. 1824. There is some confusion at times, particularly by Toole in his dispatches to Warrington, when he discusses the hostage affair with reference to the Sheikh of 'Calme'. Here Toole perhaps means 'Kanemi', but in any case, appears to be mistaken given that the rest of the body of information in the consular correspondence references Sheikh Abd' al-Jalil Saif al-Nasser in the affair.
93 TNA, FO 76/21, Warrington to Hay, 7 Nov. 1827.
94 Ibid.
95 TNA, FO 76/29, Warrington to Hay, 5 Oct. 1831, in ElGaddari, *Letters and Reports*, 305–6.
96 TNA, FO 76/29, Warrington to Goderich, 27 Aug. 1831, in ElGaddari, *Letters and Reports*, 301–2.
97 Ibid.
98 TNA, FO 76/29, Warrington to Hay, 5 Oct. 1831, in ElGaddari, *Letters and Reports*, 305–6.
99 TNA, FO 76/29, Warrington to Saif al-Nasser, 20 Dec. 1831.
100 R. Collins, 'Bagirmi, Wadai and Darfur', in K. Shillington (ed.), *Encyclopedia of African History, A-G* (New York: Fitzroy Dearborn, 2005), 203–4. Cf. J. E. Flint, *The Cambridge History of Africa: Volume 5: From 1790 to 1870* (Cambridge: Cambridge University Press, 1977); G. Nachtigal, *Sahara and Sudan: Volume 1: Tripoli and Fezzan, Tibesti or Tu*. Translated from German by A. G. B. Fisher and H. J. Fisher (New York: Barnes and Noble, 1974).
101 TNA, FO 76/22, Salt to Dudley, 13 July 1827; D. Manley and P. Rée, 'Salt, Henry (1780–1827)', *Oxford Dictionary of National Biography* (Oxford University Press, Jan. 2008). Available online: https://doi.org/10.1093/ref:odnb/24563.
102 TNA, FO 76/22, Salt to Planta, 13 July 1827.
103 Ibid.
104 TNA, FO 76/22, Salt to Dudley, 13 July 1827. D. R. Fisher, 'Ward, John William, earl of Dudley (1781–1833)', *Oxford Dictionary of National Biography* (Oxford University Press, Jan. 2008). Available online: https://doi.org/10.1093/ref:odnb/28696.
105 TNA, FO 76/22, Salt to Dudley, 13 July 1827; see also TNA, FO 76/22 Warrington to John Barker, 13 June 1827; and Barker to Salt, 10 July 1827; various other correspondences on the subject of the Prince in TNA, FO 76/23.
106 For an account of the funeral of the 'Great Chief' Mohamed Haleefa, extracted from TNA, FO 76/29, and included in, TNA, FO 76/29, Warrington to Hay, 27 Sept. 1831, in ElGaddari, *Letters and Reports*, 302–4.
107 Ibid.
108 Ibid.
109 TNA, FO 76/34, Warrington to Hay, 4 Sept. 1833, in Folayan, *Tripoli during the Reign of Yusuf Pasha Qaramanli*, 153.

Chapter 8

1 TNA, FO 76/13, Maitland to Burghersh 31 Jan. 1819, and Warrington to Bathurst, 15 Apr. 1819; TNA, FO 76/14, Warrington to Bathurst, 17 July 1820, in ElGaddari, *Letters and Reports*, 170–1; TNA, FO 76/18, Warrington to Wilmot, 14 Dec. 1820; TNA, FO 76/15, Warrington to Burghersh, 20 Apr. 1821; and TNA, FO 76/20, Warrington to Bathurst, 19 Feb. 1826, in ElGaddari, *Letters and Reports*, 241.
2 TNA, FO 8/12, Hay to Hill, 12 Apr. 1826.
3 Kirk-Greene, 'Towards a History', 108.

BIBLIOGRAPHY

Primary sources

Manuscript

The National Archives, London (TNA)
War and Colonial Department, FO 8:

1–14: General Correspondence before 1906, Barbary States.

Foreign Office and Predecessors: Political and Other Departments, FO 76:

5–39: General Correspondence before 1906, Tripoli Series I and II.

Foreign Office and Foreign and Commonwealth Office: Protocols of Treaties, FO 93:

141: Treaties and agreements with Tripoli.

Foreign Office and Predecessors: Political and Other Departments: Miscellanea, Series I, FO 95:

1/3: Despatches to consuls in the Barbary States.
9/3: Supplementary correspondence.

Foreign Office: Political and Other Departments: General Correspondence before 1906, Tripoli, Series II, FO 101:

6: Case of Captain James Perkins Chatten; *La Fortuna*.

Foreign Office and Predecessor: Consulate, Tripoli, Libya, FO 160:

35–55: General Correspondence and Letter Books.

Foreign Office and Diplomatic Service Administration Office: Chief Clerk's Department and successors: Records, FO 366:

329: Register of Service.
542: Establishment: Orders in Council.

543: Journeys: Outfits: Correspondence, etc.
770: Journeys: Expenses of: Regulations and Miscellaneous Correspondence, etc.

War and Colonial Department and Colonial Office, CO 161:

10–11: Malta, Sessional Papers: Council of Government.

Colonial Office Records, Mediterranean Despatches and Entry Books of Correspondence, etc., CO 173:

5: Précis of in-letters from Tangier, Algiers, Tunis, Tripoli, Gibraltar and Malta.

Colonial Office and predecessors: Confidential General and Confidential Original Correspondence, CO 537:

152: Mohamed Hassuna D'Ghies's petition to the House of Commons. Remarks, with appendix, 1834.

Court of Chancery Records, C 13:

83/31: *Templeman v. Thornhill*. Bill and five answers, 1807.
2101/9: *Templeman v. Warrington*. Examination, 1810.

Home Office Records, HO 46:

16/112: Memorial of Simon Lucas to Grenville, 20 Aug. 1790.

Probate Records, PRO 11:

1414/268: Will of Simon Lucas, 25 Sept. 1804.
1609/238: Will of William Wass Langford, 18 Oct. 1818.
1999/237: Will of Hanmer George Warrington, 22 May 1844.

Maps and Plans, MFQ 1:

102: Watercolour of Consul Hanmer Warrington's country house near Tripoli, 1820.

Gibraltar Government Archives, Gibraltar

Letters to Consuls and Ambassadors: Tripoli, Tunis and Algiers, 1769–97.
Letters from Consuls: Malaga, 1773–76; Barbary, 1776; Tunis and Tripoli, 1765–74; Algiers, 1769–72.

Bodleian Library, Oxford

Correspondence and papers of Francis Werry, Consul at Smyrna, and his son Francis Peter, Diplomat, c.1800–30, MS. Eng. hist. c. 1032, fols 1–230 and MS. Eng. hist. b. 238, fols 1–185.

British Library, London

Admiralty Charts, MP17.0000145303, Smyth, Capt. W. H. 'Plan of the Harbour of Tripoli', 1826 and 1835.
Heytesbury Papers, Add. MSS. 41512.

The School of Oriental and African Studies, London

Bovill, E. W., Notebooks and files. MS. 28253.

University College London, London

Bentham MSS, Box 24.

Contemporary Works (to 1846)

African Society [Association], *The Journal of Frederick Horneman's Travels, from Cairo to Murzouk, the Capital of the Kingdom of Fezzan, in Africa in the Years 1797–8*. London: Bulmer, 1802.
Aravantinos, P., Ιστορία Αλή πασά του Τεπελενλή, Εκ του Τυπογραφείου των Καταστημάτων Σπυρίδωνος Κουσουλίνος. Athens, 1895.
Betham, W., *The Baronetage of England: Volume 5*. London: Warde & Betham,1805.
Blacquiere, E., *Letters from the Mediterranean; Containing a Civil and Political Account of Sicily, Tripoli, Tunis, and Malta: Volumes 1–2*. London: Henry Colburn, 1813.
Bowring, J. (ed.), *The Works Of Jeremy Bentham: Volume 1: Principles of Morals and Legislation, Fragment on Government, Civil Code, Penal Law*. London: Simpkin, Marshall, 1843.
Caillié, R., *Journal D'un Voyage á Tembouctou et á Jenné Dans l'Afrique Central, Volumes 1–3*. Paris: à l'Imprimerie royal, 1830.
Comstock, J. L. (ed.), *History of the Greek Revolution: Compiled from Official Documents of the Greek Government*. New York: William W. Reed, 1828.
Della Cella, P., *Narrative of an Expedition from Tripoli in Barbary, to the Western Frontier of Egypt, in 1817, by the Bey of Tripoli*. Translated from Italian by A. Aufrer. London: John and Arthur Arch, 1822.
Denham, D., H. Clapperton and W. Oudney, *Narrative of Travels and Discoveries in Northern and Central Africa in the Years 1822, 1823, and 1824, Volumes 1–2*, 3rd edn. London: John Murray, 1828.
D'Ghies, H., 'A Letter Addressed to James Scarlett, Esq. M.P. and Member of the African Institution on the Abolition of the Slave Trade'. Translated from French by Dr Kelly. Haymarket: J. Brethell, 1822.

Efendi, I. M., *Mémoires sur la Grèce et l'Albanie Pedant le Gouvernement d'Ali-Pacha*, 2nd edn. Paris: D'Auguste Berthelemy, 1828.

Gavin, R. J., *Aden under British Rule 1839–1867*. London: C. Hurst, 1975.

Greenhow, R., *The History and Present Condition of Tripoli, with Some Accounts of the Other Barbary States: Originally Published in the 'Southern Literary Messenger'*. Richmond, NJ: T.W. White, 1835.

Grosvenor, R., *Extracts from the Journal of Lord R. Grosvenor: Being an Account of His Visit to the Barbary Regencies in the Spring of 1830*. London: Darf, 1986.

Hallett, R., *Records of the African Association, 1788–1831* (RGS: Edinburgh 1964), n.l.

Hertslet, L. (ed.), *A Complete Collection of the Treaties and Conventions at Present Subsisting Between Great Britain and Foreign Powers*. Volumes 1 and 2. Whitehall, London: T. Egerton, 1820.

Jackson, G. A., *Algiers: Being a Complete Picture of the Barbary States; Their Government, Laws, Religion, and Natural Productions; and Containing a Sketch of Their Various Revolutions, a Description of the Domestic Manners and Customs of the Moors, Arabs, and Turks*. London: R. Edwards, 1817.

Jackson, J., *Reflections on the Commerce of the Mediterranean*. London: W. Clarke, 1804.

L. J. E. G. (ed.), *Notice Biographique sur le Chevalier Jacques Gråberg de Hemsö*. Florence: Pezzati, 1831.

Lyon, G. F., *A Narrative of Travels in Northern Africa in the Years 1818, 19, and 1820; Accompanied by Geographical Notices of the Sudan, and of the Course of the Niger*. London: John Murray, 1821.

Marshall, J., *Royal Naval Biography; or, Memoirs of the Services of the All the Flag-Officers, Superannuated Rear-Admirals, Retired-Captains, Post-Captains, and Commanders, Whose Names Appeared on the Admiralty List of Sea-Officers at the Commencement of the Year 1823, or Who Have since Been Promoted*. Volume 3, part 1. London: Longman, Rees, Orme, Brown, and Green, 1831.

Noah, M. M., *Travels in England, France and the Barbary States in the Year 1813–14 and 15*. London: John Miller, 1819.

Pieri, M. P. C. (ed.), *Compendio della storia del Risorgimento della Grecia dal 1740 al 1824: Volume 1*. Legros: Marazzani, 1858.

Pinkerton, J. (ed.), *A General Collection of the Best and Most Interesting Voyages and Travels in All Parts of the World; Many of Which Are Now First Translated into English: Digested on a New Plan*, Volume 10. London: Longman, Hurst, Rees, Orme, and Brown; and Cadell and Davies, 1811.

Purdey, J. (ed.), *The New Sailing Directory for the Strait of Gibraltar and the Western Division of the Mediterranean Sea: Comprehending the Coasts of Spain, France, and Italy, from Cape Trafalgar to Cape Spartivento; the Balearic Isles, Corsica, Sardinia, Sicily, and the Maltese Islands; with the African Coast, from Tangier to Tripoli*. London: R. H. Laurie, 1832.

Richardson, J., 'Reports on the Commerce of Northern Africa', in *Bristol Selected Pamphlets*, 1846. Bristol: University of Bristol Library, 2010.

Salamé, A. V., *Narrative of the Expedition to Algiers, in the Year 1816, under the Command of the Right Honorable Admiral Viscount Exmouth*. London: John Murray, 1819.

Smyth, W. H., *Memoir Descriptive of the Resources, Inhabitants, and Hydrography of Sicily and Its Islands*. London: John Murray, 1824.

Tully, Miss. (ed.), *Letters Written during a Ten Year's Residence at the Court of Tripoli; Published from the Originals in the Possession of the Family of the Late Richard Tully, Esq*. 3rd edn. London: Cox and Baylis, 1819.

Warrington, G. H., 'Extract from *A Short Account of Tripoli in the West*', *Journal of the Royal Geographical Society of London*, 14 (1844): 106.
Zoological Society, *Reports of the Council and Auditors of the Zoological Society of London*. London: Mills, Jowett, and Mills, 1833.

Contemporary Journals, Serials and Newspapers (to 1846)

The Aberdeen Journal
The Annual Register
Asiatic Annual Register
The Athenaeum Journal
Blackwood's Edinburgh Magazine
The Caledonian Mercury
Cobbett's Annual Register
Freeman's Journal and Daily Commercial Advertiser
The Galignani's Messenger
Gazzetta del Governo di Malta
The Gentleman's Magazine
Jackson's Oxford Journal
The Literary Panorama and National Register
The London Gazette
The London Quarterly Review
The Monthly Magazine
The Morning Chronicle
The Morning Post
Museum of Foreign Literature and Science
The Royal Cornwall Gazette
Southern Literary Messenger
St. James's Chronicle
The Standard Magazine.
The Sydney Herald
The Times
The Westminster Review
Whitehall Evening Post

Proceedings, etc., of Governments and Other Bodies

Foreign and Commonwealth Office Collection, *A View of the Relative State of Great Britain and France, at the Commencement of the Year 1796*. London: 1796.
Foreign Office, *British Foreign and State Papers, 1812–1814*. Volume 1, part 1. London: James Ridgway, 1841.
House of Commons, *Reports from the Committees: Volume 2. Report from the Committee Appointed to Inquire into the Consular Departments*. London: 1835.
House of Lords Sessional Papers: *Report from the Select Committee (of the House of Commons) on Consular Establishment; together with the Minutes of Evidence, and Appendix*. Volume 26 (22 August 1835), 1–204.

Royal Kalender; and Court and City Register. London: Longman, Rees, Orme, Brown, and Green, 1795 to 1835.

Unpublished Theses

Altaleb, Amal M., 'The Social and Economic History of Slavery in Libya (1800–1950)'. PhD thesis. University of Manchester, 2015.
El-Nagar, O. A. R., 'West Africa and the Muslim Pilgrimage: An Historical Study with Special Reference to the Nineteenth Century'. PhD thesis. School of Oriental and African Studies, University of London, 1969.
Lafi, N., 'Tripoli de Barbarie, 1795–1911: Genese et perennite de l'institution municipale'. PhD thesis. Université de Provence-Aix-Marseille 1, 1999.
Meriwether, M. L., 'The Notable Families of Aleppo, 1770–1830: Networks and Social Structure'. PhD thesis. University of Pennsylvania, 1981.
Musteen, J. R., 'Becoming Nelson's Refuge and Wellington's Rock: The Ascendency of Gibraltar during the Age of Napoleon (1793–1815)'. PhD thesis. Florida State University, 2005.
Paschalidi, M., 'Constructing Ionian Identities: The Ionian Islands in British Official Discourses; 1815–1864'. PhD thesis. University College London, 2009.
Russell, I. S., 'The Later History of the Levant Company, 1735–1825'. PhD thesis. University of Manchester, 1935.

Secondary works (after 1846)

Abou-el-Haj, R. A., 'The Social Uses of the Past: Recent Arab Historiography of Ottoman Rule', *International Journal of Middle East Studies*, 14, 2 (1982): 185–201.
Abou-el-Haj, R. A., 'An Agenda for Research in History: The History of Libya between the Sixteenth and Nineteenth Centuries', *International Journal of Middle East Studies*, 15, 3 (1983): 305–19.
Abu-Lughod, J. L., *Before European Hegemony: The World System AD 1250–1350*. Oxford: Oxford University Press, 1991.
Abulafia, D., *The Great Sea: A Human History of the Mediterranean*. London: Allen Lane, 2011.
Abulafia, D., 'Mediterranean History as Global History', *History and Theory*, 50, 2 (2011): 220–8.
Abun-Nasr, J. M., 'The Beylicate in Seventeenth-Century Tunisia', *International Journal of Middle East Studies*, 6, 1 (1975): 70–93.
Abun-Nasr, J. M., *A History of the Maghrib*, 2nd edition. Cambridge: Cambridge University Press, 1975.
Akinjogbin, I. A., 'Archibald Dalzel: Slave Trader and Historian of Dahomey', *Journal of African History*, 7, 1 (1966): 67–78.
Akyeampong, E. K., and H. L. Gates Jr. (eds), *Dictionary of African Biography: Volume 1: ABACH-BRAND*. Oxford: Oxford University Press, 2012, 371–2.
Anderson, L., 'Nineteenth-Century Reform in Ottoman Libya', *International Journal of Middle East Studies*, 16, 3 (1984): 325–48.
Anderson, M. S., *The Eastern Question, 1774–1923: A Study in International Relations*. London: Macmillan, 1966.

Anderson, M. S., 'Great Britain and the Barbary States in the Eighteenth Century', *Historical Research*, 29, 79 (1956): 87–107.
Anderson, M. S., *The Rise of Modern Diplomacy*. London: Longman, 1993.
Anderson, R. C., *Naval Wars in the Levant, 1559–1853*. Liverpool: Liverpool University Press, 1952.
Anderson, S. P., *An English Consul in Turkey: Paul Rycaut at Smyrna 1667–1678*. Oxford: Clarendon Press, 1989.
Anstey, R. T., 'Capitalism and Slavery: A Critique', *Economic History Review*, 21, 2 (1968): 307–20.
Arnold, D., *Colonizing the Body: State Medicine and Epidemic Disease in Nineteenth-Century India*. Berkeley: University of California Press, 1993.
Arrighi, G., B. J. Silver and I. Ahmad, *Chaos and Governance in the Modern World System*. Minneapolis: University of Minnesota Press, 1999.
Arthur, B., *How Britain Won the War of 1812: The Royal Navy's Blockades of the United States, 1812–1815*. Woodbridge: Boydell Press, 2011.
Baer, G., 'Slavery in Nineteenth Century Egypt', *Journal of African History*, 8, 3 (1967): 417–41.
Baghdiantz McCabe, I., G. Harlaftis and I. Pepelasis Minoglou (eds), *Diaspora Entrepreneurial Networks, Four Centuries of History*. Oxford: Berg, 2005.
Ballantyne, T., 'The Changing Shape of the Modern British Empire and Its Historiography', *Historical Journal*, 53, 2 (2010): 429–52.
Baring, E., *Political and Literary Essays, 1908–1913*. London: Macmillan, 1913.
Bartlett, C. J., *Great Britain and Sea Power, 1815–1853*. Oxford: Clarendon Press, 1963.
Bayly, C. A., *The Birth of the Modern World, 1780–1914: Global Connections and Comparisons*. London: Wiley-Blackwell, 2004.
Bayly, C. A., *Empire and Information: Intelligence Gathering and Social Communication in India, 1780–1880*. Cambridge: Cambridge University Press, 1996.
Bayly, C. A., *Imperial Meridian: the British Empire and the World, 1780–1830*. Harlow: Longman, 1989.
Bayly, C. A., S. Beckert, M. Connelly, I. Hofmeyr, W. Kozol and P. Seed, 'AHR Conversation: On Transnational History', *American Historical Review*, 111, 5 (2006): 1441–64.
Barua, P. P., 'Maritime Trade, Seapower, and the Anglo-Mysore Wars, 1767–1799', *Historian*, 73, 1 (2011): 22–40.
Beaton, R., and D. Ricks (eds), *The Making of Modern Greece: Nationalism, Romanticism & the Uses of the Past (1797–1896)*. London: Routledge, 2009.
Bennison, A. K., 'Liminal States: Morocco and the Iberian Frontier between the Twelfth and Nineteenth Centuries', *Journal of North African Studies*, 6, 1 (2001): 11–28.
Bennison, K., 'Dynamics of Rule and Opposition in Nineteenth Century North Africa', *Journal of North African Studies*, 1, 1 (1996): 1–24.
Ben Srhir, K., *Britain and Morocco During the Embassy of John Drummond Hay*. London: RoutledgeCurzon, 2004.
Berridge, G. R., *British Diplomacy in Turkey, 1583 to the Present: A Study in the Evolution of the Resident Embassy*. Leiden: Martinus Nijhoff, 2009.
Berridge, G. R., 'English Dragomans and Oriental Secretaries: the Early Nineteenth Century Origins of the Anglicization of the British Embassy Drogmanat in Constantinople', *Diplomacy & Statecraft*, 14, 4 (2003): 137–52.
Berridge, G. R., *Gerald Fitzmaurice (1865–1939), Chief Dragoman of the British Embassy in Turkey*. Leiden: Martinus Nijhoff, 2007.

Bertram, A., *The Colonial Service*. Cambridge: Cambridge University Press, 1930.
Bhabha, H. K., *The Location of Culture*. London: Routledge, 2004.
Bickers, R. (ed.), *Settlers and Expatriates: Britons over the Seas*. Oxford: Oxford University Press, 2010.
Bindoff, S. T., *Trade, Empire and British Foreign Policy, 1689-1815: Politics of a Commercial State*. London: Taylor & Francis, 2007.
Bindoff, S. T., 'The Unreformed Diplomatic Service, 1812-60': (The Alexander Prize Essay), *Transactions of the Royal Historical Society*, 18 (1935): 143.
Bindoff, S. T., and C. K. Webster (eds), *British Diplomatic Representatives, 1789-1852*. Camden Third Series. London: Royal Historical Society, 1934.
Birks, J. S., 'The Mecca Pilgrimage by West African Pastoral Nomads', *Journal of Modern African Studies*, 15, 1 (1977): 47-58.
Black, J., *Britain as a Military Power, 1688-1815*. Abingdon, Oxon: Routledge, 2014.
Blanning, T. W. C., *The Culture of Power and the Power of Culture*. Oxford: Oxford University Press, 2003.
Blanning, T. W. C., *The French Revolutionary Wars, 1787-1802*. London: Arnold, 1996.
Blondy, A., 'The Barbary Regencies and Corsair Activity in the Mediterranean from the Sixteenth to the Nineteenth Century', *Journal of Mediterranean Studies*, 12, 2 (2002): 241-8.
Blyth, R. J., *The Empire of the Raj: Eastern Africa and the Middle East, 1850-1947*. Basingstoke: Palgrave Macmillan, 2003.
Boahen, A. A., *Britain, Sahara and Western Sudan, 1788-1861*. Oxford: Oxford University Press, 1964.
Boahen, A. A., 'The Caravan Trade in the Nineteenth Century', *Journal of African History*, 3, 2 (1962): 349-59.
van den Boogert, M. H., *Capitulations and the Ottoman Legal System: Qadis, Consuls and Beraths in the 18th Century*. Leiden: Brill, 2005.
Bottari, S., 'Geopolitical and Commercial Interests in the Mediterranean Sea. The Reports of Angelo Rutter, English Vice-Consul in Malta (1769-1771)', *Journal of Mediterranean Studies*, 12, 2 (2002): 249-57.
Bowen, H. V., *The Business of Empire: The East India Company and Imperial Britain, 1756-1833*. Cambridge: Cambridge University Press, 2008.
Bowen, H. V., 'Sinews of Trade and Empire: the Supply of Commodity Exports to the East India Company during the Late Eighteenth Century', *Economic History Review*, 55, 3 (2002): 466-86.
Bovill, E. W., *Caravans of the Old Sahara*. London: Oxford University Press, 1933.
Bovill, E. W., 'Colonel Warrington', *Geographical Journal*, 131, 2 (1965): 161-6.
Bovill, E. W., *The Golden Trade of the Moors*. London: Oxford University Press, 1958.
Bovill, E. W., 'Mohammed El Maghili', *African Affairs*, 34, 134 (1935): 27-30.
Bovill, E. W., 'The Moorish Invasion of the Sudan', *African Affairs*, 26, 103 (1927): 245-62.
Boyce, G., and R. Gorski (eds), *Resources and Infrastrcutures in the Maritime Economy, 1500-2000*. St. Johns, Newfoundland: International Maritime Economic History Association, 2002.
Braudel, F., *The Mediterranean and the Mediterranean World in the Age of Philip II*, Volumes 1-2. Translated from French by S. Reynolds, Fontana: London, 1975.
Brett, M., 'Great Britain and Southern Morocco in the Nineteenth Century', *Journal of North African Studies*, 2, 2 (1997): 1-10.

Brett, M., 'Problems in the Interpretation of the History of the Maghrib in the Light of Some Recent Publications', *Journal of African History*, 13, 3 (1972): 489–506.
Broers, M., *Napoleon: Soldier of Destiny*. London: Faber & Faber, 2014.
Brown, C. L., *Imperial Legacy: The Ottoman Empire and Early Modern Europe*. Cambridge: Cambridge University Press, 1996.
Brown, C. L., *Tunisia under Ahmad Bey*. Princeton, NJ: Princeton University Press, 1974.
Brown, D., 'Palmerston and Anglo–French Relations, 1846–1865', *Diplomacy and Statecraft*, 17, 4 (2006): 675–92.
Brown, J. A. O. C., 'Anglo-Moroccan Relations and the Embassy of Ahmad Qardanash, 1706–1708', *Historical Journal*, 51, 3 (2008): 599–620.
Brown, J. A. O. C., *Crossing the Strait: Morocco, Gibraltar and Great Britain in the 18th and 19th Centuries*. Leiden: Brill, 2012.
Brown, K. and J. Passon (eds), *Across the Sahara: Tracks, Trade and Cross-Cultural Exchange in Libya*. Cham, Switzerland: Springer International, 2020.
Brown, M. (ed.), *Informal Empire in Latin America: Culture, Commerce and Capital*. Oxford: Blackwell [for the] Society for Latin American Studies, 2008.
Bullard, R., *Britain and the Middle East: From the Earliest Times to 1950*. London: Hutchinson's University Library, 1951.
Burke, A., *A Genealogical and Heraldic Dictionary of the Peerage and Baronetage of the British Empire*. 26th edition. London: Henry Colburn, 1864.
Burke, E., 'The Mediterranean before Colonialism: Fragments from the Life of 'Ali bin 'Uthman al-Hammi in the Late Eighteenth and Nineteenth Centuries', *Journal of North African Studies*, 6, 1 (2001): 129–42.
Burke, E., and Prochaska, D. 'Rethinking the Historical Genealogy of Orientalism', *History and Anthropology*, 18, 2 (2007): 135–51.
Burton, A., *Archive Stories: Facts, Fictions and the Writing of History*. Durham, NC: Duke University Press, 2005.
Burton, A. (ed.), *After the Imperial Turn: Thinking with and through the Nation*. Durham. NC: Duke University Press, 2004.
Byrd, P. 'Regional and Functional Specialisation in the British Consular Service', *Journal of Contemporary History*, 7, 1 (1972): 127–45.
Cain, P. J., and A. G. Hopkins, *British Imperialism, 1688–2000*, 2nd edn. Harlow: Longman, 2001.
Cain, P. J., and A. G. Hopkins, 'Gentlemanly Capitalism and British Expansion Overseas I. The Old Colonial System, 1688–1850', *Economic History Review*, 39, 4 (1986): 501–25.
Cain, P. J., and A. G. Hopkins, 'The Political Economy of British Expansion Overseas, 1750–1914', *Economic History Review*, 33, 4 (1980): 463–90.
Calaresu, M., F. de Vivo and J.-P. Rubiés (eds), *Exploring Cultural History: Essays in Honour of Peter Burke*. Farnham, Surrey: Ashgate, 2010.
Cannadine, D., *Ornamentalism*. Oxford: Oxford University Press, 2002.
Candido, M. P., 'Sub-Saharan Africa: Jihads, Slave Trade and Early Colonialism in the Long Eighteenth Century', *Journal for Eighteenth-Century Studies*, 34, 4 (2011): 543–50.
Canning, S., *The Eastern Question, by the Late Viscount Stratford De Redcliffe*. London: John Murray, 1881.
Carlin, C., *William Kirkpatrick of Málaga, 1764–1837: Consul, Négociant and Entrepreneur, and Grandfather of the Empress Eugénie*. Glasgow: Graimsay Press, 2011.
Chandler, D., *The Campaigns of Napoleon*. London: Weidenfeld & Nicolson, 1998.

Chater, K., 'La Méditerranée vue du Maghreb au XVIIIe siècle', *Maghreb Review*, 33, 2-3 (2008): 151-8.
Chessell, C. I., 'Britain's Ionian Consul: Spiridion Foresti and Intelligence Collection (1793-1805)', *Journal of Mediterranean Studies*, 16, 1-2 (2006): 45-61.
Choueiri, Y. M., *A Companion to the History of the Middle East*. London: Wiley-Blackwell, 2008.
Clammer, J., *Beyond the New Economic Anthropology*. Basingstoke: Macmillan, 1987.
Clancy-Smith, J. A., *Mediterraneans: North Africa and Europe in an Age of Migration, c.1800-1900*. Berkeley: University of California Press, 2010.
Clancy-Smith, J. A., *Rebel and Saint: Muslim Notables, Populist Protest, Colonial Encounters (Algeria and Tunisia, 1800-1904)*. Berkeley: University of California Press, 1994.
Clark, P., *British Clubs and Societies, 1580-1800: The Origin of an Associational World*. Oxford: Oxford University Press, 2000.
Clayton, G. D., *Britain and the Eastern Question: Missolonghi to Gallipoli*. London: University of London Press, 1971.
Coats, A., 'The British Navy's Victualling Board, 1793-1815: Management Competence and Incompetence', *Economic History Review*, 64, 3 (2011): 1036-8.
Cole, J. R., *Napoleon's Egypt: Invading the Middle East*. New York: Palgrave Macmillan, 2007.
Collar, A., 'Network Theory and Religious Innovation', *Mediterranean Historical Review*, 22, 1 (2007): 149-62.
Coller, I., *Arab France: Islam and the Making of Modern Europe, 1798-1831*. Berkeley: University of California Press, 2011.
Colley, L., 'Going Native, Telling Tales: Captivity, Collaborations and Empire', *Past & Present*, 168 (2011): 170-93.
Collins, R., 'Bagirmi, Wadai and Darfur', in K. Shillington (ed.), *Encyclopedia of African History, A-G*. New York: Fitzroy Dearborn, 2005, 202-5.
Cooper, F., and A. L. Stoler (eds), *Tensions of Empire: Colonial Cultures in a Bourgeois World*. California: University of California Press, 1997.
Crawley, C. W., *The Question of Greek Independence: A Study of British Policy in the Near East 1821-1833*. Cambridge: Cambridge University Press, 1930.
Crouzet, F., 'Toward an Export Economy: British Exports during the Industrial Revolution', *Explorations in Economic History*, 17 (1980): 48-93.
Cunningham, A. B. (ed.), *The Early Correspondence of Richard Wood, 1831-1841*. Camden Fourth Series, Volume 3. London: The Royal Historical Society, 1966.
Cunningham Wood, J., 'JA Hobson and British Imperialism', *American Journal of Economics and Sociology*, 42, 4 (1983): 483-500.
Cummins, D. *The Wahhabi Mission and Saudi Arabia*. London: I.B. Tauris, 2009.
Curtin, P. D., *The Atlantic Slave Trade: A Census*. Madison: University of Wisconsin Press, 1969.
Curtin, P. D., *Cross-Cultural Trade in World History*. Cambridge: Cambridge University Press, 1984.
Curtin, P. D., *Death by Migration: Europe's Encounter with the Tropical World in the Nineteenth Century*. Cambridge: Cambridge University Press, 1989.
Curtin, P. D., *The Image of Africa: British Ideas and Action, 1780-1850*. Madison: University of Wisconsin Press, 1964.
Curto, J. C., and R. Soulodre-La France (eds), *Africa and the Americas: Interconnections During the Slave Trade*. Trenton, NJ: Africa World Press, 2005.

Dakhlia, J. *Lingua Franca: Histoire d'une langue métisse en Méditerranée*. Arles: Actes Sud, 2008.
Daloz, J-P., *The Sociology of Élite Distinction: From Theoretical to Comparative Perspectives*. Basingstoke: Palgrave Macmillan, 2012.
Daly, M. W. (ed.), *The Cambridge History of Egypt: Volume 2: Modern Egypt from 1517 to the End of the Twentieth Century*. Cambridge: Cambridge University Press, 2008.
Dalzel, A., (ed.), *The History of Dahomy, an Inland Kingdom of Africa, Compiled from Authentic Memoirs*. London: T. Spilsbury, 1793.
D'Andrea, D., 'Gould Francis Leckie and the "insular strategy" of Great Britain in the Mediterranean, 1800–1815', *Journal of Mediterranean Studies*, 16, 1–2 (2006): 79–89.
D'Angelo, M., 'In the "English" Mediterranean (1511–1815)', *Journal of Mediterranean Studies*, 12, 2 (2002): 271–85.
Darwin, J., *After Tamerlane: The Rise and Fall of Global Empires, 1400–2000*. London: Penguin, 2008.
Darwin, J., *The Empire Project: The Rise and Fall of the British World-System, 1830–1970*. Cambridge: Cambridge University Press, 2011.
Darwin, J., 'Imperialism and the Victorians: The Dynamics of Territorial Expansion', *English Historical Review*, 112, 447 (1997): 614–42.
Davey, J., 'Supplied by the Enemy: the Royal Navy and the British Consular Service in the Baltic, 1808–12', *Historical Research*, 85, 228 (2012): 265–83.
Dearden, S., *A Nest of Corsairs: The Fighting Karamanlis of the Barbary Coast*. London: John Murray, 1976.
Dearden, S. (ed.), *Tully's Ten Years' Residence at the Court of Tripoli: Reigning Bashaw, Moors, Arabs and Turks*. London: Arthur Baker, 1957.
Deringil, S., *The Well-Protected Domains: Ideology of Power in the Ottoman Empire 1876–1909*. London: I.B. Tauris, 2011.
Devereux Coates, P., *The China Consuls: British Consular Officers in China, 1843–1943*. Oxford: Oxford University Press, 1988.
Dodwell, H., *The Founder of Modern Egypt – A Study of Muhammad 'Ali*. Cambridge: Cambridge University Press, 1931, reprinted 1977.
Driessen, H., 'Mediterranean Port Cities: Cosmopolitanism Reconsidered', *History and Anthropology*, 16, 1 (2005): 129–41.
Driver, F., 'Distance and Disturbance: Travel, Exploration and Knowledge in the Nineteenth Century', *Transactions of the Royal Historical Society*, 14 (2004): 73–92.
Driver, F., *Geography Militant: Cultures of Exploration and Empire*. Oxford: Blackwell, 2001.
Dupuis, H. L., *The Holy Places: A Narrative of Two Years Residence in Jerusalem and Palestine, Volumes 1–2*. London: Hurst and Blackett, 1856.
Duffy, M., 'World-Wide War and British Expansion, 1793–1815', in P. J. Marshall (ed.), *The Oxford History of the British Empire: Volume 2: The Eighteenth Century*. Oxford: Oxford University Press, 1998, 184–207.
Duffy, M., 'British Naval Intelligence and Bonaparte's Egyptian Expedition of 1798', *Mariner's Mirror*, 84 (1998): 278–90.
Dykstra, D., 'The French Occupation of Egypt', in M. W. Daly (ed.), *The Cambridge History of Egypt: Volume 2: Modern Egypt from 1517 to the End of the Twentieth Century*. Cambridge: Cambridge University Press, 2008, 133–8.
Eden, A., *Full Circle: The Memoirs of Sir Anthony Eden*. London: Cassell, 1960, 424.

Edwards, E. J., *A Concise History of Small-Pox and Vaccination in Europe*. London: H. K. Lewis, 1902.
Edwards, W., *Notes on British History: Part IV: 1793–1901*. London: Rivingtons, 1958.
Eldridge, C. C. (ed.), *British Imperialism in the Nineteenth Century*. New York: St. Martin's Press, 1984.
ElGaddari, S., 'Hanmer Warrington and Imperial Intelligence-Gathering in Tripoli, 1814–46', in O. Wright and M. Suonpää (eds), *Diplomacy and Intelligence in the Nineteenth-Century Mediterranean World*. London: Bloomsbury Academic, 2019.
ElGaddari, S., 'His Majesty's Agents: The British Consul at Tripoli, 1795–1832', *Journal of Imperial and Commonwealth History*, 43, 5 (2015): 770–86.
ElGaddari, S., *The Letters and Reports of British Consular and Diplomatic Agents in Tripoli, 1793–1832*. Camden Series. London: The Royal Historical Society and Cambridge University Press, 2020.
El-Hasnawi, H. W., *Fazzan under the Rule of the Awlad Muhammad: A Study in Political, Economic, Social, and Intellectual History*. Sabha, Libya: Centre for African Researches and Studies, 1990.
El Mansour, M., 'Ceuta in Anglo-Moroccan Relations (1806–1815)', *Maghreb Review*, 4, 4–6 (1979): 129–33.
Eltis, D., 'The Export of Slaves from Africa, 1821–1843', *Journal of Economic History*, 37, 2 (1977): 409–33.
Eltis, D., and S. L. Engerman (eds), *The Cambridge World History of Slavery: Volume 3: AD 1420–AD 1804*. Cambridge: Cambridge University Press, 2011.
Erzini, N., 'Hal yaslah li-taqansut (Is He Suitable for Consulship?): The Moroccan Consuls in Gibraltar during the Nineteenth Century', *Journal of North African Studies*, 12, 4 (2007): 517–29.
Erzini, N., *Moroccan-British Diplomatic and Commercial Relations in the Early 18th Century: The Abortive Embassy to Meknes in 1718*. Durham: Institute of Middle Eastern and Islamic Studies, University of Durham, 2002.
Esdaile, C. J., *The Wars of Napoleon*. London: Routledge, 2019.
Ewald, J. J., *Soldiers, Traders and Slaves: State Formation and Economic Transformation in the Greater Nile Valley, 1700–1885*. Madison: University of Wisconsin Press, 1990.
Fabunmi, L. A., *The Sudan in Anglo-Egyptian Relations, A Case Study in Power Politics, 1800–1956*. London: Oxford University Press, 1961.
Fage, J. D., 'Slavery and the Slave Trade in the Context of West African History', *Journal of African History*, 10, 3 (1969): 393–404.
Fahmy, K., *All the Pasha's Men: Mehmed Ali, His Army and the Making of Modern Egypt*. Cairo: American University in Cairo Press, 2002.
Fahmy, K., 'The Era of Muhammad 'Ali Pasha', in M. W. Daly (ed.), *The Cambridge History of Egypt: Volume 2: Modern Egypt from 1517 to the End of the Twentieth Century*. Cambridge: Cambridge University Press, 2008, 139–79.
Farah, C. E., *The Sultan's Yemen: 19th Century Challenges to Ottoman Rule*. London: I.B. Tauris, 2002.
Faroqhi, S. *The Ottoman Empire and the World around It*. London: I.B. Tauris, 2007.
Féraud, C., and A. Bernard, *Annales Tripolitaines*. Tunis: Librairie Tournier, 1927.
Fieldhouse, D. K., *Economics and Empire*. London: Palgrave Macmillan, 1984.
Fieldhouse, D. K., *The Theory of Capitalist Imperialism*. London: Longman, 1967.
Fisher, G., *Barbary Legend: Trade and Piracy in North Africa, 1415–1830*. Oxford: Clarendon Press, 1957.
Fisher, H. J., *Slavery in the History of Muslim Black Africa*. London: Hurst, 2001.

Fleming, P., *The Siege at Peking*. Oxford: Oxford University Press, 1984.
Flint, J. E., *The Cambridge History of Africa: Volume 5: From 1790 to 1870*. Cambridge: Cambridge University Press, 1977.
Folayan, K., *Tripoli during the Reign of Yusuf Pasha Qaramanli*. Ile-Ife: University of Ife Press, 1979.
Folayan, K., 'Tripoli-Bornu Political Relations, 1817–1825', *Journal of the Historical Society of Nigeria*, 5, 4 (1971): 463–71.
Foucault, M., *The Archaeology of Knowledge*. London: Routledge, 2002.
Frangakis-Syrett, E., 'Networks of Friendship, Networks of Kinship: Eighteenth Century Levant Merchants', *Eurasian Studies*, 1–2 (2002): 189–212.
Frangakis-Syrett, E., *Trade and Money: The Ottoman Economy in the Eighteenth and Early Nineteenth Centuries*. Istanbul: Isis Press, 2007.
Freitag, S., and P. Wende (eds), *British Envoys to Germany 1816–1866*, Volumes 1–2. Camden Fifth Series, Volume 15. Cambridge: Cambridge University Press and The Royal Historical Society, 2000.
Fusaro, M. 'Representation in Practice: The Myth of Venice and the British Protectorate in the Ionian Islands (1801–1864)', in M. Calaresu, F. de Vivo and J.-P. Rubiés (eds), *Exploring Cultural History: Essays in Honour of Peter Burke*. Farnham, Surrey: Ashgate, 2010, 309–26.
Fusaro, M., C. Heywood and M.-S. Omri (eds), *Trade and Cultural Exchange in the Early Modern Mediterranean: Braudel's Maritime Legacy*. London: I.B. Tauris, 2009.
Le Gall, M., and K. Perkins (eds), *The Maghrib in Question: Essays in History and Historiography*. Austin: University of Texas Press, 1997.
Gallagher, J., and R. Robinson, 'The Imperialism of Free Trade', *Economic History Review*, 6, 1 (1953): 1–15.
van Gelder, G. J., and E. de Moor (eds), *Middle East and Europe: Encounters and Exchanges. Orientations: A Multidisciplinary Annual of the Dutch Association for Middle Eastern & Islamic Studies*. Rodopi B.V.: Amsterdam, 1992.
Ghislain de Diesbach and Robert Grouvel, *Échec à Bonaparte: Louis-Edmond de Phélippeaux, 1767–1799*. Paris: Perrin, 1979.
Gilbar, G. G., 'The Mysterious Death of a Commercial Agent and the Kārguzār of Mashhad, 1890', *Iran and the Caucasus*, 15, 1–2 (2011): 79–98.
Gilbar, G. G., 'Resistance to Economic Penetration: the Kārguzār and Foreign Firms in Qajar Iran', *International Journal of Middle East Studies*, 43, 1 (2011): 5–23.
de Goey, F., *Consuls and the Institutions of Global Capitalism, 1783–1914*. London: Pickering & Chatto, 2014.
Glaisyer, N., 'Networking: Trade and Exchange in the Eighteenth-Century British Empire', *Historical Journal*, 47, 2 (2004): 451–76.
Gräberg di Hemsö, Jacopo, 'Prospetto del Commercio di Tripoli d'Africa, e delle sue relazioni con quello dell'Italia', *Antologia*, 30 (1827): 3–29.
Graham, G. S., *The Politics of Naval Supremacy: Studies in British Maritime Ascendency*. Cambridge: Cambridge University Press, 1965.
Grainger, J. D., *The British Navy in the Mediterranean*. Woodbridge: Boydell Press, 2017.
Greene, M., 'Beyond the Northern Invasion: The Mediterranean in the Seventeenth Century', *Past & Present*, 174, 1 (2002): 42–71.
Greene, M. (ed.), *Minorities in the Ottoman Empire*. Princeton, NJ: Markus Wiener, 2005.
Guenther, L., 'The British Community of 19th Century Bahia: Public and Private Lives', University of Oxford Centre for Brazilian Studies, Working Paper 32-02, 2004.

Haddad, G. A., 'A Project for the Independence of Egypt, 1801', *Journal of the American Oriental Society*, 90, 2 (1970): 169–83.
Haggerty, S., 'The Life Cycle of a Metropolitan Business Network: Liverpool, 1750–1810', *Explorations in Economic History*, 48, 2 (2011): 189–206.
Haggerty, S., *'Merely for Money?' Business Culture in the British Atlantic, 1715–1815*. Liverpool: Liverpool University Press, 2012.
Haggerty, J., and S. Haggerty, 'Visual Analytics of an Eighteenth-Century Business Network', *Enterprise and Society*, 11, 1 (2009): 1–25.
Hallet, R., 'The European Approach to the Interior of Africa in the Eighteenth Century', *Journal of African History*, 4, 2 (1963): 191–206.
Hallet, R., *The Penetration of Africa: European Enterprise and Exploration Principally in Northern and Western Africa up to 1830: Volume 1: To 1815*. London: Routledge and Kegan Paul, 1965.
Hallet, R. (ed.), *Records of the Africa Association*. London: Nelson, 1964.
Hamilton, A., A. de Groot and M. H. van den Boogert, *Friends and Rivals in the East*. Leiden: Brill, 2000.
Hamilton, C. I. 'Naval Power and Diplomacy in the Nineteenth Century', *Journal of Strategic Studies*, 3, 1 (1980): 74–88.
Hamilton, D. J., *Scotland, the Caribbean and the Atlantic World, 1750–1820*. Manchester: Manchester University Press, 2005.
Hamilton, K., and P. Salmon (eds), *Slavery, Diplomacy and Empire: Britain and the Suppression of the Slave Trade, 1807–1975*. Brighton: Sussex Academic Press, 2009.
Harding, N. B., 'North African Piracy, the Hanovarian Carrying Trade, and the British State, 1728–1828', *Historical Journal*, 43, 1 (2000): 25–47.
Harlaftis, G., and C. Vassallo (eds), *New Directions in Mediterranean History*. St. Johns, Newfoundland: International Maritime Economic History Association, 2004.
Harland-Jacobs, J., *Builders of Empire: Freemasons and British Imperialism, 1717–1927*. Chapel Hill, NC, 2007.
Harlow, B., and M. Carter (eds), *Orientalism: The East as a Career*. London: Blackwell, 1999.
Harlow, V. T., *The Founding of the Second British Empire, 1763–93, Volumes 1–2*. London: Longmans, 1964.
Harris, N. H. (ed.), *The Dispatches and Letters of Vice Admiral Viscount Nelson*. Volume 5. Cambridge: Cambridge University Press, 2011.
Hassan, H. al-Faqih, *Al-Yawmiyat al-Libiyya: 958*–1248h./*1551–1832*. Tripoli: Manchurat Jami'at al-Fatah, Markaz Jihad, 1984.
Hazbun, W., 'Mediterranean Crossings: The Politics of an Interrupted Modernity', *Journal of North African Studies*, 13, 4 (2008): 565–7.
Herold, J. C., *Bonaparte in Egypt*. New York: Harper & Row, 1962.
Heywood, C., 'Fernand Braudel and the Ottomans: the Emergence of an Involvement (1928–50)', *Mediterranean Historical Review*, 23, 2 (2008): 165–84.
Heywood, C., 'The Frontiers of the Ottoman World', *Proceedings of the British Academy*, 156 (2009): 493–508.
Hill, G., and H. Luke, *A History of Cyprus: Volume 4: The Ottoman Province. The British Colony, 1571–1948*. Cambridge: Cambridge University Press, 1952.
Hinde, W., *George Canning*. London: Collins, 1973.
Hobsbawm, E. J., *The Age of Revolution: Europe, 1789–1848*. London: Weidenfeld and Nicolson, 1962.
Hobson, J. A., *Imperialism: A Study*. London: Allen & Unwin, 1948.

Hoek, P., 'Parallel Arc Diagrams: Visualizing Temporal Interactions', *Journal of Social Structure*, 12, 7 (2011): 1–25.
Hoock, H., 'The British State and the Anglo-French Wars over Antiquities, 1798–1858', *Historical Journal*, 50, 1 (2007): 49–72.
Holland, R. *Blue-Water Empire: The British in the Mediterranean since 1800.* London: Penguin, 2013.
Holland Rose, J., A. P. Newton and E. A. Benians (eds), *Cambridge History of the British Empire: Volume 1: The Old Empire from the Beginnings to 1783.* Cambridge: Cambridge University Press, 1929.
Holland Rose, J., A. P. Newton and E. A. Benians (eds), *Cambridge History of the British Empire: Volume 2: The Growth of the New Empire 1783–1870.* Cambridge: Cambridge University Press, 1940.
Hopkins, A. G., *An Economic History of West Africa.* New York: Columbia University Press, 1973.
Hopkins, A. G., 'The New Economic History of Africa', *Journal of African History*, 20, 2 (2009): 155–77.
Hopkins, A. G., 'The Victorians and Africa: A Reconsideration of the Occupation of Egypt, 1882', 27, 2 (1986): 363–91.
Horden, P., and S. Kinoshita (eds), *A Companion to Mediterranean History.* London: Wiley Blackwell, 2014.
Horden, P., and N. Purcell, *The Corrupting Sea: A Study of Mediterranean History.* London: Wiley-Blackwell, 2000.
Horn, D. B., 'The Board of Trade and Consular Reports, 1696–1782', *English Historical Review*, 54, 215 (1939): 476–80.
Horn, D. B., *The British Diplomatic Service 1689–1789.* Oxford: Clarendon Press, 1961.
Horn, D. B., 'The Cost of the Diplomatic Service, 1747–52', *English Historical Review*, 43, 172 (1928): 606–11.
Hourani, A. 'Ottoman Reform and the Politics of Notables', in A. Hourani, P. S. Khoury and M. C. Wilson (eds), *The Modern Middle East.* Berkeley: University of California Press, 1993, 83–110.
Hourani, A., P. S. Khoury and M. C. Wilson (eds), *The Modern Middle East.* Berkeley: University of California Press, 1993.
Huessler, R., *Yesterday's Rulers: The Making of the British Colonial Service.* London: Oxford University Press, 1963.
Hume, L. J., 'Preparations for Civil War in Tripoli in the 1820s: Ali Karamanli, Hassuna D'Ghies and Jeremy Bentham', *Journal of African History*, 21, 3 (1980): 311–22.
Hyam, R., *Britain's Imperial Century, 1815–1914: A Study of Empire and Expansion.* Basingstoke: Palgrave, 2002.
Hyam, R., 'British Imperial Expansion in the Late Eighteenth Century: Review Article', *Historical Journal*, 10, 1 (1967): 113–24.
Hyam, R., *Understanding the British Empire.* Cambridge: Cambridge University Press, 2010.
Inalcik, H., S. Faroqhi, B. McGowan, D. Quataert and Ş. Pamuk (eds), *An Economic and Social History of the Ottoman Empire, 1300–1914.* Cambridge: Cambridge University Press, 1994.
Ingram, E. (ed.), *Anglo-Ottoman Encounters in the Age of Revolution: Collected Essays of Allan Cunningham*, Volumes 1–2. London: Frank Cass, 1993.
Ingram, E., *Empire-Building and Empire-Builders.* London: Frank Cass, 1995.

Ingram, E., 'From Trade to Empire in the Near East: 1: The End of the Spectre of the Overland Trade, 1775–1801', *Middle Eastern Studies*, 14, 1 (1978): 3–21.
Ingram, E., *In Defence of British India: Great Britain in the Middle East, 1775–1842*. London: Frank Cass, 1984.
Ingram, E., 'A Preview of the Great Game in Asia – I: The British Occupation of Perim and Aden in 1799', *Middle Eastern Studies*, 9, 1 (1973): 1–18.
Insoll, T., and B. Lecocq, *The Hajj from West Africa from a Global Historical Perspective (19th and 20th Centuries)*. London: Brill, 2012.
Issawi, C., *An Economic History of the Middle East and North Africa*. New York: Columbia University Press, 1982.
Al-Jabarti, A. R. H., S. Moreh, R. L. Tignor, E. W. Said and L. A. Fauvelet de Bourriene, *Napoleon in Egypt: Al-Jabarti's Chronicle of the French Occupation, 1798*. Princeton, NJ: Markus Wiener, 2004.
Jarrett, M., *The Congress of Vienna and Its Legacy: War and Great Power Diplomacy after Napoleon*. London: I.B. Tauris, 2013.
Jasanoff, M., *Edge of Empire: Conquest and Collecting in the East, 1750–1850*. London: HarperCollins, 2009.
Jeffreys, A. (ed.), *The Indian Army in the First World War: New Perspectives*. Solihull: Helion, 2018.
Jeffries, C., *The History of the Colonial Empire and Its Civil Service*. Cambridge: Cambridge University Press, 1938.
Jeppie, S., and S. Bachir Diagne (eds), *The Meanings of Timbuktu*. Cape Town: Human Sciences Research Council of South Africa Press, 2008.
Johnston, H. A. S., *The Fulani Empire of Sokoto*. London: Oxford University Press, 1967.
Jones, R. A., *The Nineteenth-Century Foreign Office: Administrative History*. London: Weidenfeld and Nicolson, 1971.
Jones, R. A., *The British Diplomatic Service, 1815–1914*. Waterloo, ON: Wilfrid Laurier University Press, 1983.
Keene, C. A., 'American Shipping and Trade, 1798–1820: The Evidence from Leghorn', *Journal of Economic History*, 38, 3 (1978): 681–700.
Kennedy, P., *The Rise and Fall of British Naval Mastery*. London: Allen Lane, 1976.
Khazeni, A., *Tribes and Empire on the Margins of Nineteenth-Century Iran*. Seattle: University of Washington Press, 2010.
Khoo, K. K., *The Western Malay States 1850–1873: The Effects of Commercial Development on Malay Politics*. Kuala Lumpur: Oxford University Press, 1972.
Khoury, P. S. 'The Urban Notables Paradigm Revisited', *Revue du monde musulman et de la Méditerranée*, 55–6 (1990): 215–30.
Kidd, J., *The Churches of Eastern Christendom*. Abingdon: Routledge, 2010.
Killingray, D., M. Lincoln and N. Rigby (eds), *Maritime Empires: British Imperial Maritime Trade in the Nineteenth Century*. Woodbridge: Boydell Press, 2004.
Kirk-Greene, A. H. M., *Britain's Imperial Administrators, 1858–1966*. Basingstoke: Palgrave Macmillan, 2000.
Kirk-Greene, A. H. M., 'The British Consulate at Lake Chad: A Forgotten Treaty with the Sheikh of Bornu', *African Affairs*, 58, 233 (1959): 334–9.
Kirk-Greene, A. H. M., *On Crown Service: A History of HM Colonial and Overseas Civil Services, 1837–1997*. London: I.B. Tauris, 1999.
Kirk-Greene, A. H. M., *Symbol of Authority: The British District Officer in Africa*. London: I.B. Tauris, 2005.

Kirk-Greene, A. H. M., 'Towards a History of the Colonial Service', *African Affairs*, 73, 290 (1974): 105–8.
Kissinger, H., *A World Restored; Metternich, Castlereagh, and the Problems of Peace, 1812–22*. Boston: Houghton Mifflin, 1957.
Kitromilides, P. M., and C. Tsoukalas, *The Greek Revolution: A Critical Dictionary*. Cambridge, MA: Belknap Press, 2021.
Kolsky, E., *Colonial Justice in British India: White Violence and the Rule of Law*. Cambridge: Cambridge University Press, 2009.
Kolsky, E., and A. Agah (eds), *Fringes of Empire*. New Delhi: Oxford University Press, 2009.
Kour, Z. H., *The History of Aden 1839–1872*. London: Frank Cass, 1981.
Kuhnke, L. V., *Lives at Risk: Public Health in Nineteenth-Century Egypt*. Berkeley: University of California Press, 1990.
Ladurie, E. L. R., *Montaillou: Cathars and Catholics in a French Village, 1294–1324*. London: Penguin, 2002.
Lafi, N., *Une Ville Du Maghreb Entre Ancien Régime Et Réformes Ottomanes: Genèse Des Institutions Municipales à Tripoli De Barbarie (1795–1911)*. Paris: L'Harmattan, 2002.
Lafi, N. (ed.), *Municipalités Mediterranéennes: Les Réformes Urbaines Ottomanes au Miroir d'une Histoire Compareée (Moyen-Orient, Maghreb, Europe Méridionale)*. Berlin: ZMO, 2007.
Lai, C-C., *Braudel's Historiography Reconsidered*. Lanham, MD: University Press of America, 2004.
Laidlaw, C., *The British in the Levant: Trade and Perceptions of the Ottoman Empire in the Eighteenth Century*. London: I.B. Tauris, 2010.
Laidlaw, Z., *Colonial Connections, 1815–45: Patronage, the Information Revolution and Colonial Government*. Manchester: Manchester University Press, 2005.
Lambert, D., and A. Lester (eds), *Colonial Lives across the British Empire: Imperial Careering in the Long Nineteenth Century*. Cambridge: Cambridge University Press, 2006.
Lambert Playfair, R., *The Bibliography of the Barbary States, Volume 2, Part 1: Tripoli and the Cyrenaica*. London: John Murray, 1889.
Lane-Poole, S., *The Life of the Right Honourable Stratford Canning Viscount Stratford De Redcliffe K.G. G.C.B. D.C.L. LL.D. & C. From His Memoirs and Private and Official Papers, Volumes 1–2*. London: Longmans, 1888.
Last, M., *The Sokoto Caliphate*. New York: Humanities Press, 1967.
Lavery, B., *Nelson's Navy: The Ships, Men and Organisation, 1793–1815*. Oxford: Osprey Publishing, 2020.
Lee, H.I., 'The Supervising of the Barbary Consuls During the Years 1756–1836', *Historical Research*, 23 (1950): 191–9.
Lester, A., *Imperial Networks: Creating Identities in Nineteenth-Century South Africa and Britain*. London: Routledge, 2001.
Lester, A. 'Imperial Circuits and Networks: Geographies of the British Empire', *History Compass*, 4, 1 (2006): 121–41.
Lloyd, C., *Mr. Barrow of the Admiralty: A Life of Sir John Barrow, 1764–1848*. London: Collins, 1970.
Lloyd, C., *English Corsairs on the Barbary Coast*. London: HarperCollins, 1981.
Lovejoy, P. E., 'Commercial Sectors in the Economy of the Nineteenth-Century Central Sudan: The Trans-Saharan Trade and the Desert-Side Salt Trade', *African Economic History*, 13 (1984): 85–116.

Lovejoy, P. E., *Transformations in Slavery: A History of Slavery in Africa*. Cambridge: Cambridge University Press, 1983.

Lovejoy, P. E., 'The Volume of the Atlantic Trade: A Synthesis', *Journal of African History*, 23, 4 (1982): 473–501.

Lowe, J., *Britain and Foreign Affairs, 1815–1885: Europe and Overseas*. London: Routledge, 1998.

Lydon, G., *On Trans-Saharan Trails: Islamic Law, Trade Networks and Cross-Cultural Exchange in Western Africa*. Cambridge: Cambridge University Press, 2009.

Lydon, G., 'Writing Trans-Saharan History: Methods, Sources and Interpretations across the African Divide', *Journal of North African Studies*, 10, 3–4 (2005): 293–324.

Lynn, M., 'Consul and Kings: British Policy, "The Man on the Spot", and the Seizure of Lagos, 1851', *Journal of Imperial and Commonwealth History*, 10, 2 (1982): 150–67.

MacLean, G., and N. Matar, *Britain & the Islamic World, 1558–1713*. Oxford: Oxford University Press, 2011.

Mahan, A. T., *The Influence of Sea Power on the French Revolution and Empire*, 2 Volumes. Boston: Little, Brown, 1894.

Mahdavi, S., 'Shahs, Doctors, Diplomats and Missionaries in 19th Century Iran', *British Journal of Middle Eastern Studies*, 32, 2 (2005): 169–91.

Magee, G. B., and A. S. Thompson, *Empire and Globalisation: Networks of People, Goods and Capital in the British World, c.1850–1914*. Cambridge: Cambridge University Press, 2010.

Mallette, K., 'Lingua Franca', in P. Horden and S. Kinoshita (eds), *A Companion to Mediterranean History*. London: Wiley Blackwell, 2014, 330–44.

Mann, M., *The Sources of Social Power: Volume 2: The Rise of the Classes and Nation States, 1760–1914*. Cambridge: Cambridge University Press, 1993.

Marshall, P. J., *Bengal: The British Bridgehead: Eastern India 1740–1828: The New Cambridge History of India*. Cambridge: Cambridge University Press, 1987.

Marshall, P. J. (ed.), *The Cambridge Illustrated History of the British Empire*. Cambridge: Cambridge University Press, 1996.

Marshall, P. J. (ed.), *The Oxford History of the British Empire: Volume 2: The Eighteenth Century*. Oxford: Oxford University Press, 1998.

Marshall, P. J., *Problems of Empire: Britain and India, 1757–1813*. London: Allen & Unwin, 1968.

Marshall, P. J., *The Making and Unmaking of Empires: Britain, India and America, c.1750–1783* Oxford: Oxford University Press, 2005.

Martin, B. G., 'Kanem, Bornu, and the Fazzan: Notes on the Political History of a Trade Route', *Journal of African History*, 10, 1 (1969): 15–27.

Martin, E. C., 'The English Establishments on the Gold Coast in the Second Half of the Eighteenth Century', *Transactions of the Royal Historical Society*, 5 (1922): 167–208.

Masters, B., *The Origins of Western Economic Dominance in the Middle East: Mercantilism and the Islamic Economy in Aleppo, 1600–1750*. New York: New York University Press, 1988.

Matar, N., *Britain and Barbary, 1589–1689*. Gainesville: University Press of Florida, 2005.

Mather, J., *Pashas: Traders and Travellers in the Islamic World*. London: Yale University Press, 2009.

Mazower, M., *The Greek Revolution: 1821 and the Making of Modern Europe*. London: Allen Lane, 2021.

McDougall, A. E., 'Conceptualising the Sahara: The World of Nineteenth-Century Beyrouk Commerce', *Journal of North African Studies*, 10, 3–4 (2005): 369–86.

McLachlan, K. S., 'Tripoli and Tripolitania: Conflict and Cohesion during the Period of the Barbary Corsairs (1551-1850)', *Transactions of the Institute of British Geographers*, 3, 3 (1978): 285-94.

McLean, D., 'Trade, Politics and the Navy in Latin America: The British in the Paraná, 1845-46', *Journal of Imperial and Commonwealth History*, 35, 3 (2007): 351-70.

McLean, D., *War, Diplomacy and Informal Empire and the Republics of La Plata, 1836-1853*. London: I.B. Tauris, 1994.

Mézin, A., *Les Consuls de France au Siècle de Lumières (1715-1792). Diplomatie et Histoire: Volume 1*. Paris: Imprimerie Nationale, 1997.

Middleton, C. R., *The Administration of British Foreign Policy, 1782-1846*. Durham, NC: Duke University Press, 1977.

Miliori, M. 'Europe, the Classical Polis, and the Greek Nation: Philhellenism and Hellenism in Nineteenth Century Britain', in R. Beaton and D. Ricks (eds), *The Making of Modern Greece: Nationalism, Romanticism & The Uses of the Past (1797-1896)*. London: Routledge, 2009, 56-77.

Moalla, A., *The Regency of Tunis and the Ottoman Porte, 1777-1814: Army and Government of a North-African Eyalet at the End of the Eighteenth Century*. London: RoutledgeCurzon, 2010.

Moatti, C., W. Kaiser and C. Pébarthe (eds), *Le Monde de l'Itinérance. Le Contrôle de la Mobilité des Personnes en Méditerranée de l'Antiquité à l'Époque Moderne III*. Bordeaux: Ausonius, 2008.

Morgan, P., *The Decline and Fall of the British Empire, 1781-1997*. London: Vintage, 2008.

Mori, J., *The Culture of Diplomacy: Britain in Europe, c.1750-1830*. Manchester: Manchester University Press, 2011.

Mosca, G., *The Ruling Class*. London: McGraw Hill, 1939.

Myint-U, T., *The Making of Modern Burma*. Cambridge: Cambridge University Press, 2001.

Mösslang, M., and T. Riotte (eds), *The Diplomats' World: A Cultural History of Diplomacy, 1815-1914*. Oxford: Oxford University Press, 2008.

Muir, R., *Britain and the Defeat of Napoleon*. London: Yale University Press, 1996.

Müller, L., *Consuls, Corsairs, and Commerce: The Swedish Consular Service and Long-distance Shipping, 1720-1815*. Uppsala: Uppsala Universitet, 2004.

Müller, L., *Swedish Consular Reports as a Source of Business Information, 1700-1800*, Helsinki: International Economic History Congress, 2006, 1-12.

Müller, L., and J. Ojala, 'Consular Services of the Nordic Countries during the Eighteenth and Nineteenth Centuries: Did They Really Work?', in G. Boyce and R. Gorski (eds), *Resources and Infrastrcutures in the Maritime Economy, 1500-2000*. St. Johns, Newfoundland: International Maritime Economic History Association, 2002, 23-41.

Nachtigal, G., *Sahara and Sudan: Volume 1: Tripoli and Fezzan, Tibesti or Tu*. Translated from German by A. G. B. Fisher and H. J. Fisher. New York: Barnes and Noble, 1974.

Neumann, I. B., 'Introduction to the Forum on Liminality', *Review of International Studies*, 38, 2 (2012): 473-9.

Newton, J., 'Slavery, Diplomacy and Empire: Britain and the Suppression of the Slave Trade, 1807-1975', *Journal of Imperial and Commonwealth History*, 38, 4 (2010): 649-51.

Norris, Robert, *Memoirs of the Reiyn of Bossa Ahadee, King of Dahomy An Inland Country of Guiney, to which Are Added the Author's Journey to Abomey, the Capital, and A Short Account of the African Slave Trade*. London, 1789.

Omissi, D. E., 'The Greatest Muslim Power in the World. Islam, the Indian Army and the Grand Strategy of British India, 1914–1916', in A. Jeffreys (ed.), *The Indian Army in the First World War: New Perspectives*. Solihull: Helion, 2018.

Onley, J., *The Arabian Frontier of the British Raj Merchants, Rulers, and the British in the Nineteenth-century Gulf*. Oxford: Oxford University Press, 2007.

Onley, J., 'Britain's Informal Empire in the Gulf, 1820–1971', *Journal of Social Affairs*, 22, 87 (2005): 29–45.

Onley, J., 'The Politics of Protection in the Gulf: The Arab Rulers and the British Resident in the Nineteenth Century', *New Arabian Studies*, 6 (2004): 30–92.

Ould Cheikh, A. W., 'A Man of Letters in Timbuktu: al-Shaykh Sidi Muhammad al-Kunti', in S. Jeppie and S. Bachir Diagne (eds), *The Meanings of Timbuktu*. Cape Town: Human Sciences Research Council of South Africa Press, 2008, 231–48.

Owen, R., and B. Sutcliffe (eds), *Studies in the Theory of Imperialism*. Oxford: Oxford University Press, 1972.

Pamuk, Ş., *A Monetary History of the Ottoman Empire*. Cambridge: Cambridge University Press, 2004.

Pamuk, Ş., *The Ottoman Empire and European Capitalism, 1820–1913: Trade, Investment and Production*. Cambridge: Cambridge University Press, 2010.

Panzac, D., *The Barbary Corsairs: Volume 29: The End of a Legend, 1800–1820*. Leiden: Brill, 2005.

Panzac, D., 'International and Domestic Maritime Trade in the Ottoman Empire during the 18th Century', *International Journal of Middle East Studies*, 24, 2 (1992): 189–206.

Panzac, D., 'Une activité en trompe-l'œil: la guerre de course à Tripoli de Barbarie dans la seconde moitié du XVIII siècle', *Revue de l'Occident musulman et de la Méditerranée*, 47 (1988): 126–41.

Pareto, V., *The Rise and Fall of the Elites: An Application of Theoretical Sociology*. New Brunswick, NJ: Transaction, 1991.

Parry, J. P., 'Steam Power and British Influence in Baghdad, 1820–1860', *Historical Journal*, 56, 1 (2013): 145–73.

Pennell, C. R., 'Accommodation between European and Islamic Law in the Western Mediterranean in the Early Nineteenth Century', *British Journal of Middle Eastern Studies*, 21, 2 (1994): 159–89.

Pennell, C. R., 'The British Consular Courts and Moroccan Muslim Identity: "Christian" Justice as a Tool', *Journal of North African Studies*, 1, 2 (1996): 172–91.

Pennell, C. R., 'A Killing in Tripoli (1843): Principle and Contingency and Personal Diplomacy', *Libyan Studies*, 36 (2005): 59–77.

Pennell, C. R., *Morocco Since 1830: A History*. New York: New York University Press, 2000.

Pennell, C. R., 'The Origins of the Foreign Jurisdiction Act and the Extension of British Sovereignty', *Historical Research*, 83, 221 (2009): 465–85.

Pennell, C. R. (ed.), *Piracy and Diplomacy in Seventeenth-Century North Africa: The Journal of Thomas Baker, English Consul in Tripoli, 1677–1685*. Rutherford, NJ: Fairleigh Dickinson University Press, 1989.

Pennell, C. R., 'The Social History of British Diplomats in North Africa', in M. Mösslang and T. Riotte (eds), *The Diplomats' World: A Cultural History of Diplomacy, 1815–1914*. Oxford: Oxford University Press, 2008, 347–79.

Pennell, C. R., 'Treaty Law: The Extent of Consular Jurisdiction in North Africa from the Middle of the Seventeenth to the Middle of the Nineteenth Century', *Journal of North African Studies*, 14, 2 (2009): 235–56.

Pennell, C. R., 'Tripoli in the Mid Eighteenth Century: A Guidebook', *Revue d'histoire maghrébine*, 9, 25–6 (1982): 91–121.
Perkyns, M., *Life in Abyssinia: Being Notes Collected during Three Years' Residence and Travels in that Country*. Volume 2. London: John Murray, 1853.
Piterberg, G., T. F. Ruiz and G. Symcox (eds), *Braudel Revisited: The Mediterranean World, 1600–1800*. Toronto: University of Toronto Press, 2010.
Platt, D. C. M., *The Cinderella Service: British Consuls Since 1825*. London: Longman, 1971.
Platt, D. C. M., 'Further Objections to an "Imperialism of Free Trade", 1830–60', *Economic History Review*, 26, 1 (1973): 77–91.
Platt, D. C. M., 'The Imperialism of Free Trade: Some Reservations', *Economic History Review*, 21, 2 (1968): 296–306.
Platt, D. C. M., 'The Role of the British Consular Service in Overseas Trade, 1825–1914', *Economic History Review*, 15, 3 (1963): 494–512.
Playfair, I. S. O. (ed.), *The Mediterranean and Middle East: Volume 2: The Germans Come to the Help of Their Ally, 1941*. London: HM Stationary Office, 1956.
Plumb, J. H., *England in the Eighteenth Century*. London: Penguin, 1990.
Pomeranz, K., *The Great Divergence Europe, China, and the Making of the Modern World Economy*. Princeton, NJ: Princeton University Press, 2000.
Porter, A., and W. R. Louis (eds), *The Oxford History of the British Empire: Volume 3: The Nineteenth Century*. Oxford: Oxford University Press, 1999.
Porter, A., 'Religion, Missionary Enthusiasm, and Empire', in A. Porter and W. R. Louis (eds), *The Oxford History of the British Empire: Volume 3: The Nineteenth Century*. Oxford: Oxford University Press, 1999, 222–46.
Porter, A., 'Commerce and Christianity: The Rise and Fall of a Nineteenth-Century Missionary Slogan', *Historical Journal*, 28, 3 (1985): 597–621.
Porter, B., *The Absent-Minded Imperialists: Empire, Society, and Culture in Britain*. Oxford: Oxford University Press, 2006.
Prevelakis, E., and K. Kalliataki Merticopoulou (eds), *Epirus, Ali Pasha and the Greek Revolution, Consular Reports of William Meyer from Preveza, Volumes 1–2*. Monuments of Greek History No. 12. Athens: Academy of Athens, 1996.
Quataert, D., *The Ottoman Empire, 1700–1922*. Cambridge: Cambridge University Press, 2005.
Quataert, D., B. Tezcan and R. A. Abou-el-Haj (eds), *Beyond Dominant Paradigms in Ottoman and Middle Eastern/North African Studies, a Tribute to Rifa'at Abou-El-Haj*. Istanbul: ISAM, 2010.
Raymond, A. *Grandes villes arabes à l'époque ottomane*. Paris: Sinbad, 1985.
Rees, T., *Merchant Adventurers in the Levant: Two Families of Privateers, Consuls and Traders, 1700–1956*. Stawell: Talbot Press, 2003.
Reimer, M. J., *Colonial Bridgehead: Government and Society in Alexandria, 1807–1882*. Cairo: American University in Cairo Press, 1997.
Rejeb, L. B., '"The General Belief of the World": Barbary as Genre and Discourse in Mediterranean History', *European Review of History: Revue europeenne d'histoire*, 19, 1 (2012): 15–31.
Richardson, D., 'The British Empire and the Atlantic Slave Trade, 1660–1807', in P. J. Marshall (ed.), *The Oxford History of the British Empire: Volume 2: The Eighteenth Century*. Oxford: Oxford University Press, 1998, 440–64.
Richardson, J., *Travels in the Great Desert of Sahara, in the Years of 1845 and 1846*, Volumes 1–2. London: Richard Bentley, 1848.

Ridley, R. T., *Napoleon's Proconsul in Egypt: The Life and Times of Bernardino Drovetti*. London: Rubicon Press, 1998.
Roberts, P. H., and R. S. Roberts, *Thomas Barclay (1728–1793): Consul in France, Diplomat in Barbary*. Bethlehem: Lehigh University Press, 2008.
Robinson, A. E., 'The Conquest of the Sudan by the Wali of Egypt, Muhammad Ali Pasha, 1820–1824. Part II', *Journal of the Royal African Society*, 25, 98 (1926): 164–82.
Robinson, R., 'Non-European Foundations of European Imperialism: Sketch for a Theory of Collaboration', in E. R. J. Owen and R. B. Sutcliffe (eds), *Studies in the Theory of Imperialism*. Oxford: Oxford University Press, 1972, 117–40.
Robinson, R., J. Gallagher and A. Denny, *Africa and the Victorians: The Official Mind of Imperialism*. Basingstoke: Macmillan, 1981.
Roded, R. 'The Syrian Urban Notables: Elite, Estates, Class?', *Asian and African Studies*, 20 (1986): 375–84.
Rodger, A. B., *The War of the Second Coalition: 1798 to 1801, a Strategic Commentary*. Oxford: Clarendon Press, 1964.
Rothman, E. N., *Brokering Empire: Trans-Imperial Subjects between Venice and Istanbul*. Ithaca, NY: Cornell University Press, 2012.
Rossi, E., 'Tripoli', in E. J. Brill, *Encyclopedia of Islam*, Volume 4. Leiden: Brill, 1934, 814–18.
Rutherford, I., 'Network Theory and Theoric Networks', *Mediterranean Historical Review*, 22, 1 (2007): 23–37.
Saad, E. N., *Social History of Timbuktu: The Role of Muslim Scholars and Notables, 1400–1900*. Cambridge: Cambridge University Press, 1983.
Said, E. W., *Culture & Imperialism*. London: Vintage, 1994.
Said, E. W., *Orientalism*, 25th edition. London: Penguin, 2003.
Said, E. W., and G. Viswanathan (ed.), *Power, Politics, and Culture: Interviews with Edward W. Said*. London: Bloomsbury, 2005.
Sainty, J. C. (ed.), *Office-Holders in Modern Britain: Volume 6: Colonial Office Officials, 1794–1870*. London: Institute of Historical Research, University of London, 1976.
Samson, J. (ed.), *The British Empire*. Oxford: Oxford University Press, 2001.
Samson, J., *British Imperial Strategies in the Pacific, 1750–1900*. London: Routledge, 2021.
Sattin, A., *Lifting the Veil: British Society in Egypt, 1768–1956*. London: Dent, 1988.
al-Sayyid Marsot, A. L., *Egypt in the Reign of Muhammad Ali*. Cambridge: Cambridge University Press, 1994.
Scammell, G. V., *The World Encompassed: The First European Maritime Empires*. London: Methuen, 1981.
Schaffer, S., L. Roberts, K. Raj and J. Delbourgo (eds), *The Brokered World: Go-betweens and Global Intelligence, 1770–1820*. Sagamore Beach, MA: Science History, 2009.
Schofield, P. (ed.), *Securities against Misrule and Other Constitutional Writings for Tripoli and Greece*. Oxford: Clarendon Press, 1990.
Scholch, A., 'The "Men on the Spot" and the English Occupation of Egypt in 1882', *Historical Journal*, 19, 2 (1976): 773–85.
Schroeder, P. W., *The Transformation of European Politics, 1763–1848*. Oxford: Clarendon Press, 1994.
Schumpeter, J. A., *Imperialism and Social Classes*. Oxford: Basil Blackwell, 1951.
Seeley, J. R., *The Expansion of England*. London: Macmillan, 1914.
Seton-Watson, R. W., *Britain in Europe: 1789–1914*. London: Cambridge University Press, 1955.

Shair, I. M., and P. P. Karan, 'Geography of the Islamic Pilgrimage', *GeoJournal*, 3/6 (1979): 599.
Shaw, S. J., *History of the Ottoman Empire*. Cambridge: Cambridge University Press, 1977.
Sherwood, M., 'The British Illegal Slave Trade, 1808–1830', *Journal for Eighteenth-Century Studies*, 31, 2 (2008): 293–305.
Shillington, K. (ed.), *Encyclopedia of African History, A-G*. New York: Fitzroy Dearborn, 2005.
Sluglett, P., 'Formal and Informal Empire in the Middle East', in R. Winks (ed.), *The Oxford History of the British Empire: Volume 5: Historiography*. Oxford: Oxford University Press, 1999, 416–36.
Smyth, W. H., *The Mediterranean: A Memoir*. London: John W. Parker and Son, 1854.
Solow, B. L., 'Capitalism and Slavery in the Exceedingly Long Run', *Journal of Interdisciplinary History*, 17, 4 (1987): 711–17.
Spencer, T. J. B., *Fair Greece! Sade relic: Literary philhellenism from Shakespeare to Byron*. London: Weidenfeld and Nicolson, 1954.
St Clair, W. *That Greece Might Still Be Free: The Philhellenes in the War of Independence*. Cambridge: Open Book, 2008.
Stearns, R. P., 'Fellows of the Royal Society in North Africa and the Levant, 1662–1800', *Notes and Records of the Royal Society of London*, 11, 1 (1954): 75–90.
Stoler, A. N., *Along the Archival Grain: Epistemic Anxieties and Colonial Common Sense*. Princeton, NJ: Princeton University Press, 2010.
Stoler, A. N., 'Imperial Debris: Reflections on Ruins and Ruination', *Cultural Anthropology*, 23, 2 (2008): 191–219.
Swanson, C. A., and D. W. Knox (eds), *Naval Documents Related to the United States Wars with the Barbary Powers, Volumes 1–6*. Washington, DC: US Government Printing Office, 1844–1939.
Syrett, D., 'Keppel at Algiers: Diplomacy and the Limitations of Naval Power' *Mariner's Mirror*, 91, 1 (2005): 13–23.
Szijarto, I., 'Four Arguments for Microhistory', *Rethinking History*, 6, 2 (2002): 209–15.
Tabak, F., *The Waning of the Mediterranean, 1550–1870: A Geohistorical Approach*. Baltimore, MD: Johns Hopkins University Press, 2008.
Tabak, F., 'Imperial Rivalry and Port-Cities: a View from Above', *Mediterranean Historical Review*, 24, 2 (2009): 79–94.
Tambo, D. C., 'The Sokoto Caliphate Slave Trade in the Nineteenth Century', *International Journal of African Historical Studies*, 9, 2 (1976): 187–217.
Tarazi Fawaz, L., and C. A. Bayly (eds), *Modernity and Culture: From the Mediterranean to the Indian Ocean*. New York: Columbia University Press, 2002.
Tawil, A. H., *Khafaya Jadid al Muthirah Takshifuha Maqbarat Tarabulus al-Burutistantiyah*. Tripoli: Markaz Jihad al-Libiyin lil-Dirasat al-Tarik hiyah, 2008.
Temperley, H. W. V., *The Foreign Policy of Canning, 1822–1827: England, the Neo-holy Alliance and the New World*. London: Frank Cass, 1925.
Temperley, H. W. V., and L. M.Penson (eds), *Foundations of British Foreign Policy: From Pitt (1792) to Salisbury (1902), or Documents, Old and New*. Cambridge: Cambridge University Press, 1938.
Thorne, R. G. (ed.), *The History of Parliament: The House of Commons, 1790–1820*. London: Secker & Warburg, 1986.
Thornton, J. K., *Africa and the Africans in the Making of the Atlantic World, 1400–1880*. Cambridge: Cambridge University Press, 1998.

Tidrick, K., *Empire and the English Character: The Illusion of Authority*. London: Tauris Parke, 2009.
Toledano, E. R., 'The Emergence of Ottoman-Local Elites (1700–1900): A Framework for Research', in I. Pappé and M. Ma'oz (eds), *Middle Eastern Politics and Ideas: A History from within*. London: Tauris Academic Studies, 1997, 145–62.
A Treatise upon the Trade from Great-Britain to Africa ... By an African Merchant. London, 1772.
Turnbull, C. M., 'Formal and Informal Empire in East Asia', in R. Winks (ed.), *The Oxford History of the British Empire: Volume 5: Historiography*. Oxford: Oxford University Press, 1999, 379–402.
Turnbull, D., 'Boundary-Crossing, Cultural Encounters and Knowledge Spaces', in Schaffer, S., L. Roberts, K. Raj and J. Delbourgo (eds), *The Brokered World: Go-Betweens and Global Intelligence, 1770–1820*. Sagamore Beach, MA: Science History Publications, 2009, 387–428.
Twells, A., *The Civilising Mission and the English Middle Class, 1792–1850: The 'Heathen' at Home and Overseas*. Basingstoke: Palgrave Macmillan, 2009.
Ulbert, J., and G. Le Bouëdec (eds), *La Fonction Consulaire à L'époque Moderne. L'affirmation D'une Institution Économique Et Politique (1500–1700)*. Rennes: Presses Universitaires de Rennes, 2006.
Ulbert, J., and L. Prijac (eds), *Consuls et Services Consulaires au XIXe Siècle /Die Welt Der Konsulate Im 19. Jahrhundert /Consulship in the 19th Century*. Hamburg: Dobu Verlag, 2010.
Ulbert, J., A. Bartolomei, G. Calafat and M. Grenet (eds), *De l'utilité commerciale des consuls. L'institution consulaire et les marchands dans le monde méditerranéen (XVIIe -XXe siècle)*. Rome: Publications de l'École française de Rome, 2017.
Urbach, K., *Bismarck's Favourite Englishman: Lord Odo Russell's Mission to Berlin*. London: I.B. Tauris, 2000.
University of Oxford, *New Hart's Rules: The Handbook of Style for Writers and Editors*. Oxford: Oxford University Press, 2005.
Valensi, L., *Le Maghreb Avant La Prise d'Alger, 1790–1830*. Paris: Flammarion, 1969.
Valensi, L., *On the Eve of Colonialism: North Africa before the French Conquest*. Translated from French by K. J. Perkins. New York: Africana, 1977.
Vanneste, T., *Global Trade and Commercial Networks: Eighteenth-Century Diamond Merchants*. London: Pickering & Chatto, 2011.
Varnava, A., *British Imperialism in Cyprus, 1878–1915: The Inconsequential Possession*. Manchester: Manchester University Press, 2009.
Vassallo, C., 'The Maltese Mercantile Diaspora in the Mediterranean in the Eighteenth and Nineteenth Centuries', *Journal of Mediterranean Studies*, 10, 1–2 (2000): 203–11.
Vergara, L. G., 'Elites, Political Elites and Social Change in Modern Societies', *Revisita de Sociología*, 28 (2013): 31–49.
Vertovec, S., and R. Cohen (eds), *Conceiving Cosmopolitanism: Theory, Context and Practice*. Oxford: Oxford University Press, 2002.
Vick, B. E., *The Congress of Vienna: Power and Politics after Napoleon*. Cambridge, MA: Harvard University Press, 2014.
Wallerstein, I., *The Modern World-System: Capitalist Agriculture and the Origins of the European World-Economy in the Sixteenth Century. Volume 1*. Berkeley: University of California Press, 2011.

Wallerstein, I., *The Modern World-System: Capitalism and the Consolidation of the European World-Economy, 1600–1750: Volume 2.* Berkeley: University of California Press, 2011.

Wallerstein, I., *The Modern World-System: Second Era of Great Expansion of the Capitalist World-Economy, 1730s–1840s: Volume 3.* Berkeley: University of California Press, 2011.

Wansbrough, J., 'The Decolonization of North African History', *Journal of African History*, 9, 4 (1968): 643–50.

Wansbrough, J., *Lingua Franca in the Mediterranean.* Richmond, Surrey: Curzon, 1996.

Webster, A., *The Debate on the Rise of the British Empire.* Manchester: Manchester University Press, 2006.

Webster, C. K., *The Congress of Vienna, 1814–1815.* London: Oxford University Press, 1918.

Winks, R. (ed.), *The Oxford History of the British Empire: Volume 5. Historiography.* Oxford: Oxford University Press, 1999.

Wood, A. C., *A History of the Levant Company.* London: Routledge, 1964.

Woodruff, P. [pseud.], *The Men Who Ruled India, Volume 1: The Founders of Modern India & Volume 2: The Guardians.* London: Jonathan Cape, 1953 & 1954.

Wright, J., *The Trans-Saharan Slave Trade.* London: Routledge, 2007.

Webb, E. A. H., *A History of the Services of the 17th (The Leicestershire) Regiment.* London: Vacher, 1911.

Y Layblich, D. B., *Voyages D'Ali Bey El Abbassi, en Afrique et an Asie, les Années 1803, 1805, 1806, et 1807.* Paris: P. Didot L'ainé. 1894.

Yapp, M. E., *The Making of the Modern Near East, 1792–1923.* Oxford: Oxford University Press, 1987.

Young, D. M., *The Colonial Office in the Early Nineteenth Century.* London: Longmans, 1961.

Zamoyski, A., *Rites of Peace: The Fall of Napoleon and the Congress of Vienna.* London: Harper Perennial, 2007.

Ze'evi, D., 'Back to Napoleon? Thoughts on the Beginning of the Modern Era in the Middle East', *Mediterranean Historical Review*, 19, 1 (2004): 73–94.

Zemon Davis, N., 'Decentering History: Local Stories and Cultural Crossings in a Global World', *History and Theory*, 50 (2011): 188–202.

Zubaida, S., 'Middle Eastern Experiences of Cosmopolitanism', in S. Vertovec and R. Cohen (eds), *Conceiving Cosmopolitanism: Theory, Context and Practice.* Oxford: Oxford University Press, 2002, 33–8.

Zubaida, S., 'Cosmopolitanism in the Middle East', Research Center for International Political Economy and Foreign Policy Analysis (RECIPE), Issue 12, Amsterdam Middle East Papers. Amsterdam International Studies, 1997.

Websites

Australian Dictionary of Biography: https://adb.anu.edu.au/.
Dizionario Biografico degli Italiani: https://www.treccani.it/.
Hansard House of Commons Debates: http://www.parliament.uk/business/publications/hansard/commons/.
History of Parliament Online: http://www.historyofparliamentonline.org/.
Geneall: http://geneall.net/pt/.

Naval, Military and Air Force Bible Society: http://www.nmafbs.org/about-us/
Oxford Dictionary of National Biography: http://www.oxforddnb.com/.
Svenskt Biografiskt Lexicon: http://sok.riksarkivet.se/SBL/Start.aspx.
The Trans-Atlantic Slave Trade Database: https://www.slavevoyages.org/voyage/database.
University of Hull Library and Learning Innovation: https://www.slavevoyages.org/voyage/database.

INDEX

abolition of slavery 15, 37, 46–7, 49, 87, 90–1
   treaties of Exmouth and Fremantle (1816) 31, 87, 106, 127
   see also slavery, slave trade (or traffic)
Abukir, Bay of 10
Abyssinia 47, 72
à Court, Sir William (1779–1860) 11, 43–4, 61, 64, 81, 123, 134 n.29, 147 n.52, 152 n.57
African Society 16, 89, 113
   African Association 1, 17, 46–7, 67, 79, 81–2, 88–90, 93, 103, 107, 109, 113, 121
Agha 35
   Omar Agha, Dey of Algiers 9, 14
agriculture 5
   agricultural reform 53
   agricultural sector 31
Albania 13
Alexandria 31, 72, 77, 79–80, 100, 113
   see also Egypt
Algiers 4–5, 9, 11, 13–15, 21–2, 25, 27–9, 31, 46, 58, 63–4, 74, 79, 80, 83, 96, 100, 104, 107, 117, 119
   see also Hassan Pasha; Dey of Algiers; Omar Agha; Dey of Algiers
Ali Bey 86
Ali Pasha (1740–1822) 105–6, 126
Ali, Mohamed (1769–1849) 11, 13–15, 17–18, 23, 31–2, 86, 99–101, 104–5, 107, 113, 122
   see also Egypt
Allied Powers 14
   see also Holy Alliance
amils, *see* qa'ids
Amor, Sidi 14
Anatolia 36–8
   see also Erzurum
antiquities 16, 101

Apsley, Lord, *see* Bathurst, Henry
Arabia 95, 100
   see also Hijaz, Jeddah, Mecca, Medina
Arabs 40, 51
Austria 14, 58, 93
   Imperial, of the Austrian Empire 33, 92–3
Awjila 32

Bagirmi, Sultanate of 83, 102, 110, 113
Bait-al-Mal, Hajj Mohamed (born c.1794) 37, 39–41, 44, 50–2, 99, 118–19, 123
Bani Waleed 30
Barqa 29–30, 73, 81, 89
Bathurst, Henry (1762–1834), Lord Apsley, 3rd Earl Bathurst 15–16, 28, 41, 43, 61, 64–8, 70, 81–3, 86, 90, 101, 109, 119, 121, 123, 142 n.70, 144 n.9, 147–8 nn.46, 58, 75, 82, 150 n.11, 151 n.39, 152 nn.61–62, 153 nn.66, 71, 78, 154 n.79, 157 nn.20, 23, 158 nn.24, 30, 35, 37, 159 nn.43, 45, 55, 160 nn.68–70, 78, 161 n.93, 163 nn.26, 40–41, 164 n.56, 165 nn.64, 73, 166 nn.90, 92, 167 n.1
Beaussier, Bonaventure (b.1748) 87, 123
Beaussier & Company 81
Beechey, Henry William (1788/1789–1862) 57, 81–2, 89, 123
Bello, Sultan Muhammad (1781–1837) 38, 40, 52, 77, 88, 94, 109–10, 121, 123
Benghazi 4, 27, 29, 30, 32, 35, 51, 53, 57, 66–7, 81, 83–6, 107–8
Benin, Bight of 78, 84, 87–8, 120
Bentham, Jeremy 36–7, 47–8, 51
   see also Civil and Constitutional Code for Tripoli
Bentinck, Lord William (1774–1839) 8, 21, 123, 134 n.29, 137 n.4
Bey, of Benghazi 35, 126–7, 141
   of Derna 35

of Tunis, *see* Hammuda Pasha
    (1759–1814)
Board of Health, Tripoli, 81, 91–2, 120
Bomba, Gulf of 14, 29, 82, 101
Bonaparte, Napoleon (1769–1821) 7,
    9–10, 95, 105
Borghul, Ali 13, 22–3, 30
Borgu 102
Bornu 27, 41, 81, 83, 89, 93, 104, 108, 113,
    124, 126
    see also Kanem-Bornu
Brazil 32
    see also d'Itabayana, Baron
Bruce, James (1730–1794) 17, 124
Bu Khalloum, Abubakr 49
Bulgaria 13
    see also Pazvanoğlu, Osman
Bunbury, Lt Col. Thomas (1791–1862)
    124, 134 n.23, 142 n.64, 150 n.16, 151
    n.40, 160 n.80
Buonaparte, *see* Bonaparte
Buttabel, 40, 124

Caillé, René (1799–1838), 110
Cairo 9, 13, 39, 77, 79, 95, 101, 108
    see also Mohamed Ali, Egypt
Camden, Earl, *see* Pratt, John Jeffreys
Candia, *see* Heraklion
Cape of Good Hope 95, 110
Caravana, Pietro (d.1832) 70, 108,
    124
cargo 25, 42, 49, 60–1, 85, 127
Carstensen, J. A. 124, 158, 165
Casalaina (d.1832) 70, 124
Castlereagh, Viscount Robert Stewart
    (1769–1822), 2nd Marquess of
    Londonderry 16, 60, 124, 135 n.56,
    136 n.64, 140 n.48, 141 n.58
cattle 28, 30, 32, 69, 84, 100
    bullocks 81, 100
    livestock 5, 14, 81, 86, 100
    sheep 81, 100
Cavendish-Bentinck, William Henry
    Cavendish (1738–1809), 3rd Duke of
    Portland 8, 21, 123
Chad, Lake 4, 79, 87–8
Chichester, Earl of, *see* Pelham,
    Lord Thomas
cholera 90–2

    see also disease, epidemic,
        plague, typhus
Church Missionary Society 72
    see also Coffin, William
church 72–3, 120
    Catholic 73
    Greek 72
Church, Mr 69
Clapperton, Lt Hugh (1788–1827) 40,
    44, 57, 81–2, 88–90, 102, 104, 108–
    10, 124
Clot, Antoine Berthelemy (1793–1868) 92
Clot Bey, *see* Clot, Antoine Berthelemy
    (1793–1868)
Codrington, Vice Admiral Sir Edward
    (1770–1851) 68, 124, 136 n.59,
    147 n.59
Coen, Joseph 39, 124
Coffin, William 72
    see also Church Missionary Society
Collingwood, Lord Cuthbert (1748–1810)
    99, 124
Concenza, House of 81
Constantinople, *see* Istanbul
Constitutional and Civil Code for
    Greece 37
    see also Bentham, Jeremy
Constitutional and Civil Code for
    Tripoli 37
    see also Bentham, Jeremy
corsairs 16, 29, 31, 86, 157 n.14, 164 n.52
    see also privateers, piracy
Corsica 7–8, 125
    Corsicans in Tripoli 24, 139 n.38
cotton 12, 31, 86
Crocilla, Dr Pietro Francesco 92, 124
Croker, John Wilson 101, 141 n56, 158
    n.34, 160 n.67, 161 n.1, 163 n.30,
    165 n.63
cruisers 28, 60, 106, 140, 164 n.52
Cyrenaica 14
    Cyrene 86
    see also Barqa, Benghazi, Derna

Dale, Commodore Richard (1756–1826)
    28
Darfur 77, 102–3, 110, 166 n.104
    Sultan of Darfur 113
dates 24, 27, 84

Delacroix, Eugène, 'Massacre at Chios' 15, 135 n.52
   see also von, Hess, P., 'Commander Panagiotis Kefalas Plants the Flag of Liberty upon the Walls of Tripolizza, after the Siege of Tripolitsa' (Tripoli in the Peloponnese) 15, 135 n.52
Denham, Maj. Dixon (1786–1828) 40, 42, 43, 57, 62, 72, 83, 89, 90, 101–2, 104, 108–10, 122, 124, 146 n.37, 148 n.78, 152 n.49, 153 n.78, 158 n.158, 160 nn.68–9, 74, 163 n.40, 165 n.66, 171
Denmark 26, 37, 49, 50, 93
Derna 14, 29, 32–3, 35, 66–7, 70, 81–2, 86, 107–8, 124, 127–8, 141 n.56
   see also Gulf of Bomba
Dey of Algiers, 28
   emissary Hamdan Ben Othman Khoja 36
   Hussein Dey 13, 23, 107
   Omar Agha 9, 14
D'Ghies, Fatima 37, 44, 47, 124
D'Ghies, Hassuna (1792–1836 or 1837) 31, 36–7, 144 nn.12–13
   ambassador in London 42, 48, 137 n.19, 147 n.63
   appeal to British government 52
   assistance to explorers 39–40, 49, 119
   complicity in murder of Laing 46, 50–1, 53, 144 n.13, 145 n.18, 146 n.37
   family 42–4, 124–5
   notable, 99, 118
   political reform 50, 52, 147 n.54
   on the slave trade 46–7, 90
   see also Jeremy Bentham, Civil and Constitutional Code for Tripoli
D'Ghies, Khadija 37, 44, 47–8, 125
D'Ghies, Mohamed (d.1826) 36, 125, 136
D'Ghies, Mohamed 36, 50, 125
D'Ghies, Seid 36, 125
Djerba 23
Dickson, Dr John 67, 92, 108, 125, 153 n.73, 161 n.87
   see also Archibald Dalzel
Dickson, Louisa Buena Parry (née Warrington) 61, 153 n.72
Dirke, Sultan of 104
disease 20, 30, 70, 89, 91–2, 161 n.161
   see also cholera, epidemic, plague, typhus
Diwan 26–7, 35, 37–41, 45–6, 49, 52–53, 70, 110–11, 118
Dorby, Mohamed 32, 100, 126, 143 n.76
Dongola 102–3, 110
drought 30–1, 34, 70, 143 n.1
   see also famine
Dundas, Henry (1742–1811), 1st Viscount Melville 13, 91, 110, 126, 134 n.35, 137 n.17, 139 n.36, 140 n.52, 144 n.9, 145 n.27, 148 n.80, 150 nn.8–9, 151 n.37, 160 nn.81–2
Dupuis, Joseph (1789–1874), 56, 107, 125, 164 n.61, 179

Egypt 4, 6–8, 13, 15, 17, 19, 23, 32, 44, 83, 86, 95, 98–9, 100, 107, 113, 115
   Battle of the Nile, 10
   Board of Health in Egypt, 92
   British invasions 11, 82, 96
   exiled Mamluks 102–3
   French expeditions to Egypt and Syria 9–10, 50, 63, 77, 80, 95–6, 105, 122
   planned invasion of the North African Regencies 100, 104, 143 n.76, 149 n.3
   slave trade 46, 100
   war with Ottoman Empire, 100
   see also Cairo, Alexandria, Mohamed Ali, Ibrahim Pasha
Elba 7
Elgin, Earl of (1766–1841) 105, 164 n.49
elite, see notables
el-Targhi, Hateeta 35, 40, 128, 144 n.8, 146 n.38
epidemics 91–2, 120, 127, 161 n.85
   see also cholera, disease, plague, typhus
Erzurum 37
   see also Anatolia
Exmouth, Viscount, see Pellew
Exmouth Treaty 31, 87, 106, 127
   see also abolition
exploratory missions 1, 12, 16–17, 20, 40–1, 52, 57, 66–8, 77–9, 81, 85, 88–90, 93, 102, 104, 107–9, 119, 121, 146 n.37

famine 20, 30, 34, 64, 91–2, 143 n.1
   see also drought

Farfara, Leon (d.1805) 25
Fezzan 5, 22, 24, 29, 30–1, 33, 35–6, 45, 66, 70, 73, 77, 80–1, 83–4, 89, 93–4, 98, 102–4, 111, 118, 123, 126, 137 n.10, 138 n.23, 139 n.37, 142 n.67, 146 n.35, 166 n.92
  see also Murzuq
Firman 22
Fornelles, Giacomina 69
  see also Church, Mr
France 2, 5–7, 9, 11, 13, 14, 24, 33, 53, 58, 65, 80, 93, 96, 99, 104–5, 110, 121, 124, 141 n.56
  Board of Health in Tripoli, 92
  bombardments against the Regencies 4
  declining trade with Tripoli, 85
  expulsion of French subjects from Tripoli 10
  occupation of Algiers, 31, 77, 162 n.20
  Revolutionary and Napoleonic Wars 31, 70, 87
  see also Allied Powers, Egypt, Mohammed Ali
Fremantle Treaty, see Exmouth Treaty
Fulani jihads 40, 145 n.24

Genoa 14, 24
Ghadames 27, 33, 35–6, 40, 67, 84, 121
Gharian 30, 36, 36, 40, 125, 129
  see also Sheikh Mohamed Haleefa and Sheikh Wooma Haleefa
Gibraltar 8, 11, 14, 28, 86, 99, 100, 105, 123, 132 n.15
Goderich, Lord Viscount Frederick John Robinson (1782–1859) 37, 92, 125, 141 n.60, 144 nn.12–13, 145 n.24, 149 n.91, 160 nn.83–4, 161 nn.87, 92, 166 n.96
Gold Coast 12, 134 n.32
gold dust 27, 83–4
Gordon, Lt Col. Sir James Willoughby (1772–1851) 27, 85, 125, 140 n.47, 163 n.24
Goulburn, Henry (1784–1856) 101, 125, 146 n.36
Gråberg of Hemsö, Count Jacob Florence (1776–1847) 71, 125, 139 n.44, 154 n.95, 181
grain 4, 15, 22, 100

Grand Seignior 21, 22
  see also Selim III, Mahmud II, Mustafa IV, Ottoman Porte
Greece 11, 13, 15, 99
  Constitutional and Civil Code 37
  Greek Question 15, 96, 135 n.50
  Greek Wars of Independence (1821–1832) 18
Grosvenor, Lord Richard (1795–1869) 25, 59, 125, 138 n.30
Gurji, Mustafa (born c.1789) 38, 40, 125

Hajj pilgrimage 3, 39, 145 n.24, 146 n.32
  pilgrims 3, 39, 83
  see also Mecca
Haleefa, Sheikh Mohamed 36, 114, 125
  see also Sheikh Wooma Haleefa
Haleefa, Sheikh Wooma 36, 129, 114
  see also Sheikh Mohamed Haleefa
Hamburg 88, 61
Hamet, Reis (born c.1754) 125
Hamet, Sidi (born c.1747) 44–5
Hammuda Pasha (1759–1814), Bey of Tunis 23, 125
Hanseatic towns 88
Hassan, Hassan al-Faqih (b.1781) 36, 144 n.3
Hausaland 38, 121
  see also Sokoto Caliphate
Hawkesbury, Lord, see Jenkinson, Robert
Hay, Robert William (1786–1861) 13, 50, 71–2, 112, 119, 126, 135 n.36, 138 n.24, n.28, 139 n.38, 141 n.60, 142 nn.65–9, 143 n.82, 144 n.9, 146 n.37, 147 n.51, n.55, 148 n.84, 152 n.44, 153 nn.67–8, 157 n.20, 158 n.31, 160 n.72, 166 nn.93–6, 98
Heraklion 106, 164
Heytesbury, Baron, see à Court, Sir William
Hijaz 39, 100, 162 n.21
  see also Jeddah, Mecca, Medina
Hillman, William 89, 126, 160 n.67
Holland 58, 124
  Anglo-Dutch bombardment of Algiers 9, 14
  tributary to Tripoli 28
Holy Alliance 31, 47
  see also Allied Powers

Hornemann, Friedrich (1772–c.1819) 146 n.35
horses 28, 81
Horton, Robert John Wilmot (1784–1841) 11, 32, 33, 43–4, 70, 82, 84, 102, 109, 126, 138, 142 n.72, 146 n.37, 148 n.76, 81, 152 nn.43, 57, 153 n.73, 157 n.18, 161 n.91, 164 n.58, 166 n.91
hostages 30, 39, 111
   hostage taking 36, 112, 166 n.92
Huskisson, William (1770–1830) 51–2, 65–6, 126, 149 n.94, 152 n.64, 153 n.71, 155 n.111
al-Hussein, Mohamed (1838–1873) 113
   see also Darfur, Sultan of

Ibrahim Pasha (1789–1848) 23, 36, 100, 122, 126
India 7–10, 12, 17, 19, 80, 88, 96, 99, 121, 125
Institute to Alleviate the Suffering of Christian slaves 106
   see also Smith, Sir Sidney
Ioannina 11, 13, 105–6
Ionian Islands 5, 7, 11, 65, 105–6, 149 n.3, 152 n.63
   Ionian neutrality 15
   see also Greece
Istanbul 4, 10, 13–14, 20, 22–3, 28, 47, 63, 99, 105, 111, 114, 125–6, 158 n.29, 164 n.49
   see also Ottoman Porte
d'Itabayana, Baron Manuel Rodrigues Gameiro Pessoa (d.1846) 32, 143
   see also Brazil
ivory 84
Izmir 47, 63, 84, 129

Jaffer, Prince 112–13, 126
   see also Wadai, Kingdom of
jama'a al'Bilad 35, 36, 38
janissary 3, 35
Jebel Akhdar 86, 100
Jebel Nafusa 36
Jeddah 39
   see also Hijaz
Jenkinson, Robert Banks (1770–1828), Lord Hawkesbury, 2nd Earl of

Liverpool 14, 22, 26, 29, 56, 58, 60, 65–7, 126, 135 n.40, 137 n.9, 166 n.89
jihad, see Fulani jihads
jurisprudence, Islamic, 24, 36
   see also Qu'ran

kahiya 35, 38, 40
Kalamas 11
Kanem-Bornu, Kingdom of 4–5, 36, 38, 40–1, 45, 49, 67, 74, 77, 80–1, 83, 89, 94, 108, 121, 124, 126
al-Kanemi, Shehu Muhammad al-Amin (1776–1837) 36, 38, 40–1, 80, 94, 124, 126, 144 n.8, 146 n.44, 166 n.92
   see also Kanem-Bornu, Kingdom of
Kano 4, 27, 39, 121
Khartoum 101
khazanader 35
Khoja, Hamdan Ben Othman, Dey of Algiers 36
Knights of Malta, Knights of St. John 4
Knudsen, Andreas Peter 49, 126, 148 n.83
Kogia, Mustafa 23, 126
Kolovos, Spiros 106, 126, 164 n.51
Kordofan 78, 102, 113
Kuka 57, 66–7, 70–1, 81–2, 93, 103–4, 107–8, 121, 128
Kunta, confederation of 38

L'ahaman, Bey Mustapha (d.1823) 124
Laing, Major Alexander Gordon (1794–1826) 41, 44, 46, 50–3, 73–4, 84, 87, 89, 108, 110, 114, 119, 126, 128, 144 nn.12, 13, 148 n.85, 159 n.60
Laing, Emma (née Warrington) 61, 66, 73, 153 n.69
   see also Emma Wood
landowners 36, 39
   insecurity of property 51
   landowning 35
   see also notables
Langford, William Wass (born c.1768) 5, 22, 28, 43, 56–8, 60, 63–9, 72, 75, 85, 98–100, 110, 119, 126–7, 132 n.13, 137 n.9, 139 nn.35–6, 142 n.64, 147 n.52, 150 nn.6, 11, 153 n.68, 154 nn.83–8, 155 n.101

recall to England 56, 70, 81, 111, 157 n.23, 158 n.25
see also slave trade (or traffic)
Leghorn, *see* Livorno
Leptis Magna 101
Levant 7–8, 10, 19, 2, 79, 82, 88, 95–6, 99
Levant Company 4, 8, 12, 63–4, 143 n.84, 149 n.3, 156 n.7
Lisbon, *see* Portugal
Liverpool, Lord, *see* Jenkinson, Robert
Livorno 13–14, 104, 110, 162
Londonderry, 2nd Marquess, *see* Castlereagh, Viscount Robert Stewart
Lords Commissioners 60, 89, 101, 106
Lucas, Simon (d.1801) 5, 8, 13, 21, 23, 26, 30, 49, 55–8, 60, 63–4, 66, 75, 85, 91, 95, 98, 100, 110, 119, 125–6, 132 n.13, 134 n.35, 137 n.4, 139 n.36, 141 nn.62–3, 144 n.9, 145 n.27, 148 n.80, 150 nn.8, 14, 152 nn.54, 59, 159 n.62
Horatio Nelson's ultimatum to the Pasha 10
Lyle, Peter, *see* Murad Rais
Lymph vaccine, *see* smallpox vaccine
see also disease; epidemic
Lyon, Lt George Francis (1795–1832) 40, 48, 59, 89, 126, 144 n.12, 146 n.35, 151 n.30

McDonogh, Bryan 21–2, 28, 30, 56–7, 67, 83, 111, 126, 132 n.13, 137 n.7, 140 n.52, 150 n.15, 153 n.76, 158 n.41, 165 n.84
makhazaniyya 35
madder root 27, 83–4
Mahmud II (1785–1839), Sultan of the Ottoman Empire 13, 15
see also Grand Seignior
Mahon 105
Mahsen, Hajj Mohamed 40, 43
Maitland, Sir Thomas (1760–1824) 64–5, 105–6, 126, 139 n.38, 150 n.23, 152 n.60, 164 n.51, 167 n.1
Malta 4, 9–10, 14, 19, 22, 29–30, 32, 48, 64–6, 68–70, 72, 82, 86, 91, 93, 99–100, 104, 105, 110, 111, 120, 123, 126, 128–9, 152 n.60, 158 n.29, 162 n.7, 163 n.32

Valletta 5, 86
Mamluks 4, 101–4, 142 n.75
see also Egypt
man on the spot 2, 5, 78, 93–4, 106, 115, 117–18, 121–2, 131 n.3, 156 n.2
marabout 38, 128
head marabout 38, 40, 124
see also Sheikh al-Mukhtar al-Saghir ibn Mohamed (d.1847)
Mecca 3, 29, 39, 83, 100, 113, 145 n.28
see also Medina
Medina 3, 39, 100
see also Mecca
Melville, Viscount, *see* Dundas, Henry
Menshia 24–5, 74, 112, 138 n.23
Milos 106
Minorca 8, 10, 19, 86, 93, 100, 105
see also Mahon
Minto, Earl of, *see* Elliot-Murray-Kynynmound, Sir Gilbert
Morea, Peloponnese Peninsula 15, 96, 126
Morier, J. Philip 126
Morocco 9, 22, 29, 31, 39, 46, 60–1, 63, 74, 119, 127, 131 n.6, 132 n.15, 142 n.69, 149 n.3, 157 n.14
al-Mukni, Hajj Mohamed (born *c*.1764) 30, 31, 123, 126, 142 n.67
mufti 38
Murad Rais (born *c*.1764) 25, 28, 38, 49, 125, 127, 138 n.32
Murray, Sir George (1772–1846) 4, 50–1, 68, 74, 107, 127, 140 n.53, 147 n.60, 148 n.85, 149 n.88, 154 n.82, 155 n.108, 165 n.69
Murzuq 4–5, 27, 30, 33, 66–7, 70, 74, 81–2, 84, 93, 101–3, 108, 111, 118, 121, 138 n.23
see also Fezzan
Mustafa, head dragoman 61, 62, 151 n.42

Naples 24, 31, 58, 88, 118, 123
al-Nasser, Sheikh Abd' al-Jalil Saif 22, 30, 31, 36, 80, 102, 111–12, 115, 118, 122, 127, 137 n.10, 142 n.68, 161 n.93
see also Fezzan, Murzuq
Naudi, Saverio/Xavier (born *c*.1768) 26, 70, 127, 138 n.34
Navarino, Bay of 15, 124

Nelson, Vice Admiral Horatio (1758–1805) 10, 87, 124, 133 n.9, 134 n.18, 159 n.57
Nepean, Sir Evan (1752–1822) 65, 127, 152 n.52, 153 n.66
neutrality 15, 81
  of Tripoli 51–2, 99
Niger, River 1, 17, 33, 38, 79, 87–9, 109–10, 121, 127, 139 n.44, 156 n.3
Nile, River 17, 79, 88, 108, 124
notables 24, 35–40, 43, 45, 47–53, 79, 89, 99, 118–20, 144 nn.2, 8, 145 n.21, 146 n.40

O'Brien, Richard Henry (1759–1824) 19, 141 n.47
oil 27, 84
ostrich feathers 84
Ottoman Porte, *see* Porte, Ottoman
  see also Grand Seignior, Selim III, Mahmud II, Mustafa IV
Ouaddai, *see* Wadai, Kingdom of
Oudney, Dr Walter (1790–1824) 40, 42–3, 66, 81–2, 89, 90, 101, 102, 104, 108–10, 124, 126–7, 146 nn.36–7, 148 n.77, 153 n.70, 158 n.35, 160 n.69, 163 n.36, 165 n.68

Palermo 104, 134 n.18
  see also Naples
Parga 11, 105–6
Park, Mungo (1771–1806) 17, 127
Paxos 105–106
Pazvanoğlu, Osman (1758–1807) 13
peace treaties with Tripoli 5, 29, 31–2, 10, 32–3, 37, 51, 65, 79–81, 86–8, 106, 118, 127, 159 n.61
  see also Exmouth Treaty
Peacocke, Sandford 67, 127, 153
Pearce, Captain Robert (c.1797–1825) 88, 127
Pelham, Lord Thomas (1756–1826), 2nd Earl of Chichester 22, 127, 137 n.6, 140 n.54, 141 n.58, 158 n.41, 165 n.85
Pellew, Admiral Edward (1757–1833), Viscount Exmouth 5, 61, 65, 106, 127, 135 n.44
Penrose, Rear Admiral Sir Charles Vinicombe (1759–1830) 101, 127, 141 n.56, 160 n.77, 161 n.1, 165 n.63

Persia 47
Persian Gulf 110
piracy 77, 164 n.52
  see also corsairs
plague 64, 91–2
  see also cholera, disease, epidemic, typhus
Pope 159
  Papal court 31, 88, 118
  Papal States 31, 88, 118
Porte, Ottoman 4, 5, 9–10, 13, 22–3, 31, 36–7, 52, 69, 80, 96, 98, 99–100, 105–7, 126, 152 n.15
  see also Grand Seignior, Selim III, Mahmud, Mustafa IV
Portelli, Clara 57, 73
Portland, Duke of, *see* Cavendish-Bentinck, William Henry Cavendish
Portugal 7, 37, 58
  Lisbon 32, 126
Pratt, John Jeffreys (1759–1840), Earl Camden 29, 64, 124, 141 n.55, 152 n.55, 154 n.84, 160 n.80
Preveza, *see* Parga
Prinsep, Charles Robert (1789–1864) 17, 136 n.64, 140 n.48
Prussia 14

qadi 26, 38, 40, 139 n.37
qa'ids 38
Qadiriyya 38, 128
Qaramanli, Ahmad 3, 4, 27, 30
Qaramanli, Ahmad ibn Yusuf 44
Qaramanli, Ali ibn Yusuf 30, 44, 48, 69, 114, 125
  see also Khadija D'Ghies
Qaramanli, Hamed ibn Ali ibn Ahmad 23, 127
Qaramanli, Mohamed ibn Mohamed ibn Yusuf 30, 74, 114–15
Qaramanli, Mohamed ibn Yusuf (d.1828) 44, 141 n.58
Qaramanli, Yusuf ibn Ali ibn Ahmad (1766–1838) 1–3, 5, 11, 22–3, 26, 35, 37, 41–42, 74, 86, 93, 111, 115, 117, 128
  becomes Pasha of Tripoli 21, 24
  conflict with Sheikh Abd' al-Jalil Saif al-Nasser 30–1, 111

debt settlement with Egypt 32, 100
exports to British garrisons 81, 100
growing instability of the Regency of Tripoli 19–20, 27, 30–1, 34, 48, 52, 67, 118
negotiations with Sir William à Court 43, 64, 80, 129
neutrality of Tripoli, *see* neutrality
relations with African powers 38, 41, 90
relations with the Ottoman Porte 20, 23, 51–2, 99
succession dispute 30, 68–9, 73, 114
trade with European states 19, 32–3, 49, 118, 230, 241
treaty with Napoleon Bonaparte 10
ultimatum from Horatio Nelson 10
war with the United States 28–9
see also Sheikh Abd' al-Jalil Saif al-Nasser; Sir William à Court
Qatrun 104
see also Fezzan
quarantine 92
Qu'ran 24, 36
al-Qusayr 39

rais al-Bahr 35, 38
Reade, Sir Thomas (1782–1849) 17, 128
see also Tunis
Red Sea 9, 12, 39, 47, 80, 162
Regigniani, Benedetto, 61, 66, 108
Ritchie, Dr Joseph (1788–1819) 40, 48, 89, 126, 128, 146 n.35
Rofsoni, Giacomo 61, 66, 108, 128
Rousseau, Jean-Baptiste-Louis-Jacques-Joseph (1780–1831) 50–1, 53, 73, 87, 119, 128
Russia 5, 8–9, 11, 13–14, 18, 58, 96, 98, 99, 104, 121

al-Sabun, Abd' al-Karim (1805–1815) 113
saffron 27, 84
al-Saghir ibn Mohamed, Sheikh al-Mukhtar (d.1847) 38, 128
salt 84, 132 n.14
Sardinia 118
  Sardinian consul 73, 104
  Sardinian vessel 44

Scarlett, Sir James, Baron Abinger (1769–1844), MP 46–8, 52–3, 119, 145 n.18, 147 n.63, 148 n.70
Schembri, Gaetano 39, 128
Selim III (1761–1808), Sultan of the Ottoman Empire 13, 18, 123, 137 n.4
  see also Grand Seignior
senna 27, 83–4, 112, 139 n.41, 159 n.47
Sennar 101–3, 113
Sicily 11, 19, 93, 101, 123, 163 n.31
Sirte, Gulf of 14
skins 84
slavery 31, 47, 87, 106
  slave trade (or traffic) 12, 15–16, 20, 27, 46–7, 49, 52, 64, 84, 90, 100, 136 n.58
  see also Exmouth treaty; abolition
smallpox vaccine 92, 161 n.85
  see also disease; epidemic
Smith, Sir William Sidney (1764–1840) 10, 99, 106, 110, 128, 133 n.17, 164 n.53, n.57
Smyrna, *see* Izmir
Smyth, Capt. William Henry (1788–1865) 25, 56, 100–1, 128, 163 n.31
Sockna 126, 128
Sokoto, Caliphate of 27, 38, 67, 121, 123, 131 n.9, 145 n.24
  see also Sultan Muhammad Bello; Fulani jihads
Sollicoffre Brothers & Wilkie, House of 87
  see also Wilkie, Pat
Somerville, James 56–7, 81, 128, 150 n.23, 158 n.25
Souza, Don Gerardo José de 43, 128, 147 n.52
Spain 4, 7, 14, 43, 61, 64, 80–1, 93, 100, 129, 140 n.52
Sudan 20, 27, 33, 38, 40–1, 45, 73, 77, 94, 100, 107, 109–10, 114, 122, 131 n.11, 146 n.35
  see also Bello, Sokoto, Kanem-Bornu
Sultan of the Ottoman Empire, *see* Mahmud II, Mustafa IV, Selim III
  see also Grand Seignior
Sweden 37, 50, 93
Syria 9–10, 18, 95, 99, 124, 126

Tarhoona 30
Tepedeleni, *see* Ionnina

Tibu 103
timber 16, 81, 86, 100
Timbuktu 4, 27, 50–1, 77, 84, 89, 102, 108–9, 110, 121, 126, 128, 136 n.64, 144 n.13, 145 n.24, 148 n.85
Toole, Ensign Ernest Stuart 57, 70, 81–2, 89, 103–4, 108–9, 163 n.45, 166 n.91
Toulon 8
treasury 27, 29, 35, 37, 49, 123
Trieste 84
Tully, Richard (d.1739) 26, 123–4, 128, 147 n.48, 151 n.37
Tunis 4–5, 11, 17, 19, 21–3, 25, 29, 31, 46, 58, 63–4, 74, 83, 86, 100, 104, 110, 117, 119, 124–8, 132 n.15
  see also Hammuda Pasha (1759–1814)
Turkey 4, 9–11, 18, 58, 149 n.3
  see also Ottoman Porte
Turkish dress 102
Tuscany 31, 34, 59
typhus 127
  see also cholera, disease, epidemic, plague
Tyrwhitt, John (d.1824) 67–8, 71, 81–2, 89, 108, 128, 142 n.75, 160 n.73, 165 n.65, 166 n.92
Tyrwhitt, Sir Thomas (1762–1833) 68, 128, 154 n.93

United States of America 7–8, 14, 19, 22, 27–9, 37, 47, 51, 55, 70, 72, 78, 93, 106, 111, 124

vaccination 17, 92, 120
  see also Board of Health, Tripoli
Valleta, see Malta
Venice 37
vessels 5, 25, 104, 112
  British 16, 31, 60, 83, 85, 121, 104
  European 16, 44
  French, 83
  Greek 106, 164 n.50
  Spanish, 91
  Tripoline 16, 22, 28, 61
Vienna, Congress of 14, 16, 31, 33, 47, 87, 126, 128, 143 n.82

von, Hess, P., 'Commander Panagiotis Kefalas Plants the Flag of Liberty upon the Walls of Tripolizza, after the Siege of Tripolitsa' (Tripoli in the Peloponnese) 15, 135 n.52
  see also Delacroix, Eugène, 'Massacre at Chios' 15, 135 n.52

Wadai, Kingdom of 4, 27, 84, 98, 101, 112–13, 122, 125, 142 n.75
  see also Prince Jaffer
al-Wahhab, Abd' 100, 126, 129
Warrington, Emma, see Laing, Emma, Wood, Emma
Warrington, Frederick 61, 66
Warrington, George 66–7
Warrington, Jane 61, 66
  see also Wood, Jane
Warrington, Julia, 73
Warrington, Hanmer George (1776–1847) 5, 13, 16–17, 24, 26–8, 30–4, 40–4, 48–53, 56–9, 61–8, 70–5, 78, 81–5, 92, 103–15, 122, 129
  see also Board of Health, Tripoli; al-Nasser, Sheikh Abd' al-Jalil Saif; man on the spot, slave trade (or traffic); Wadai, Kingdom of; vaccination
Warrington, Louisa, see Dickson, Louisa Buena Parry
Warrington, Walter Bornou 66, 153 n.70
Wellesley, Sir Henry (1773–1847) 129, 147 n.52, 157 n.23
Werry, Francis (1745–1832) 129, 171
West Indies 9, 12, 28, 121
Wilkie, Patrick (Pat) (d.1813) 56, 72, 81, 87, 128–9, 150 n.23, 158 n.25, 159 n.58
Windham, William (1750–1810) 56–8, 72, 98, 129, 150 n.9
Wood, Emma (née Laing) 66, 153 n.69
Wood, Jane (née Warrington) 66
Wood, Thomas 66, 67, 108, 153 n.69
wool 32, 83, 84

Yemen 9, 18, 100, 126

Zuwara 69